BEATING THE
COLLEGE BLUES

BEATING THE
COLLEGE BLUES

Paul A. Grayson, Ph.D.
Philip W. Meilman, Ph.D.

Facts On File
New York • Oxford

Beating the College Blues

Copyright © 1992 by Paul A. Grayson, Ph.D. and Philip W. Meilman, Ph.D.

Facts On File, Inc.
460 Park Avenue South
New York, NY 10016
USA

Facts On File Limited
Collins Street
Oxford OX4 1XJ
United Kingdom

Library of Congress Cataloging-in-Publication Data
Grayson, Paul A.
Beating the college blues / Paul A. Grayson, Philip W. Meilman
p.   cm.
Includes bibliographical references and index.
ISBN 0-8160-2455-3 (hc)
ISBN 0-8160-2832-X (pbk)
1. College students—United States—Psychology. 2. Stress (Psychology) 3. Adjustment (Psychology) I. Meilman, Philip W. II. Title.
LA229.G74   1992
378.1'98—dc20   91-24341

A British CIP catalogue record for this book is available from the British Library.

Facts On File books are available at special discounts when purchased in bulk quantities for businesses, associations, institutions or sales promotions. Please contact our Special Sales Department in New York at 212/683-2244 (dial 800/322- 8755 except in NY, AK, or HI) or in Oxford at 865/728399.

Text design by Donna Sinisgalli
Jacket design by Victore Design Works
Composition by Facts On File, Inc.
Manufactured by the Maple-Vail Book Manufacturing Group
Printed in the United States of America

10 9 8 7 6 5 4 3 2 1

This book is printed on acid-free paper.

CONTENTS

NOTE TO
READERS

This book is intended as a general guide. While every effort has been made to ensure the accuracy of the information included here, the reader should consult qualified professionals for answers regarding specific situations. Neither the publisher nor the authors are engaged in rendering psychological, psychiatric, medical or legal services to the reader. If such expert assistance is required, the services of a competent professional, with knowledge of the reader's situation, should be sought.

ACKNOWLEDGMENTS

Without the enthusiasm of Bob Silverstein this project might never have gotten off the ground. We are also grateful to our editor, Deirdre Mullane, who's been equally enthusiastic as well as supportive throughout.

Many readers were kind enough to read early drafts of chapters and help point us in the right direction. Our thanks go to Gerald Amada (and daughters one and two), Leigh Anderson, Ron Buchheim, Clarke Carney, Georgeanne Du Chossois, Heather Earle, Kathy Emmett (thanks twice), Elyse Getzler, Jay Gottlieb, Julie Grayson, George Higgins, Randolph Lee, Jacqueline Lopez, Kevin Maly, JoAnne Medalie, Alice Meilman, Diana Pace, Richard Raskin, Antonia Salmere, Allan Schwartz, Emanuel (Skip) Sturman, Mel Thrash and Leighton Whitaker. In addition, thank you Michele Wheeler and Elaine Ramos for your assistance in preparing the manuscript.

Finally, we'd like to express our appreciation to our college student clients. This book captures the flavor of the fascinating questions they ask, but it can't do justice to the satisfactions we experience daily in counseling them.

INTRODUCTION

If you are a college student, or are about to become one, no doubt you have questions about how you will adjust to college life. Possibly you haven't voiced these questions to anyone, because you're afraid they sound silly or awkward. The questions may be about shyness, a failed relationship, procrastination, homosexual feelings, a drinking problem or your parents' divorce. In *Beating the College Blues* you will find discussions about more than 300 of the common concerns that privately trouble college students.

The questions in this book have been culled from our combined professional experience counseling more than 4,000 students at half a dozen colleges and universities. (All students' names and identifying details have been changed, of course.) As you will see, the questions range over a diversity of categories. No single problem is "typical" for all college students; rather dozens of problems are common. You are not the only one to experience certain fears or doubts, to have certain self-defeating habits, to harbor certain painful memories. Whatever may be troubling you, rest assured that many other college students are secretly struggling along with you.

In the discussions that follow, you will notice three main features. First, the basic problem is outlined—its definitions, distinguishing features and underlying causes. For example, you will learn what anorexia and bulimia are, how to recognize signs of these eating disorders, and what factors may account for them. This information can help you view your concerns with perspective, cutting exaggerated fears down to size while opening your eyes to problems you may be underestimating. With any problem, the first step in coping is to see it for what it is.

Second, you will read suggestions about what to do for common problems. In some cases we suggest actions for you to take; in other cases we propose fresh ways of thinking about the problem. These are not in-depth solutions, they're not tailored to your particular personality or circumstances, and of course they're no substitute for personal counseling. They are quick "self-help" remedies, no more or less. But although self-help methods have built-in limitations, sometimes a tip or two can show the way out when you're feeling stuck on a problem.

Though not panaceas, these suggestions are reasonable steps to take if you want to try to solve a problem on your own.

What if you follow the suggestions and they don't work, or if trying them seems easier said than done? In that case, professional assistance may be required. The third feature of this volume is information about counseling (see especially Chapter 11). The general, commonsense advice running like a refrain throughout these pages is to seek professional help for a problem whenever your own efforts aren't achieving results.

This book is about problems, but it's not written in a spirit of pessimism. We know from years of experience that college students' problems are not trivial. But we also have learned that college students are blessed with the resources needed to work on these problems. Consider your assets compared to those younger and older than yourself. Unlike an early adolescent, you have the maturity to reflect on problems, to discover motives and recognize patterns of behavior. You also are at a stage where your family holds comparatively little sway, you're freer than ever before to try out new ways of thinking and relating, to become your own person. But while you're old enough now to apply insight and take responsibility for yourself, still you're young, with a future rich in possibilities. Compared to an older person, your behavior hasn't settled in and become a permanent part of your basic makeup. In a nutshell, you can change.

With these advantages, you are at an ideal age while at college to address personal concerns. The progress you make now will carry over for the rest of your life. We hope this book helps guide you in the right direction.

The problems and concerns of college students are diverse. If you have questions or subjects that you would like to see included in a future edition of *Beating the College Blues*, please address them to:

Dr. Paul Grayson   or   Dr. Philip Meilman
University Counseling Services   Counseling Center
3 Washington Square Village #1M   240 Blow Memorial Hall
New York University   College of William and Mary
New York, NY 10012   Williamsburg, VA 23187-8795

GETTING
STARTED AND
FITTING IN

Living on your own with other college students is exciting, liberating and enriching. You may love being at college from day one. But not everyone adjusts so smoothly. The first few days in particular—encountering a blur of new faces, finding your way among unfamiliar buildings, standing in endless lines—can feel overwhelming; it's not surprising if you have fleeting thoughts about packing up and taking the first bus home. Then there's the ongoing challenge of maintaining good relations with your roommate. Thrown together as if in an arranged marriage, you and this person have to live together—even if you never would have chosen each other as friends. Another task is to find your place in the college community, to adapt to the bustling campus social scene. Despite the fact that you see fellow students everywhere you look, it can be hard to make friends and feel comfortable. Groups in particular may discomfort you, or you may wonder about the best groups to join.

These are the themes we develop in this chapter, the common concerns about getting started and fitting in at college.

FIRST DAYS

Q: I'm really worried about going off to college. What can I do to make this easier?

A: For starters, be patient with yourself. If you're scared now and in the first days after arrival, so are half your classmates. Feelings of anxiety, loneliness and disorientation are typical for new students—that's why colleges conduct orientation programs. So expect these feelings, and comfort yourself when you have them. Don't be self-critical if in the beginning life at college feels difficult.

In addition, here are some other suggestions for making the first few days easier:

- To keep perspective on what's happening, think back to previous major transitions, such as when your family moved or you started high school. Remind yourself that at first the going was bumpy then too. You made it, though, and you can make it now.
- Rely on the familiar coping devices that work for you during times of stress. Go for walks, play the guitar, write in your journal, play a game of pool—do whatever you usually do to help you through trying times.
- Organize your room (or your half of it) the way you like it—arranging your desk, putting up posters, displaying photographs, buying a plant. This will give you a reassuring feeling of being in control, of bringing order and familiarity into your new home.
- Familiarize yourself with the campus and the neighboring community. Stop in at the library, bookstore, gym, student center and major classroom buildings, as well as banks, drugstores, movie theaters and pizza parlors. The sooner you know your way around, the sooner you'll feel at home.
- Most important, actively make social connections right from the start. Make sure to join your roommate or the people next door for dinner, and visit the students you met during orientation. An early sense of belonging, of knowing people, will make the transition much easier.

Q: After three weeks here, I'm still miserable and I want to go home. Is this a bad decision?

A: At this point, it probably is. If you still feel this way weeks and months from now, then by all means consider leaving school. There's no point subjecting yourself to prolonged suffering. But homesickness and unhappiness often ease up after a while. It would be a pity to give up during the predictably rough beginning when it's quite possible your outlook will change before very long.

Q: Why do I feel so unhappy?

A: There are many reasons. You may feel shy around your classmates and despair of making friends. New classes, academic requirements and the sheer size of the college may seem intimidating, and you may feel lost with the relative lack of structure, unsure how to manage being on your own so much of the time. You may miss your family, your high school friends, your dog, your own bedroom, your car, your hometown. Your family may likewise miss you and subtly signal for you to return—or, equally bad, they may seem to have forgotten about you.

As if any of these reasons weren't enough, you may feel embarrassed and ashamed of your feelings, as if homesickness were only for children (it isn't). Embarrassment and shame only make matters worse and reinforce your urge to go home.

Q: What should I do if I'm so unhappy?

A: Very often all you have to do is hang on, because the roughest part may come to an end within a few weeks. By then you may have made a friend, survived your first test or become excited about an extracurricular activity, and you'd hate the thought of leaving college. In the meantime, get as much support from home as you need. Going to college needn't be a radical break from family and friends. It's okay to call, exchange letters and plan weekend visits. With backing from home you may feel encouraged to throw yourself into college.

On the other hand, not everyone is ready to go away to college or chooses the right college to go to. So if your spirits don't brighten by, say, the midpoint of the term, discuss options with your family and perhaps a counselor. Next term it may make sense to go on leave or transfer to another college, possibly one where you can live at home. There's nothing shameful about taking one of these steps. The important thing is to do what's best for you.

If your reaction to college is extreme—if you are feeling suicidal or are unable to study or carry out other responsibilities—this decision shouldn't wait. Speak to your parents and a counselor about the pros and cons of leaving college right away.

Q: How do I get a good night's sleep around here?

A: It isn't easy. For one thing, dormitory life is remarkably noisy. If you're lucky enough to go to bed without an electric guitar playing or a fire alarm going off, then expect to be awakened at dawn by an alarm clock or your roommate doing calisthenics.

But noise is only one of the enemies of sleep at college. You also may lie awake at night because of stress and worry, depression, poor sleep habits or physical problems. Fortunately, losing sleep isn't dangerous, and for a short while it shouldn't hurt you in class or on tests. While prolonged sleep loss does dull performance (and too many all-nighters are a bad idea), you can probably work up to capacity after a night or two of tossing and turning.

Here are some suggestions to help you sleep:

- Don't panic about losing sleep. Worrying about sleep loss only keeps you awake. Instead of thinking "this is terrible" and "I must get to sleep!" and frantically checking the clock every 10 minutes, remind yourself that you can perform fine tomorrow even if you don't sleep a wink tonight.
- Keep regular sleep habits. Wake up at roughly the same time each morning, and go to bed at roughly the same time each night. Avoid oversleeping the next day after a poor night's sleep. This way you train yourself to fall asleep at a set time each night.
- Avoid taking afternoon naps—unless for some reason they help you sleep at night.
- Stay away from sleeping pills (after a few days they make insomnia worse) and avoid street drugs. In the afternoon or evening, abstain from alcohol, coffee, caffeinated soft drinks, chocolate and smoking.
- Stay active and exercise during the day, but don't exercise at night.
- Try not to eat heavily before bedtime. A light snack may help you fall asleep, however.
- Use your bed for sleeping rather than reading, watching TV or writing. The bed is then associated with falling asleep rather than wakeful activity.
- Make time early in the evening to think about worries and plans rather than saving heavy thinking for bedtime.
- Don't force yourself to sleep. If you can't fall asleep, get up, do something relaxing and try again later when you're drowsy.
- Buy earplugs, or use an electric fan or white noise machine to mask noise.
- If after a week of trying these methods you still can't sleep well, perhaps the cause is psychological or medical. Consider making appointments at your college's counseling center and health center.

Q: At home I never had to do the laundry or make the bed. How do I learn things like this now?

A: Well, we're not talking about organic chemistry here. If you're smart enough to get into college, you should be able to decipher the mysteries of the washing machine and the hospital corner. The biggest hurdle to overcome will be your embarrassment at having to ask. See if your roommate, RA (resident assistant) or a friend can give you a crash course on laundry and such, or go home for a weekend and have your parents teach you. If you need to, have them also explain the basics of ironing, dry cleaning, cooking, shopping, balancing a checkbook and cleaning up in the kitchen and bathroom.

ROOMMATES

Q: My roommate Matt borrowed my tennis racket without asking and he always leaves his dirty dishes in the sink. How do I let him know I'm annoyed?

A: The best way is the direct way. Mention the tennis racket and the dirty dishes, and ask that he get your permission before borrowing your things and clean up after himself in the kitchen.

Your effectiveness with this message will depend on how assertively you deliver it. Try not to sound apologetic, as if you're being petty for speaking up; then he may dismiss your concerns. But try not to sound blaming and angry either, as if he's a horrible person; that will make him defensive.

In both your choice of words and tone of voice, strive to come across as one friendly, reasonable adult talking to another friendly, reasonable adult. You have something important you want to say, and you assume he'll listen. Make sure to respect his point of view, too. Approach the conversation not as an indictment, but a two-way exchange.

Some colleges encourage roommates to write up a contract at the beginning of the term spelling out living arrangements. Agreements are drawn up about sharing things, cleaning up, the use of drugs, alcohol and tobacco and having overnight guests of the same or opposite sex. Even if your college doesn't have this policy, you and Matt may want to sit down and draft your own written agreement, or at least discuss ground rules.

Q: But shouldn't Matt know to be considerate? Why do I have to tell him or put it into a contract?

A: You can't take for granted that your roommate, or anyone else, will do what you think he should. You can't assume he will know how you feel and what you want. To get what you want, you must take responsibility for yourself and communicate assertively. Assertiveness means speaking up when necessary to express your wishes, feelings and needs and to exercise your rights. At the same time, assertiveness involves considering the wishes, feelings and needs of others and respecting their rights as well.

What happens if you're not assertive? One alternative is to be passive—to suppress your point of view. For example, you might complain to your friends about Matt's transgressions but not say a word to him, or you might drop little hints around Matt, give him the cold shoulder, roll your eyes or utter meaningful sighs. You might wash his dishes while muttering under your breath, or leave your own dishes unwashed and hope he gets the idea. The trouble with any of these ploys is that you remain frustrated. Passivity keeps the peace, but you don't get what you want. Eventually, your frustration may get the better of you and you'll blow up at him over a small matter.

The other alternative to assertiveness is to be aggressive—to fight for your rights while trampling on others' rights. You'd be aggressive with Matt if you called him names ("You're selfish and a slob"), made threats ("You'd better not take my stuff anymore or else"), threw in loaded side issues ("You're really a jerk with women, too"), shouted at him or retaliated by taking his clothes or breaking his dishes. Obviously, these actions cause their own problems. Aggressiveness may yield short-term results; you may strong-arm Matt into respecting your wishes. However, at the very least he'll resent you, and very possibly you'll have a fight on your hands. You also may feel guilty after attacking him and hesitate to speak up next time you have something to say.

Finding the middle ground between passiveness and aggressiveness takes some practice. A useful rule of thumb is to ask yourself what you want, need and feel, and then say so directly: "Matt, I'd like you to return my racket and clean up your dishes." Such direct expression lies at the heart of assertive communications. Remember, too, that you can get your points across in a friendly, calm, reasonable manner.

Q: But when I tried talking to my roommate before about the dishes, he screamed at me. How can I stop him from yelling?

A: You can't, at least not with certainty. Friendly, calm, reasonable language usually brings a like response, but not always. Your roommate may be someone who can't stand to be confronted and automatically goes on the attack. His style may be aggressive.

We still think you should express your concerns. Aggressiveness shouldn't bully you into silence. But if he does attack you, it's important to know how to protect yourself. These two techniques may come in handy:[1]

- Keep repeating your main point no matter what your roommate says or how loudly he says it. Don't let yourself get sidetracked by unfair criticisms, irrelevant points or baiting questions. If he shouts at you "You're so small-minded" or sarcastically asks "How do you know those are my dishes?," stick to your guns, again and again: "I'd like you to return my racket and clean up your dishes." This method is called the broken record technique, and it's a powerful defense against unfair attacks.
- Refuse to deal with your roommate while he's attacking you. Say, "We can talk about this later, when you've calmed down," or "I won't talk about this until you stop yelling at me."

These techniques let him know that you will address the issue but that his manner is out of line.

Q: My roommate Nancy has this New York accent that drives me crazy. How can I let her know it bothers me?

A: We're not sure you should. While we encourage you to speak up assertively when basic needs and rights are at issue, sometimes with little annoyances you have to look—or listen—the other way. This is especially true when the problem is beyond your roommate's ability to change, such as the way she talks. You can't make Nancy be just what you'd like her to be. You're probably not everything she wants you to be, either.

When your roommate gets on your nerves, sometimes the best medicine is to visit a friend, study in the library or spend a weekend off campus. Afterward you may be glad to see her, the annoyance forgotten. It also may help to remind yourself of the good times you've had and the interests and activities you share. Now may be the time to suggest a game of cards or to go out together to a movie.

Q: Why doesn't my roommate like me?

A: Her feelings may have less to do with you personally than with your situation. Dormitory rooms are a breeding ground for annoyances. You and your roommate are cooped up in a small living space, both of you are under considerable pressure, and under these conditions little irritations and even animosity can surface. If the two of you didn't live together, you might get along fine.

Q: But what should I do about her? She never includes me when she goes out with her friends, and when she talks to me it's always in a sarcastic, condescending tone of voice.

A: Certainly speak to her about this problem, if you haven't already done so. Maybe she's upset over solvable issues—the personal questions you ask, or your smoking in the room. Once the issues are out in the open and solutions are discussed, she may soften toward you.

But if her dislike isn't based on a specific complaint—if she's made up her mind against you—then there's not much you can do. You can't force her to invite you along. You can't write up a contract mandating her to be your friend.

What you can do, though, is insist on civil treatment. You have a right to be treated with respect, especially in your own room. If your roommate is sarcastic and condescending, speak to her about it. Point out what she's doing, and ask her to change: "Please don't make comments about my clothes. If you don't like what I wear, I'd rather not know about it."

Sometimes roommates get along fine even though they're not friends. They work out a harmonious living arrangement while satisfying their friendship needs elsewhere. So try focusing on your ties to other people. Perhaps then you'll be less upset when she's unfriendly, she won't need to push you away, and the tension in the room may abate.

Q: I've tried everything to get along with my roommate, but it's still not working out. Now what?

A: Perhaps a third party can help. Have you asked your RA or a friend to act as a mediator? With someone else present, you and your roommate may be able to speak honestly, hear one another out and reach appropriate and acceptable agreements.

If even mediation doesn't help, the next step is a "divorce." Arrange through the housing office for a change of rooms. If you feel this needs to be done right away, explain your reasons to the housing office. If the change can be postponed until next semester, in the meantime spend time apart from your roommate. When you are together, try to make the best of a bad situation. A strained but peaceful coexistence is much better than open warfare.

FITTING IN

Q: My friend Cheryl and I used to spend all our free time together, but lately she's been hanging out with a new crowd and saying she needs more time to herself. How can I get her back?

A: Are you sure you've lost her? All friendships have ups and downs, periods of more or less involvement. Cheryl's pulling away for now doesn't prove your friendship is disintegrating.

Actually, one of you was due to back off sooner or later. Any inseparable, we-do-everything-together relationship is bound eventually to feel confining. When you limit yourself to one person, you do just that—limit yourself. You don't learn from other points of view, you don't express all sides of your personality and you don't feel like an autonomous person.

Q: What then should I do about Cheryl?

A: Give her space. Don't resent her for having other friendships. Enjoy the time she does spend with you without making a production out of the time she spends apart.

Meanwhile, try to develop other associations of your own. Not everyone can be your best friend or even a true friend, but you will find that many persons have something to offer: a shared interest, the same sense of humor, common experiences in your backgrounds. With more people in your life, you won't have to depend on Cheryl to supply all your needs.

One more thing: Don't try to make Cheryl feel guilty. If you flaunt your unhappiness and blame her for backing away, she may feel bad about hurting you, she may even spend more time with you for a while—but she won't feel good about it. Playing on her guilt will cause her resentment and sour your friendship.

Q: In high school I was never one of the cool people, and it really bothered me. I thought all that would be over in college, but I see there's an in-crowd on my hall pledging the same few fraternities. Doesn't this in-group, out-group stuff ever end?

A: No, not entirely. Whenever human beings socialize, they congregate into groups and some people get left out. It's the same in employee cafeterias or health clubs or senior citizen communities. At every stage of life and in every setting, you'll find people vying to be accepted and jockeying for social position.

But, happily, the social setup at college is looser than the one-party system you remember from high school. Football stars, cheerleader-type women and party-goers have status at college, but they're not alone at the top—or rather, there's more than one top. At most colleges there are also social sets for actors and musicians, radio jocks and computer whizzes, politicians and scholars, and an assortment of other like-minded individuals. No single group dominates the collegiate social scene. So if you don't make it with one clique, odds are you can find your place with another.

One question to ponder is your sensitivity to social rankings. Why did it bother you so in high school not to be cool? Perhaps as you mature and gain confidence you'll become less concerned about in-crowds and social standing. With a stronger sense of yourself, you may not need validation by high-ranking peers.

Q: I envy this one girl on my floor, Renee, who's got it all together. Why can't I be like her?

A: This question raises issues both about her and about you. About her, you need to understand that, impressive as she is, there's more to her than meets your eye. She may be brilliant, poised, charismatic, beautiful—fill in your own superlatives—but for her, as for every student, there also exists an undercurrent of doubt and insecurity. Take the word of two seasoned college counselors: there are no college students who feel, in their heart of hearts, that they've got it all together.

As for you, the issue concerns self-esteem (see page 53). It's not unusual to admire a classmate, to wish you had some of her qualities. But when you elevate her above you, you correspondingly lower yourself. Envy for her erodes your self-respect. It would be healthier to see Renee and you—and everyone else—as different in particulars but fundamentally equal. Call this a democratic view of human nature. Ideally, you should regard all of your classmates as in some respects your superior and in other respects your inferior, but in terms of basic human worth, no better or worse than yourself.

Q: Everyone at this college seems different from me.

A: In what way? Do you mean you're one of the few Latinos? Southerners? Older students? Gays? Nondrinkers? If so, then on one level maybe you're right. Though every college and university contains disparate groups, each one does have its own character. Especially at smaller schools, where sometimes there's less room for diversity, it's possible to be in a small minority and feel out of your element.

However, many students who say they feel "different" mean something more basic than being Latino, gay or whatever. They feel *radically* different, alienated and dissimilar to the core, as if there were two kinds of people on campus—themselves and everyone else. This basic sense of "differentness" transcends categories like ethnicity or sexual orientation; it's a pervasive attitude carried to each new situation. Students who have this attitude typically feel like outsiders wherever they go. Unless given lots of reassurance, they assume people don't like them. The eminent psychoanalyst Karen Horney described this alienated mind-set as an "all-pervading feeling of being lonely and helpless in a hostile world."[2]

Feeling different can become a self-fulfilling prophecy. If you assume others are unlike you and won't accept you, your manner will be standoffish. Most people will then view you as conceited or unfriendly and won't bother with you. And so the assumption that you don't fit in becomes a reality. Your sense of differentness has the effect of keeping others away.

Are we describing you here? If so, it's time to reevaluate. Whether or not your present college is right for you, an "everyone is different from me" attitude needs to be addressed for the sake of your future adjustment.

Q: But why should I waste my time with people here if I don't like them?

A: It may help to think of your classmates as an educational opportunity. Throughout your life, particularly at work settings, you'll be faced with all sorts of personalities, from all sorts of backgrounds. Like it or not, you're going to have to get along with them. College gives you a chance to learn how to do this. If you can figure out how to make connections here, even to deal with people you don't especially like, then you've got a head start on future success and personal happiness. The relationship skills you develop at college will prove as valuable as anything you learn in a textbook.

Besides, we predict that some people you initially don't take to will surprise you once you get to know them. They may even become your friends.

Q: I find it hard to resist doing what everyone else does on my hall. Is that a problem?

A: Like so much else, it depends on the degree. Conformity is a universal human process, and ordinarily it's no cause for alarm. Doing what others do is an almost instinctive way to fit in. That's why certain expressions and hairstyles and fads sprout up on campus, and why in some circles everyone wears a uniform of trendy black. Nobody has to twist your arm to speak or act or dress that way. You follow the crowd almost automatically, because quite naturally you want to belong.

Doing what your hallmates do is okay, as long as they're not up to anything self-destructive. Obviously, it's not a great idea to play copycat if that means excessive drinking or taking other drugs. It's not a great idea to have sex, especially unprotected sex, simply because everyone else seems to be doing it, or because you want to be liked and can't tell somebody no. It's not a great idea to be coerced into joining a cult (more about this later in this chapter). Especially in these areas, you need to have a mind of your own.

It's also not desirable to have ready-made values and opinions. Because you want to fit in, you may find yourself almost unthinkingly spouting your group's party line, being scrupulously politically correct, tailoring your ideas to fit the latest campus fashion. But that's not what an education is about. You are in college, after all, to learn to reason for yourself.

To help you locate your own voice and keep peer influences in perspective, you may want to write down your thoughts and experiences in a journal. This is your chance to make sense of the happenings in your life and draw your own conclusions. We also recommend venturing outside your social circle. You're less likely to tag along mindlessly if you expose yourself to diverse people and points of view.

Q: I find it very difficult to talk to anyone new. Why am I so shy?

A: You can blame your genes or your upbringing. Scientific studies have found that some people are genetically predisposed to be shy. Timid and passive even as toddlers, they have a biologically based tendency to retreat from unfamiliar situations. Other people become shy because of early life experiences. Bullied or teased by siblings or other children, ridiculed by parents or raised by uptight parents who modeled fearfulness, they learned to be afraid of people and back away.

Does it seem that no one else is as shy as you? Don't you believe it. Most people know how to disguise social discomfort and put up a confident front, but that doesn't mean they feel inwardly relaxed. Surveys have found that 40% of the population rate themselves generally shy, while an additional 15% are shy in specific situations, such as going to parties or delivering a speech.

Q: But can I do anything about my shyness?

A: Absolutely. You may not metamorphose into the life of the party, but you can certainly come out of your shell. Here are some tips:

- Place yourself in a variety of social situations: Talk to your roommate and the guys down the hall; join clubs, committees and teams; make yourself go to parties; take speech classes or join assertiveness groups. Through these efforts, you gain social experience and give yourself the chance to grow comfortable. By taking risks, you break your lifelong pattern of running away from social situations.
- Set yourself small, attainable social goals. For instance, if you go to a party, plan to say hello to at least one person, to smile at somebody once or at least to stick around for one hour. Achieving small goals encourages you and makes it easier to continue developing social skills.
- After an event, focus on your social successes and strong points rather than dwelling on possible failures or weak points. Many students get this backward, and brood afterward about the supposedly stupid things they said or the one person who snubbed them. Focus instead on the conversation you initiated and the person who was friendly.
- To reduce anxiety and self-consciousness during an event, direct your attention to the conversation you're having rather than how you're coming across. Every time your mind wanders back to your performance, focus again on what others are saying and what you want to say. Socializing is like ice-skating. The goal is to concentrate on what you're doing rather than observe yourself doing it.
- Consider making an appointment at your college's counseling center. Individual or group counseling can be helpful for shyness.

Q: You say focus on social successes, but when I approach people I always get shot down. What am I doing wrong?

A: It could be a number of things. At the risk of increasing your self-consciousness—which we *don't* want to do—here are some suggestions to consider:

- If you want others to like you, first you need to show that you like *them*. Many friendships get started primarily because one person conveys an interest in the other. To express interest, you can suggest getting together with someone, pay a compliment or ask questions about the person. There are many channels that can communicate interest. Even joking or playfulness can deliver the winning message, "I like to be with you."
- Make sure you listen well and pick up on what the other person is saying. How often do you find someone who *really* listens to you? It's an appealing quality, don't you think?
- Refrain from self-promotion. Don't brag about your grades or your parents' connections, and don't monopolize the conversation with jokes and cleverness. The goal isn't to knock people's socks off. Act natural. Let others discover for themselves what makes you worthwhile.
- On the other hand, don't send off "I'm nothing" signals either. Don't imply that nobody else likes you and confess that you're boring. If you refer to yourself—and too many "I" statements are tiresome anyway—do so with self-respect.
- Similarly, don't prematurely open up about problems. Your difficulties with your family or your history of psychotherapy are not appropriate topics for a first meeting.
- Don't come on too strong too fast. Yes, display an interest if you like someone, but don't back the person into a corner as if to say, "Are we friends now? I need to know immediately." Let your friendships evolve naturally.
- In spite of all these "don'ts," try not to censor yourself. Better to make some social gaffes—we all do—than to weigh everything you might say and rule out most of it. To connect with someone, you needn't produce flawless conversation. Simply feel out the other person for common areas of interest—baseball, jazz, classes, the opposite sex, how you both hate small talk—and you're halfway there. Discover your shared interests, and let yourself freely talk about them.
- Evaluate your nonverbal behavior. Do you establish good eye contact, generally meeting someone's gaze but without staring? Do you stand appropriately close, neither crowding the person nor backing

away in retreat? Do you speak clearly, with some animation and at the appropriate volume? Do you smile readily, and sincerely?

- We don't want this to sound too mechanical. Pasting a smile on your face won't assure you love and attention. But nonverbal behaviors do have an impact. So try to imagine yourself as others see you, or ask someone you trust to give you feedback on how you come across. If there's an area that needs work—let's say you have a characteristic down-in-the-mouth facial expression—see what you can do to improve.

- Finally, consider your grooming and cleanliness. There's no dress code for success in college, but that doesn't mean you should neglect washing your clothes, cleaning your fingernails or taking a shower. Even in the permissive collegiate atmosphere, the way to make friends and influence people is not with body odor.

Q: Sooner or later, I always blow people off. Why do I do this?

A: Blowing people off affords a surge of satisfaction. For a short while, you enjoy the power of getting back at people who've hurt you and showing you don't need them. They can't fire you, you quit! Or you may want to jettison people who've fallen short of your standards. You can do better than them, you tell yourself.

But after the satisfaction fades, an empty feeling typically follows. You made your point and got rid of them—and now you're alone. For this reason, we urge you to hesitate before writing someone off. If the person is really wrong for you, by all means cut the tie. But if you're just feeling a bit disillusioned or temporarily hurt or angry or uncomfortable—and with everyone, sooner or later, these feelings will come up—give the matter some thought before you toss the relationship away. The friendship may well be worth saving.

Q: How can I make friends when I'm a commuting student?

A: Some commuters do it simply by approaching people after class, at the student center or in the library. If you're not that bold, then we recommend participating in extracurricular activities. These let you meet other students naturally and can lead to binding friendships. Every college offers a full menu of possibilities: the campus newspaper and radio station; academic and career interest clubs; religious, ethnic and cultural clubs; informal theater groups; varsity and intramural athletics; fraternities and sororities; volunteer organizations; campus government; and on and on. Ask at the office of student affairs for a rundown of your campus's offerings.

GROUPS, ORGANIZATIONS AND CLUBS

Q: I don't consider myself shy one-to-one, but I'm uncomfortable in groups. Why is that?

A: Group dynamics are quite different from one-to-one interactions. When you're alone with one person, your role is assured. Either you're speaking or you're listening; either way, you are a participant. But in a group, the spotlight can be off you. You may not get to speak often or even be noticed very much, and you may feel ignored and out of it. When you do speak, it can feel strange to have everyone's eyes on you. In a group, you can never tell for sure how each individual is privately reacting to you.

Yes, groups can feel uncomfortable, but it's important not to write them off. You'll be in many group situations in college and later in life, and so it pays to learn group skills. We urge you to keep working at groups until your comfort level increases.

One group skill is knowing how to inject yourself into the conversation. The trick is to react quickly when there's an appropriate opening, but not to interrupt anyone or hog the attention. Pay close attention to what's being said and then follow up on others' comments: "The same thing happened to me once. I was visiting this guy . . ." If someone cuts you off, don't brood and take it personally. Group discussions naturally have a disorderly, rough-and-tumble quality. Simply wait for a good moment and pipe up again.

Equally important, and in some ways tougher, is reacting appropriately when you're not speaking or being spoken to. When this happens you need to remind yourself, and convey to others, that you're still very much part of the group. This you do by the quality of your listening. Show by your eye contact and body language, and by your comments when you get around to them, that you're following the exchanges. The spotlight is elsewhere, but you're still involved.

Q: I want to join a fraternity, but some of my friends oppose them. What do you think?

A: Fraternities and sororities have their good points. They provide a pool of potential friends, they run parties and events you may like and they give members a feeling of belonging. After you graduate, they may furnish business contacts and ongoing social connections. Additionally, in recent years many "Greeks" have raised money for charities and done volunteer work for social causes.

Yet fraternities and sororities also have a potential dark side. Many of them have a history of excluding blacks and Jews—not to mention the opposite sex—and in a subtler way they still exclude those who don't fit their particular image of jock, party animal or whatever. These practices raise ethical questions—are exclusionary clubs inherently discriminatory and wrong?—and they limit members' social opportunities. Diverse people attend your college, but in some social houses, though not all, you may never get to know them.

Another problem is that some houses have promoted or at least tolerated irresponsible drinking and sexual behavior. Some have subjected "pledges" to hazing—physical abuse, humiliation and dangerous drinking practices—as rites of passage toward becoming full-fledged "brothers" or "sisters."

Your friends are not alone in questioning the value of fraternities and sororities. Some colleges have abolished them entirely, others have pressured them to go coed and have regulated their activities, and virtually all colleges have made hazing illegal. In response to criticism, many fraternities and sororities have adopted more enlightened practices.

In making your decision, first weigh your feelings about fraternities in general, carefully considering the pros and cons we've outlined. Then if you remain interested, we suggest taking your time to investigate the particular fraternities on your campus. Each house is different, and it's critical to find one that fits your values and interests.

Q: Someone I never met before came up to me and invited me to join her at a prayer meeting. What's this about?

A: Her purpose may not be clear. Though she may want you to join a legitimate prayer meeting, she also may be recruiting for a cult. Most cults appear outwardly respectable and associate themselves with religion, presenting themselves at first just like any other prayer meeting.

Q: But what's wrong with her group if its purpose is religious?

A: The problem is not with the supposed cause, but with methods and effects. Legitimate prayer meetings—and there are many on college campuses—respect your right to think for yourself. Cults, by contrast, tell you how to think and behave and set themselves apart as having the Truth. Cults use mind-control techniques of persuasion. They apply group pressure, isolate you from your usual social contacts, deceive you about their true purpose and invalidate your objections.

Once they get you committed, cults may alienate you from family and friends. They may demand unquestioning adherence, cause you to neglect school work and provoke psychological problems. All of this tends to happen without your recognizing it.

Q: But how can I know if this group is a cult?

A: Do members discourage other points of view? Are you prevented from leaving the group? Is manipulation used to get you to join? Are you pressured into staying and spouting the party line? If the answers are yes, it's probably a cult.

Q: How can I resist being sucked in?

A: Here are five suggestions:

- Retain a critical capacity when others try to persuade you. Don't stop thinking for yourself. Listen to what others say if you're interested, but remind yourself that no one has a monopoly on the truth.
- Don't let yourself be pressured into joining. Meet with the group if you want, but make sure you feel free to leave and to decline invitations. In other words, retain the capacity to say "no."
- Stay open to many points of view. You're in college to learn from many sources, not to listen to one dogma.
- If you're uncomfortable with any group or organization, leave it.
- If in doubt about what to do, discuss your concerns with an independent person you trust. Ask parents, a friend, a professor, a minister, priest or rabbi, or a counselor at the counseling center. This person may help you sort out whether the group is a cult. Your college may also have educational programs about cults. At the University of California at Berkeley, 10 former student members of cults have

formed the Student Cult Awareness Team to spread the word about cults' dangerous appeal.

WOMEN AT COLLEGE

Q: Am I at a competitive disadvantage as a female student in college?

A: Unfortunately, you may be. Research studies have found that professors are more likely to remember the names of male students than female students and to take the answers of male students more seriously. And males are quicker to participate in class discussions than females.[3]

But you don't have to play along with this unequal arrangement. Without becoming abrasive, you can be firm and persistent in asserting your right to be heard in class. If a professor seems to ignore or devalue you, you can privately point this out to him—or her!—and if that doesn't help, you can discuss the problem with the department chair.

Q: What should I do if the men at this college are sexist?

A: No doubt some of them are. There are males on college campuses, as there are men in society at large, who don't respect women and who treat them offensively. Our advice on this score is that you should be aware of sexist behavior, address it when you can and combat it when necessary. If a male friend seems to take you lightly, talk to him about it. If a campus newspaper article puts down women, write a rebuttal. If someone verbally harasses you, report it to college authorities.

But while taking up the cudgels against sexism, try to have an open mind about men—who are, after all, as human as women. Don't prejudge an entire sex. Though some of your male classmates are sexist, most are not, and you sell them and yourself short if you fail to recognize this.

SOME PROBLEMS MINORITY STUDENTS MAY FACE

Q: How can I deal with the prejudice against African-Americans on campus?

A: Fortunately, your college is also probably concerned about this issue. Some colleges sponsor educational programs about cultural differences. At the University of Pennsylvania, for example, entering students participate in a daylong Diversity Education Program, and at the University of Michigan and at Stanford University students are required to take courses pertaining to diversity. Many colleges also have professional offices, student political associations and social clubs for African-American, Latino and Asian students. In addition, every college has explicit policies to handle instances of discrimination, harassment and abuse. If you are ever victimized because of your race or cultural background, you have plenty of places to turn.

Colleges are trying, but that's not to say racism is nonexistent on campus. Nobody will march down fraternity row wearing a white hood, but it's possible you'll encounter instances of patronizing or unfair treatment, even a rare expression of open hostility. College policies and practices, for example in admissions or faculty hiring, may strike you as unjust. So your question about the proper response to racism is a valid one.

In our opinion, your best course is to be sensitive to racism, but not to confuse it with other issues. In other words, by all means take instances of prejudice seriously. You need to know when bias is happening, when to fight for your rights. With major instances of discrimination, whether on campus, in the community or in society as a whole, you may want to join others in making strong responses, such as participating in demonstrations.

But at the same time, it's crucial that you see others, white or black, for who they really are. You do yourself and whites a disservice if you mistrust them in general and read racism into actions that aren't meant that way. A white professor may give you a low grade or a white classmate may not smile at you, and it may have nothing to do with your skin color. A white may not understand you very well; that's frustrating, but it's not necessarily racism either. Mistrust, as we said before, can become a self-fulfilling prophecy. If you suspect whites of racism, they'll sense that and back away, and then you will think: "See, whites are racists."

Our advice also applies to Asian, Latino and Jewish students, to gays, the obese and the disabled, to religious Catholics and Protestants, and to anyone else on campus who feels in the minority. Whatever your affiliation, you have the right and the duty to oppose prejudice against you. Anti-Semitic graffiti on one campus, for example, quite properly provoked students to conduct meetings to reevaluate their views.

But try to be fair in your assessments. Don't assume prejudice lurks behind every smile. When you lie in wait for Christians or heterosexuals or whomever to reveal themselves as bigots, you've formed your opinion about them beforehand—a form of prejudice in itself. You also box yourself in socially. There are so many "others" in this world. Can any of us really afford to exclude them all?

Q: I'm a Latino, and sometimes I want to be around my own kind. Is there anything wrong with that?

A: Not at all. While it's good to know many kinds of people, it's also fine and healthy to socialize with others from your background. Associating with fellow Latinos declares that you have self-esteem, are proud of who you are. Likewise, women who like to be with other women, blacks who like to be with blacks, and Jews who like to be with Jews are, by and large, at peace with their identity. Those who scorn their own kind, by contrast, often have a low opinion of themselves.

FOR FURTHER READING

Robert E. Alberti and Michael L. Emmons, *Your Perfect Right*, third edition. San Luis Obispo, Calif.: Impact Publishers, 1978.

Philip G. Zimbardo, *Shyness*. Reading, Mass.: Addison-Wesley, 1977.

YOUR STUDIES

No matter how well everything else is going at college, you can't feel fully comfortable unless you're getting what you want out of your studies. Studies are central in your life; they're the college student's equivalent of an occupation. Doing well in studies doesn't just mean maintaining an acceptable grade point average. Academic well-being also implies enjoying learning, studying efficiently, keeping grades in perspective and making sensible academic decisions.

Throughout this chapter we propose many straightforward remedies for academic problems. Dozens of how-tos are offered to help you manage your time, avoid procrastination, and be more effective in reading, writing, memorizing, participating in class and taking tests. In some of these areas our tips may do the trick, while in other areas you'll need to experiment with techniques of your own. The only good study methods, of course, are ones that work for you.

Employing these methods alone, however, is no guarantee of academic success. Many study problems are not the result of inadequate study skills but of internal conflicts. Your studies may suffer because you prevent yourself from getting ahead, like a driver with one foot on the gas pedal and the other foot on the brake. Therefore we also call attention to the psychological side of academics, to the restraining tug of hidden wishes and fears and resentments. If you can understand why you hold yourself back from academic success, perhaps you can free yourself to do the work you're capable of.

TIME MANAGEMENT

Q: I'm always doing assignments at the last minute. How can I learn to organize my time?

A: Here are some suggestions to help you budget your time:

- To manage your daily schedule, use an appointment book. Fill in all your standing commitments for classes, meetings and appointments as well as due dates for tests, papers and projects. For example, on Tuesday, September 30, you might write "English" in the space between 10:00 and 12 noon, "Math" between 1:00 and 2:30, "Debating club" between 4:00 and 5:00 and, in the margin at the top, "English paper due." This way you'll always know exactly where you have to be, what you have to do, and when.

- To organize your studying, make up a list of everything you have to do. This "to do" list provides an overview of all your responsibilities—papers, homework assignments, materials to study before a test. When a new responsibility comes in, promptly add it to the list.

- In using the list, it's helpful to break down each task into its component parts. For example, rather than simply putting down "history paper," write on consecutive lines: "Choose history paper topic." "Research topic." "Write outline." "Write first draft." "Revise." "Type—due October 18." Then as you finish each part of the project, cross it off the list. Crossing off tasks lets you chart your progress and affords you the satisfaction of making headway on the project.

- When a given list becomes unusable because you've crossed off too many items and have others to add, start over on a fresh sheet. The very process of compiling a new list will help you get organized.

- Go through the list often to decide priorities: which items should be tackled promptly and which ones can be put off. High-priority items are ones that are due soon, require a great deal of time and are most important. Working out priorities gives you a general battle plan, an overall strategy for completing the assignments on your list.

- Finally, use a second sheet of paper to figure out a specific time budget for each major project you tackle. To do this you need to consider the actual time you have available. Suppose you've set aside five days for a history paper. Though seemingly a wealth of time, five days is a misleading figure, like gross income before taxes. When you subtract time for sleeping, eating, socializing, attending class, traveling to class and so forth, your actual working time may shrink to 20 hours. Now decide how to apportion those precious 20 hours among the various stages of the project. For example: "Choosing and researching a topic—7 hours." "Outlining—1 hr." "Writing—6 hrs." "Revising—3 hrs." "Typing—3 hrs." Such a time budget helps you work efficiently and keeps you from exceeding your time resources.

Q: I tried keeping a daily schedule but soon gave it up. I just can't stick to schedules.

A: Perhaps your system was too rigid and unforgiving. Time organizers should feel like aids rather than burdens, helpers rather than
enslavers. If you attempt to control your time too exactly—if you set
up a strict daily schedule accounting for every waking minute—pretty
soon you'll naturally want to escape this straitjacket, or you'll feel like
a failure if even temporarily you get off schedule.

The three-part system—using the appointment book, the "to do" list
and specific time budgets for each project—is meant to be flexible. You
can modify your plans or goof off an hour or a day and still get back on
course; though if you're really behind, you'll have to accelerate your
pace to catch up. But whether you use our system or experiment with
one of your own, allow some freedom in organizing your time.

PROCRASTINATION AND MOTIVATION

Q: I'm a procrastinator and I don't always feel motivated to work. Do you have any
suggestions?

A: Yes. Here's a grab bag of tips:

- Since success breeds success, it helps when stuck on a large task to
  polish off some small, easy part of it. So clean your desk, make an
  appointment with your professor, take out a library book as a
  reference or write down ideas for paper topics. Accomplishing one
  preliminary chore may motivate you to tackle the rest.
- Similarly, make use of small chunks of time. Put to use a 20- or
  30-minute interval between classes or before dinner; challenge
  yourself at the library to make the next 45 minutes productive. It's
  relatively easy to work well for a short time, and, again, your success
  may inspire you to keep going.
- Make yourself fully aware of your excuses for avoiding work. Do you
  tell yourself it's too late to hand in an assignment, you're too tired or
  the work is too hard? Expose and challenge such rationalizations by
  reasoning with yourself: "It's better to turn this in late than never,"
  or "Yes, I'm tired and this is hard, but if I finish this chapter I'll be
  caught up with my reading for the week." Once you start exposing
  weak excuses, it's easier to stick to your study plans.
- Be aware of your usual escapes from working—eating popcorn,
  reading a magazine, watching television, visiting a friend. The tendency with escape routes is to take them automatically, without

thinking about what you're doing. Instead, catch yourself at the moment you're tempted to escape and ask yourself, "Is this really what I want to do?" or "Do I really need to watch this 'Star Trek' rerun again?" Full awareness of your avoidance behaviors may enable you to resist them and stay with studying.

- Adopt an active perspective regarding your education. Instead of treating coursework as slave labor imposed by professors, remind yourself that *you* decided to go to college, *you* chose these courses. What's more, you are constantly able to make further choices. Tonight, for example, you can decide what subject to study and what aspects of the material to emphasize. Reminding yourself of your role in your own education may melt your resistance to studying.
- Similarly, try to recapture the love of learning for its own sake. No subject is intrinsically boring if you let yourself be open to it. The more you learn about a field, any field, the more you'll enjoy it. Remind yourself, too, that college is a soon-to-be-exhausted opportunity. Never again in your whole life will you be as free to indulge yourself in learning.
- To help make learning fun again, you can approach studies in a playful spirit. You might challenge yourself to see how many formulas you can memorize within a half hour. You can learn quotations or esoteric words to spring on your friends, fun facts that will make you unbeatable in Trivial Pursuit ™.
- Find connections between your studies and long-term goals. Will your psychology course help you someday as a business manager, or a parent? Will your term paper in history be good preparation for writing briefs as a lawyer? Will you use German on a future vacation? You'll enjoy studies more if you can make such connections and see the relevance of your courses.
- Learn to pace yourself when you study. True, you need to push yourself somewhat or else you'll fall behind and become anxious. But don't drive yourself through exhausting all-nighters or force yourself to keep going when you've really had it. Jog along at a steady pace that feels comfortable.
- Pay attention to where and when you work best. Arrange the room and your desk just the way you like them, or find the library carrel that best suits you. Work at times when you have peak energy. With these conditions on your side, studying is more rewarding.
- Encourage yourself when you have to. If a task comes slowly or a grade is disappointing, acknowledge your effort and tell yourself you'll do better next time. Reward yourself when you deserve it, too.

Before a three-hour stint of studying, promise yourself a visit to a friend when you're finished.

Q: I don't think even with these suggestions that I'll feel motivated or get work done on time. Isn't it possible I'm just lazy?

A: We doubt that it's pure laziness. In our opinion, inside every lazy student there's an enthusiastic learner struggling to get out. Think back to when you were a child. Weren't you eager to learn how to read, to ride a bicycle, to find out about people and nature and how things work? How come you weren't too lazy to learn back then? Your innate love of learning has been stifled for some reason, but it's still there, waiting to be released.

There are many reasons besides laziness why you may procrastinate or feel unmotivated. For example, you may never have learned to persist when you run into obstacles. This isn't laziness on your part; it's not having learned to tolerate frustration. (Perhaps your parents gave up easily too and served as role models.) Or you may avoid studies as an act of rebellion. Suppose your parents want you to study engineering, while you prefer liberal arts, or you're angry at them for being unsupportive or for planning a divorce. Neglecting studies is then like a strike against management, your protest against their actions. Or perhaps you lack confidence in your abilities. You'd very much like to get good grades but fear you can't, and so you procrastinate or make a half-hearted effort as an excuse for mediocre performance. "Why should I expect an A," you tell yourself, "when I put in so little effort? Just think what I could do if only I tried."

To understand your reasons for procrastination, we suggest asking yourself some key questions:

- How prepared are you to persist when you confront obstacles?
- Did *you* choose your course of study, or are you resentfully fulfilling your parents' expectations?
- Are there other reasons why you're upset with your family?
- How much confidence do you have in yourself as a student? How confident are you in general?
- What else is going on in your life that may be troubling you and interfering with your ability to study?

These questions may be enlightening. However, the sources of procrastination and motivation problems are often difficult to pinpoint and still more difficult to work through. If you continue to fall behind in your courses, by all means talk to an academic advisor and also consider consulting a counselor.

READING

Q: I'm a slow reader and I don't retain what I read anyway. What do you recommend?

A: It may be that you're concentrating too much on each individual word. Maybe you even go back over words to make sure you haven't missed any. Not only does this painstaking, perfectionist approach slow you down, but you can lose the main argument this way; you miss the forest for the trees. Instead, try speeding up your pace and reading for overall comprehension, even if you miss a detail or two. You'll not only read faster but probably retain more in the bargain.

Some experts recommend breaking down the task of reading into separate steps. Modifying their approach, we recommend a three-stage process: "pre-reading," "reading," and "post-reading":

Pre-reading gives you a head start in comprehending what you later read. To pre-read, quickly skim the material, paying special attention to headings, first paragraphs within a heading and first and last sentences within a paragraph. Look over the chapter summary, too. Pre-reading is like reading newspaper headlines before you read the article. You don't have the full story yet, but at least you've got the basic idea.

Next *read* the material. As you proceed, make sure you understand what you're reading. Key in on main points by selectively underlining critical sentences or selectively jotting down notes in a notebook or the book margins. Let us stress the word "selectively." If you underline or write down everything, you waste time and fail to discriminate between essential points and peripheral material.

Finally, at the *post-reading* stage, go back and ask yourself questions about the material. If you don't understand or can't recall what you've read, briefly review the unclear sections.

The key to successful reading is actively engaging the material rather than passively plodding along from first word to last. Reading should be an interaction; you are both taking in and questioning what you read. Experiment with methods of pre-reading, reading and post-reading to see what works best for you.

TAKING NOTES

Q: What's the best way to take notes in class?

A: The trick is to decide what's important enough to write down. Recording the professor's every last syllable is not recommended, because then you're not really concentrating on what's being said or distinguishing what's important. But you have to write down the essential points or else you'll forget them. Most professors make it easy to identify essential points by putting them on the blackboard or calling attention to their significance.

While you don't have to be a calligrapher, legible writing is a must. To write quickly, it also helps to employ symbols and abbreviations. Some examples are: w/ for "with," w/o for "without," = for "equals," ll for "looks like," re: for "regarding" or "about," > for "greater than," < for "less than," i.e. for "that is," Eng. for "English," WW1 for World War One, WW2 for—well, you get the idea.

Also valuable are symbols or comments in the margins, whether you're writing class notes or taking notes from reading. For example, you might enter the number "3" in the margin when three points are being made, write "Q" for important quotations, write "Def" for a definition, write "?" when a point is unclear and write "!" for critical points. You can also underline or draw boxes around key points, or draw arrows to link related concepts.

Be inventive. Any abbreviation or sign that helps you make sense of the material is useful to employ.

Experts recommend reviewing your notes regularly throughout the week and throughout the term. That way you'll learn the material as you go along rather than depending on heroic exertions right before the exam. Also, reviewing your notes right away alerts you if there's a topic you don't understand.

MEMORIZING

Q: What do you suggest to improve a lousy memory?

A: Is your memory really lousy or is it untrained? Many memory researchers believe that a good memory isn't an inborn capacity but a skill that can be developed. Here are some methods to strengthen your memory:[1]

- Put material from different sources—books, papers and classnotes—onto summary sheets. It's much easier to memorize material condensed onto a few pages than material scattered over many sources.
- Make sure you understand the material. Clear understanding makes material easier to remember.
- Organize the material into meaningful clusters or subunits. For example, you might not be able to memorize all 50 states in random order, but you'll improve your chances if you divide them into the six New England states, five Middle Atlantic States and so forth.
- Make an *effort* to remember. An active process, memory doesn't just happen through reading or listening. You have to concentrate on remembering to commit material to memory.
- Use mnemonic devices. These are word or association tricks to aid memory. One trick is to arrange the first letters of a set of items into easily remembered names, nonsense words or acronyms. Experiment with mnemonic devices that work for you.
- Question yourself on what you've learned. Ask, "What are the six New England states?" "What are the five Middle Atlantic States?" The more you recite answers, the stronger your recall.
- If during a test you're stuck trying to recall something, don't panic or give up. Try to remember any part of the missing material or any related material. Once any piece comes back to you, you may be able to retrieve the rest. ("It was Connecticut, Rhode Island,. . . Oh yes, Massachusetts . . .") Also, try to visualize how the material looked on the study sheet. Being able to "see" a missing item may help you to recall it.

WRITING

Q: Do you have any advice for someone who hates writing?

A: First of all, we advise practicing it as much as you can. Through practice you can build up skills and confidence and make writing a natural activity. You may even find yourself starting to enjoy it. So sign up for courses that emphasize writing, and look for additional opportunities to write, like keeping a journal.

In addition, we suggest the following:

- Efficient writing, like efficient time management or reading, benefits from a plan. Here's ours:

- First, give careful thought to your topic. Exactly what do you want to write about? Topics that are too broad or hazy are setups for failure. Equally bad are topics that don't interest you. To succeed at writing, you need to find something specific you want to write about.
- Next, research the topic. Take notes on what you read. While you're doing the research, jot down your ideas stimulated by the reading.
- After the research is finished, write down or enter into the computer all the ideas you can think of to go in the paper. Be inventive; put down everything that comes to mind. What might you possibly say—what's interesting—about this topic?
- Next, play with these ideas. Which ones belong together? (Draw arrows.) Which ones are primary and should go first? (Note them.) Which ones are irrelevant and should be excluded? (Cross them out.) From this exercise you should start forming an image of your paper, like an architect's preliminary sketches of a building.
- Continue manipulating your ideas, starting on new sheets, until you've put together an outline. This is a step-by-step plan, from introduction to conclusion, of what you intend to convey.
- Now, follow your outline and put down your thoughts, section by section. This should be done quickly and fluently, without worrying about perfect expression or consistency.
- Finally, set aside ample time for revising. Check your draft for clarity, consistency, logic, spelling and grammar. When a section needs rewriting, try it again. It may take considerable reworking before you've got the paper pretty much as you want it, every idea snugly in place. You'll probably be quite relieved and even proud of your product and motivated to write again.
- Don't go crazy with self-criticism, especially during the writing phase. Some students can't write down two successive sentences without thinking "This is no good" and crumpling the paper. Needless to say, writing's no fun that way. If you can, silence this critical inner voice. Allow yourself while writing to put down ideas as if you're speaking to someone, letting words and sentences come to mind and flow onto the paper. The time to be somewhat critical—but not too critical—is during the revision phase.
- If you use a personal computer, the whole process becomes easier because it is simple to make corrections, additions and deletions. You can even cut and paste parts of your text, print a new draft, and then edit all over again if necessary. With word processing there is less pressure to produce a polished version right away, and you can let ideas flow onto the paper. Editing can come afterward, as you rework each successive draft of the paper.

- Don't strain for an elevated vocabulary or lofty style. Not only does the paper come out stilted and possibly difficult to understand, but you turn writing into an artificial, arduous exercise rather than a natural means of expression.

PARTICIPATING IN CLASS

Q: A quarter of my grade is based on class participation, but I'm terrified to raise my hand.

A: Talking in class, a great concern to many students, is like standing on the proverbial high diving board. The longer you hesitate, the harder it is to jump in. Our commonsense advice is to forget about being brilliant and simply get something out. Resolve to make a contribution, preferably at the beginning of the very next class. Ask a question (you probably have some), ask the instructor to repeat a comment or state your opinion. Breaking the ice is what's important here. Once you've made your speaking debut, silently congratulate yourself—you did it! Then do it again, making another utterance later that same class. Now you've set the precedent, establishing yourself as a participant, and it should be easier to follow up with more contributions from here on in.

If this doesn't do the trick, you may want to talk to a sympathetic professor about the problem. Perhaps he or she can help you make a contribution in the classroom. Also, see the information on performance anxiety (pages 70–72), where we make several suggestions that also apply to talking in class.

TEST ANXIETY AND TEST TAKING

Q: Whenever I take a test I go into a panic and freeze. Are there any remedies?

A: Yes. Most likely you're psyching yourself out with negative thoughts like "I'll never be able to do this," "Oh no, I'm getting anxious again," "I can't think," "Everybody else is getting ahead of me" and "I'm going to fail." To reduce test anxiety, try instead to talk to yourself in a confidence-building manner. Say to yourself, "Good. I know I got that one right," "I'm doing fine" and "This test isn't as bad as I thought." If negative thoughts make you anxious, constructive thoughts can calm you.

Test anxiety can begin long before you enter the classroom. Hours or days in advance, you may make yourself frantic by imagining all sorts of catastrophic scenarios: "Suppose I botch up this exam. Then I'll fail this course, my academic record will be ruined, I'll never make medical school." Try not to let such thoughts go unchallenged. For example, say to yourself, "This test won't decide my chances for medical school." Corrective reasoning will ease your pre-test jitters, and you'll be in a calmer frame of mind when you actually take the exam.

It also helps to be prepared for some rough moments during the exam. Of course you'll be anxious—who isn't?—so there's no point getting upset when it happens. You also will run into questions you can't answer, so here again there's no reason for alarm.

Relaxation exercises may alleviate test anxiety before the exam (see pages 83–84). For anxiety during the test itself, you can spend a moment taking slow, deep breaths and silently reciting the word "relax."

Another source of test anxiety is unrealistic goals and overemphasis on grades. More about this later in the chapter.

Q: What good are constructive thinking and relaxation techniques if I haven't studied for the test?

A: Good point. The best anxiety-reduction method of all is solid preparation for the exam. Trying to cram material the night before gives you good reason to be anxious, whereas studying thoroughly and knowing the material instills confidence.

In studying for exams, it may help to consolidate your lecture and textbook material onto summary sheets. Include on these summary sheets the course's essential points rather than every last detail. Don't just read the sheets; question yourself about them: "What were the main causes of World War I?" "What do these French verbs mean?"

Q: Do you recommend any strategies for test-taking?

A: Yes. Try the following:

- Scan the whole test at the beginning to work out a time budget for each question. For example, an hour's exam containing four equally weighted questions allows you roughly 15 minutes per question; an hour's exam with 60 questions allows you one minute per question.

On any given item try not to spend much more time—or much less—than you've planned.

- Read the overall directions and the exact wording of each question. If the question asks for "two causes" or "three examples" or wants you to "compare and contrast," make sure you provide just what's requested.
- When you draw a blank on an item, skip it and come back to it later. Answering the easy questions first puts you in a confident, effective frame of mind. You may also see clues or get reminders from subsequent questions that enable you to answer the ones you've skipped.
- If there's no penalty for wrong answers, put down something for every question, even if you're unsure of the answer. You may guess right on a multiple choice question or get partial credit on an essay.
- With multiple-choice questions, eliminate the obviously incorrect answers first. Watch out for overstatements containing words like "all," "none," "always" and "never." These choices are usually—but not always—wrong.
- Essay questions are like miniature term papers, and like papers they benefit from a plan. First, briefly outline your answers on scrap paper. Second, write the essay. Third, check and revise it as necessary and as time allows.
- In writing essays, make sure you're clear about what you're trying to say. Sometimes it's helpful to explain what you will say, then say it, then summarize what you have said.
- Don't rush to be the first person out the door. If you go through the test quickly, put extra time to good use by going back over the exam and checking your answers.

MATH ANXIETY

Q: What do you suggest for math anxiety?

A: With math anxiety—or science, computer or language anxiety— part of the problem is a vicious cycle of fear, avoidance and more fear. You're afraid of the material and so give up; by giving up, you remain afraid of the material. Coupled with avoidance is a defeatist mind-set in which you tell yourself you can't do math and so set up failure when you do try. Another factor behind math anxiety is the cumulative nature of the material. Since each topic in math builds on preceding topics, any last-ditch attempt to catch up is bound to seem too little, too late.

Overcoming math anxiety requires a combination of steady work and self-encouragement. From the earliest days of the course, you need to read material closely, ask questions in class, attend tutoring sessions and do anything else it takes to ensure your grasp of the coursework. You need to stay on top of the material. At the same time, it's critical not to give in to self-defeating thoughts. Tell yourself you *can* do math. Keeping up throughout the course and maintaining a positive attitude can turn around math anxiety.

LEARNING DISABILITIES

Q: You're giving advice to work harder in weak areas, but no matter how hard I try I can't succeed in writing classes or keep up with my reading.

A: Then it's possible you have a learning disability. A learning disability is a chronic, presumably neurological condition—your nervous system is somehow impaired—that can frustrate your efforts no matter how hard you work. A variety of abilities can be affected—reading speed, reading comprehension, understanding of instructions, writing, organizational ability, spelling, memory, math, etc. As a learning-disabled person, you may perform badly in certain areas despite having a normal or high IQ.

Given your marked weaknesses in writing and reading skills, you should consider being tested. Your college may have an office that provides assessment for learning disabilities, and if not you can get a referral for testing off campus by contacting the Orton Dyslexia Society chapter in your state or the national office at 724 York Road, Towson, MD 21204 [(301) 296-0232, (800) 222-3123]. You also can contact the Learning Disability Association at 4156 Library Road, Pittsburgh, PA 15234 [(412) 341-1515]. Even if it turns out you're not learning disabled, testing will give you a clearer understanding of your academic strengths and weaknesses. And if you are discovered to be learning disabled, you'll probably feel a sense of relief—there's a *reason* why you've been academically frustrated—and then you can pursue a strategy to help yourself.

Q: What can I do if I'm diagnosed as learning disabled?

A: A lot depends on what your campus has to offer. Many colleges, notably Curry College and New York University, have specialists, even whole offices and programs, designed to aid learning-disabled students. Tutors may be available to assist you in areas such as note taking, understanding assignments, checking papers and developing other compensatory strategies. Specialists may act as a liaison with faculty, helping professors understand and respond to your special needs. Courses and workshops may be offered on study skills, and counseling and support groups may exist to deal with the emotional side of learning disabilities.

In addition to your college's special provisions for the learning disabled, there are steps you can take on your own to compensate for deficits.[1] It may benefit you, for example, to tape record your professors' lectures, to use a word processor with a spell check or to have material read aloud to you; there are even tape-recorded textbooks available. You may be able to arrange with professors to take exams in a separate classroom or to have more time to complete them. Deans or department chairpersons may let you substitute alternative educational experiences for requirements you are unable to handle. You also can talk to someone at your college's counseling center to discuss the embarrassment, anger, low self-esteem or discouragement that your disability may have caused you.

GRADES

Q: I'm a good student but I can't stop worrying about my grades.

A: Actually, some concern about grades is inevitable, even desirable. After all, grades do have an importance in your life. You need to maintain a certain grade point average (GPA) to be accepted at graduate or professional schools, to keep a financial scholarship and simply to satisfy yourself that you've mastered course material. So you should take grades and studying seriously—up to a point.

What you shouldn't do, though, is overvalue grades. When you attach meaning to grades that they don't have, you cause yourself needless worry. So don't make the mistake of using grades as the yardstick to measure self-worth, as if your entire identity could be condensed into a few letters and numbers assigned by professors—or, for that matter, as if your entire identity rested on intellectual ability alone. Remember that although grades say some things about you, they leave out most of what makes you human. There are no grades to assess your creativity, sensitivity and judgment, no grades for your special interests, physical grace, integrity, warmth, humor, dreams. Remember too that grades are subjective ratings assigned by fallible human beings who base their judgments on only a sample of your coursework. Professors can only make an estimate of what you've learned.

Also, bear in mind that your entire future does not turn on whether you get a B or a B+ in French. Yes, graduate and professional schools do consider performance in college, but grades are only one among several factors that enter into their admissions decisions. And in the long run, your college GPA will fade in importance. When you're a dentist, teacher, editor or parent some day, nobody will care what grades you made in college.

Q: But I've always had this need to be perfect, to get straight A's.

A: Aspirations are fine. By all means set goals for yourself in academics as well as other areas. Wanting to be perfect, though, is a treacherous aim. Perfectionism limits you as a person and can pave the way to anxiety and academic underachievement.

One trouble with perfectionism is that you become single-minded and driven in the pursuit of your goal. Like a miser who only cares about hoarding money, your attention is so much on your grade point average that you lose sight of whatever and whomever falls outside your narrow line of vision. Besides, you probably won't even enjoy a perfect 4.0 GPA if you get it, because the pressure will be on for a repeat performance next term. You can never relax, never pat yourself on the back when you feel driven to be the best.

When you strive to be perfect, it's difficult knowing where to draw the line. You may read course material over and over, endlessly rewrite sentences, try to memorize every fact, all because you're afraid of getting some tiny detail wrong. And since you'll never get everything just right, you're apt to be anxious and dissatisfied no matter how hard you try or how well you do.

Ironically, perfectionism often leads to underachievement. Since it's such a long shot that you'll do perfectly, the natural tendency is to get scared and procrastinate or give up studying altogether. Better not to try hard, you may erroneously think, than to do your best and almost certainly fall short of perfection.

Q: But if I give up trying to be perfect, aren't I settling for mediocrity?

A: Nobody is saying you have to settle. You can still set goals and push to do your best, but the trick is to do *your* best, to compete with yourself, rather than worrying about being perfect or outperforming everyone else. As long as you continue to make progress, you have reason to be pleased with yourself whether or not you're perfect or better than others. It also may help to base your goals on knowledge and skills rather than grades. You can't guarantee a particular GPA, but you certainly can set your sights on mastering new material.

You might also want to consider the loaded word "mediocrity." Do you regard good results, or even very good results, as mediocre? In our view, there's a huge gap between conscientious work and sloppy work, between good performance and so-so performance. Something you do well, though not perfectly, hardly deserves to be dismissed as mediocre.

Q: No one else besides me seems to work so hard to get good grades.

A: Don't be too sure. It's no fun being called a grind or a geek, and for that reason many of your classmates keep their studying a secret. They'd like you to think their good grades just materialize somehow, no effort necessary. But no one, no matter how bright, can succeed at college without hard work. You can't bluff your way through term papers and final exams merely by flashing superior intelligence. And what goes for college holds doubly for your future. Though not glamorous, effort and persistence are indispensable qualities that often separate the successes from the also-rans in life. So it's fine to work hard. Usually it's necessary.

Q: Yes, but I'm at the library 10 hours a day 7 days a week. Am I overdoing it?

A: Probably. Everything has its limits, hard work included. When you overwork, your performance eventually deteriorates. You get so weary and tired or so tense and distraught that you're unable to concentrate, and eventually you may feel burnt out and want to drop studying altogether. Completing an academic semester is like running the marathon. You have to pace yourself or else you'll never make it to the finish line. Besides, working to excess causes you to miss out on other sides of the college experience. You need time for socializing, clubs, activities and exercise, too.

Overstudying is a driven behavior, not unlike overeating, overspending, starving yourself or feeling compelled to drink or have casual sex. Like these behaviors, it's probably rooted in personal issues—like low self-esteem—and may cause you greater anxiety if you try to stop it. You may want to review the section on self-esteem in Chapter 3, and you may also want to consider consulting a counselor.

CHEATING

Q: I'll never meet the deadline in my history class unless I copy my friend's paper. Everyone else cuts corners to get good grades. Why shouldn't I do it?

A: While it's not true that everyone does it, admittedly cheating—let's call it by its right name—is widespread at college. According to one study, more than 30% of college students plagiarized work within a recent year.[2] The usual reason is the pressure to get good grades, and the usual excuse is "Everyone else does it too." Cheating isn't very hard to do, whether you're copying a friend's paper or copying answers on a test. You can even cheat without realizing it. Using information in a paper without noting or citing the source is cheating; so is citing references you haven't read to pad a bibliography.

But even though cheating is fairly common and easy, it's still not in your best interests. For one thing, you might get caught. Every year on every college campus there are students who suffer the humiliation of being accused of cheating, and often they wind up flunking classes or getting expelled. Second, cheating short-changes you. When you use someone else's work rather than your own, you deprive yourself of an opportunity to learn, and if you don't learn, then what's the point of paying thousands—or tens of thousands—of dollars for college? Third, you probably won't like yourself if you cheat. Inevitably, cheating causes you to think of yourself as a cheater. No matter how strenuously you defend your actions or varnish the truth, on some level cheating chips away at your self-respect. Bottom line: It's not worth it.

FAILING

Q: I'm already on probation, and now I think I'm about to flunk out. What now?

A: Before you do anything, first see if there's a way to salvage the term. Can you drop a course? Get extra help? Take an incomplete? Get an extension? We suggest that you talk to your professors and your dean before any more time goes by. Possibly you don't have to flunk out after all.

But if failing is inevitable, don't let yourself panic. There's nothing disgraceful or catastrophic in what has happened. You're not the first college student to flunk out, and you won't be the last. At least now after a long struggle you know where you stand and can get on with your life.

Your immediate task is to decide how to use your time productively after the term is over. Will you enroll at another school? Take time off to go to work? Travel? Join the military? The sooner you make sensible plans, the better you'll feel.

In planning for the future, it helps to analyze what went wrong this time. Possibly you were enrolled in a program of study or at a college too difficult for you. If so, you're wise to face up to this now rather than planning to come back later—and failing all over again. It's also possible that college itself isn't right for you; it's not for everyone. Being honest with yourself about this will enable you to make realistic career decisions that don't require a college education.

Maybe you failed because of your attitude about studies. Perfectionist standards, lack of self-confidence, a passive approach to studies, rebellious feelings toward your parents—any of the psychological issues we've mentioned may account for your poor performance. If you've failed for some such reason, we urge going into counseling before resuming a full-time course of study. You need to understand and work through your inner resistances before you'll be ready to resume college.

ACADEMIC DECISIONS

Q: I'm a second-term sophomore studying economics, but I want to switch to biology. Should I change majors?

A: Of course. As a sophomore you're certainly not locked into your original major. Many students change majors, sometimes more than once, in an ongoing process of discovering their academic interests. It's much better to start on a desirable new path than to continue trudging in an unwanted direction.

There may be a few obstacles to overcome. When you switch to a new major, you need to work out distribution requirements—minimum course totals in the humanities, social sciences and natural sciences—to make sure you're on track for graduation. Sometimes it's necessary to take an extra term to meet the requirements for a new major. Deans or advisors can help in setting up a new program.

Our advice would be different if you were a first-term senior, because working out distribution requirements would be unlikely at that late point. As a senior, your best bet would be to complete your present major. After graduation, you could then take an additional year or two of courses to pursue your new interest.

Our advice would also be tempered if you were contemplating, say, a *third* change of majors. This would suggest a fear of committing to one area, or a fear of finishing college. We'd suggest then that you talk this over with your advisor and a counselor if necessary.

Q: My college doesn't have an engineering program, and I realize now that's what I want to study. Should I consider transferring?

A: Yes, provided you're pretty certain about engineering. No college can meet everyone's academic needs. If your current school doesn't offer the program of your choice, then switch to another college that does.

However, transferring to another college is a big decision that shouldn't be made lightly. Suppose you were going through a personally unhappy or difficult spell or you had vague doubts about your college's suitability for you. Our suggestion then would be to take your misgivings seriously but not to transfer right away. Instead, allow time for the problem to resolve itself, and in the meantime try to gain perspective by speaking to parents, a friend, a dean, an advisor or a counselor. You also might go on leave for a term and take classes at another college that interests you.

Transferring *is* sometimes the right thing to do. But be confident about the move before you burn your bridges behind you.

Q: I only came to this college because I didn't make my top choices. I like it here now, but I'm still considering transferring. What do you think?

A: We think it would help to shed light on your motives. Do you want to transfer to improve your education? Are you hoping to take advantage of intellectual and cultural features lacking at your current college? For example, you may prefer a bustling urban environment to your current rural setting, or want a school with a more pronounced intellectual atmosphere. In our opinion, these are valid reasons to transfer, even though you're not dissatisfied where you are now.

But suppose after all is said and done your reason for transferring boils down to prestige. Your current college provides a stimulating education, you've made close personal ties—but another college has a more elite reputation. Here we would caution you to think twice before transferring. Academic satisfaction and personal happiness are a lot to give up solely for the sake of prestige. It may not be worth it to move on simply because of another college's name value.

TAKING TIME OFF

Q: I'm burnt out with school and would love to take time off. But if I do this, I'm afraid I'll never make my way back to college.

A: There's no assurance, of course. Once out of academia, it's possible you'll settle into your new life and never want to be a student again. However, most students who spend a semester or a year away from college do make a successful return. The time off lets them recharge their batteries, clarify their priorities and come to appreciate, if they didn't before, the value of education and a diploma. Not only that, the working or traveling engaged in while on leave often proves a valuable educational experience in its own right.

Your parents may be uncomfortable with your taking time off, fearing, as you do, that the detour will become permanent. It may help to reassure them about your long-term educational objectives and inform them, as we mentioned, that most students who leave college eventually go back. Point out that it's foolish to put time and money into college when you're not really taking advantage of it. You'll return when you're ready to make full use of the opportunity.

Q: I'm under a lot of stress for personal reasons, and I can't study for my finals. What should I do?

A: You have several options. You can talk directly to your professors, who may let you postpone assignments or tests until later in the term, or grant you an incomplete to finish the work after the term. Alternatively, you can speak to a dean or faculty advisor, who may be able to work out an arrangement with your professors. Either way, it's important to act quickly rather than waiting until after assignments are due.

Another possibility is to go to the counseling center to work on the emotional problems that are interfering with your academics. With help from counseling, you may feel strong enough to handle coursework. If counseling alone doesn't suffice, then your counselor— with your permission, of course—may recommend to a dean or faculty member that you take an incomplete or drop a course.

The counselor may also recommend a medical leave of absence. This option lets you drop the term's classes and so preserves your grade point average. Because the term "medical leave" is nonspecific and can refer to anything from pneumonia to a broken leg, your permanent record is not blemished. No one can tell later from inspecting your transcript that you went on leave because of emotional difficulties.

FOR FURTHER READING

William H. Armstrong and M. Willard Lampe II, *Study Tactics*. Hauppage, NY: Barron's, 1983.

Albert Ellis and William Knaus, *Overcoming Procrastination*. New York: Signet, 1979.

Sara Gilbert, *How to Take Tests*. New York: William Morrow & Co., 1983.

Kenneth A. Green, *Making the Grade in College*. Hauppage, NY: Barron's, 1990.

Charles T. Mangrum and Stephen S. Strichart, eds., *Peterson's Guide to Colleges with Programs for Learning Disabled Students*, second edition. Princeton, N.J. Peterson's Guides, 1988.

Barbara Scheiber and Jeanne Talpers, *Unlocking Potential: College and Other Choices for Learning Disabled People—A Step-by-Step Guide*. Bethesda, Md.: Adler & Adler, 1987.

FEELING DOWN AND GETTING BACK UP

It's fitting that we introduce the concept of depression early in this book, because it overlaps with nearly every other problem area we discuss. If you feel homesick at college, if you feel academically overstressed, if you have concerns about romance or sex or diet or career, then you can end up depressed. Conversely, if you are depressed, then you may be below par in socializing, studies, romance, sexual performance and so forth. Depression is both a cause and a consequence of personal difficulties. It is a common denominator, sometimes unrecognized, of widely differing concerns.

In this chapter we explain the nature of depression, distinguishing it from sadness. We show how to recognize depression's warning signals, and give strategies for combating it. We also cover the related topics of mood swings, low self-esteem and identity confusion. Finally, we discuss the critical subject of suicidal feelings.

DEPRESSION VS. SADNESS

Q: I get sad a lot. Is that normal?

A: It depends on what you mean by "sad" and "a lot." If all you have are passing downshifts in mood, episodes of feeling blue, then you're probably no different from anyone else. If, however, you have long bouts of feeling downcast or your down periods are intense and incapacitating—you can't study, eat, sleep, socialize—that's different. You probably are depressed.

45

Q: But what's the difference between sadness and depression?

A: It's not entirely clear if sadness and depression come from the same root, or if they're essentially unrelated phenomena. Either way, it's important not to confuse the two. Sadness—a temporary state of feeling down—is a limited experience, and for that reason it's not a problem. In fact, it can feel satisfying sometimes to feel sad and have a good cry, to listen to melancholy music or watch a tragic drama. Sadness adds a fitting solemnity to human existence; life would seem shallow without it. Sadness also has lessons to teach. Through recognizing sadness you may discover that a relationship is empty, a need is unfulfilled, a potential has been wasted. You can discover when you're sad who and what matters to you.

Depression is on a different scale. Depression isn't satisfying; it doesn't uplift or teach. A debilitating condition, depression casts a pall over every aspect of life. In its stronger forms, depression can make you unable to continue in college, and can cause you to think about suicide.

You can't eliminate sadness from your life. You can, and should, take steps to fight off depression.

Q: I've known lots of people who say they're being treated for depression, but they don't all seem the same to me. Are there different kinds of depression?

A: Yes, there are. Here's a thumbnail description of some of the most important types:

A *depressive reaction* is, as its name implies, a reaction to some negative event, such as failure at school, a romantic breakup or the death of a parent. A depressive reaction is "normal" in the sense that anyone facing the same circumstances would naturally feel bad. However, depressive reactions certainly don't feel normal. Like any other kind of depression, they can be intense and profound, can last many weeks or even longer and in severe cases are disabling. But they are related to a specific cause, and ordinarily the depression will abate with time.

Other forms of depression aren't due to negative circumstances alone. The person who experiences them also has an underlying biological and/or psychological vulnerability to depression; the cause lies at least partly within. Of these forms, *dysthymia* refers to a long-lasting but comparatively mild form of depression. Dysthymic persons manage to get by from day to day, they can bring themselves to study and socialize, but they view whatever they turn to through gray-colored glasses. One psychologist compares dysthymia to "a low-grade infection. Dysthymics never really feel good."[1]

By contrast, a *major depression* has a relatively sudden onset and lasts several weeks to many months. It is paralyzing. College students who suffer a major depression find themselves unable to function and often must withdraw from school. This is the most severe form of "unipolar" depression, meaning that the extreme moods only go in one direction; depression does not alternate with elevated, or high, moods.

With *manic-depressive disorder*—also called bipolar disorder—episodes of being uncontrollably high ("mania") alternate with episodes of depression. Both the up and down extremes are grave problems, although in the manic phase the person has no insight into the dangers. During manic episodes judgment is impaired and inhibitions melt away, and the person may act recklessly by perhaps gambling away money or running away from responsibilities. During depressive episodes he or she despairs and may be suicidal.

A less extreme up-and-down mood pattern is called *cyclothymia*. If even less pronounced, we simply refer to mood swings—which isn't a disorder at all. Neither cyclothymia nor mood swings should be confused with a full-fledged manic-depressive disorder.

WARNING SIGNS

Q: Sometimes I wonder if I'm depressed and don't know it. Is that possible?

A: Very much so. You may not recognize depression if it creeps up on you, or if you're chronically depressed (dysthymic) and so have no normal emotional baseline as a comparison. And if you're severely depressed, your thinking may be so clouded that you don't recognize your condition.

Here are some classic signs and symptoms to identify depression:

- Prolonged sad or depressed mood; crying spells; irritability; or an inability to feel anything at all. (Note: You can be depressed without feeling sad).
- Loss of interest and pleasure in activities and other people.
- Significant weight loss or weight gain, or marked increase or decrease in appetite.
- Low self-esteem; feelings of worthlessness, guilt and self-blame.

- Poor concentration; you can't read, write or study for a test.
- Difficulty making decisions.
- Feelings of hopelessness; a belief that the future won't be any better than the present.
- Fatigue and loss of energy, or agitation and restlessness.
- Problems with sleep: inability to fall or stay asleep, waking up early and being unable to get back to sleep, or sleeping too much.
- Worries about health, and physical symptoms such as digestive disorders and nonspecific aches and pains.
- Recurrent thoughts of death or suicide.

FAMILY INFLUENCE

Q: Both my parents sometimes get depressed. Will the same thing happen to me?

A: It could. Research shows that being the child of a depressed parent may double or triple the risk of depression in later life.[2] Sometimes this happens because of genetic transmission. Studies suggest that a vulnerability to major depression and particularly to manic-depressive disorder can be inherited.[3] Parents also can transmit depression if they serve as role models demonstrating how to be miserable, or if they don't provide the love, attention and structure that children need.

However, there is nothing certain about any of this. Children take after each parent in some respects, not in others. It's good to be aware of the risk of depression so you'll seek treatment if the need ever arises. But don't assume because of your parents' history that your own fate has been sealed.

Some students are so afraid of following in their depressed parents' footsteps that they won't let themselves feel sad or upset. One student we know wore a constant smile, as if a cheerful face could ward off evil moods. She was determined not to be like her mother, who'd once been hospitalized for depression. Then this student's boyfriend broke up with her, and she could no longer muster the smile. This terrified her. Did her sorrow indicate severe depression? Was she turning into her mother after all? Thanks to several counseling sessions, she finally saw that suffering after a breakup is normal, not a sign of emotional illness.

SEASONAL DEPRESSION

Q: I often seem to feel bad in the winter months and then start improving when the days grow longer. Is that normal?

A: It sure is. In recent years researchers have found that in colder climates perhaps 5% of the population have a rather serious form of depression during the winter, while an additional 20% suffer mild depressive symptoms. Those who are seriously affected have what is called seasonal affective disorder, or SAD. Common symptoms of SAD are chronically depressed mood, social withdrawal, excessive sleep and a voracious appetite that leads to weight gain.

Researchers' best guess is that winter blues are caused by the relative lack of sunlight. In other words, your outlook could be dark and gray because it's dark and gray outside your window. If you are severely impaired, you should consult a professional, who may refer you to a specialist in treating SAD (the new, recommended treatment involves light therapy). If instead you have a mild case of cold-weather blahs, then treatment is not usually necessary.

HELPING YOURSELF

Q: What should I do if I'm feeling down?

A: If it's just a question of sadness—a low mood—then no major remedies are necessary. Time is your ally. No matter how bad you feel, chances are it will all be better in a day or two. In the meantime, you might let out what's troubling you to someone you trust. A bit of support and blowing off steam can work wonders for a down emotional state. You may also want to take a break from the usual routine by going to a movie or leaving campus for the weekend.

Choose wisely, however, when you select a break. Don't soothe bad feelings by getting drunk, taking other drugs, bingeing on food, missing classes, having careless sexual experiences or buying clothes you can't afford. Such excesses may distract you for the moment, but you're only substituting a new, larger problem for the one that got you down in the first place.

We should emphasize that alcohol is particularly troublesome when you're down. As a depressant drug, alcohol has chemical properties that may make you feel even worse than before. Since it lowers inhibitions, alcohol also increases the likelihood of risky or self-destructive acts, such as unprotected sex or suicide attempts.

Q: How about more serious, lasting depression? Is there anything I can do on my own?

A: Yes. One method, popular among counselors and therapists, is to identify and challenge self-defeating thoughts and beliefs. According to this "cognitive" approach, depression is caused by talking yourself into disturbed feelings and self-defeating behaviors. You have distorted, negative views about yourself, the world and the future, you repeat these views to yourself, and that's why you're depressed. What's more, these internal communications are so familiar, so automatic, that you may not be aware of them; you're giving yourself subliminal messages to be unhappy. To battle depression, then, you need to replace the messages.

The first step with the cognitive approach is to discover your depression-inducing thoughts. So pay close attention next time you feel down or discouraged. What thoughts were crossing through your mind? What were your thoughts when your down mood began? Keep a written record of these thoughts. The goal is to expose hidden thinking to the bright light of conscious awareness.

Next, evaluate the thoughts. How realistic do they look on paper? Chances are you'll notice that your thinking isn't really objective or reasonable. Specifically, you may find yourself falling into some of the following problem thinking patterns:[4]

- *Dwelling on the negative*: You zero in on the negative aspects of a situation while downplaying or explaining away positive details:
  "Sure I got three B's, but that D is going to ruin my average."
  "I only got an A because the test was easy."
  "He's only being nice because he feels sorry for me."
  "She only goes out with me because she doesn't really know me very well."
- *Thinking in all-or-nothing terms*: You interpret things as all-good or all-bad. Either you perform perfectly (which is unlikely) or you perform horribly; events are either completely wonderful (also unlikely) or they're terrible:
  "I said something stupid in that seminar. The whole class must think I'm an idiot."
  "I've gained five pounds. Now, I'm so fat!"
  "Jan and I had a fight. That's the end of our friendship."
- *Overgeneralizing*: You draw general conclusions based on minimal information. Absolute-sounding words like "always," "never," "only," "just," "everyone," "everything" and "completely" are clues to this type of thought:
  "I knew I wouldn't make the tennis team. I always screw up at tryouts."

"This C proves it. I never do anything well at college."
"Of course Vicki wouldn't go out with me. Everyone thinks I'm a loser."

- *Catastrophizing*: You expect the worst outcomes imaginable and dwell on disastrous future possibilities:
  "I'll never make any good friends here."
  "What if I fail this test?"
  "My parents will blow up when they see my grades."
  "What if I never make it to medical school?"

- *Overassuming*: In the absence of real proof, you assume you know what people are thinking and feeling. In particular, you assume their actions have personal, negative meaning for you. (Taken to an extreme, overassuming becomes paranoia):
  "Mike didn't call me tonight. He must think I'm boring."
  "Serena is always talking to that other guy. I bet she wants to go out with him."
  "Alice didn't return my sweater yet. She probably plans to keep it."

- *Having unrealistic expectations*: You refuse to accept other people, yourself or conditions as they really are. Instead you are so angry and distraught that reality isn't what you want it to be. You use words like "should" and "shouldn't" and phrases like "it's awful," "I can't believe" and "it's not fair" to express your indignation:
  "Larry should treat me better than he does."
  "It's awful that I'm so short."
  "I can't believe this graduate school rejected me."
  "It's not fair that I got sick right before that party."

Once you recognize your negative thinking patterns, the next step is to challenge and replace flawed thoughts whenever they occur. Counter each one by asking yourself, "Is this an accurate view of the situation?" and "Am I being fair and reasonable?" Then replace the original thought with a realistic alternative. In other words, use your reasoning abilities to restore perspective and ward off depression.

Q: How can I use this cognitive approach?

A: Here's an example:

When Monica didn't smile as they crossed paths on campus, Jerry kept thinking about her expression (dwelling on the negative) and concluded that she didn't like him anymore (overassuming). He overlooked their recent friendly talk, and never considered the possibility that she hadn't noticed him or might be preoccupied with something else. Dwelling on the incident, he decided that most people didn't like him (overgeneralizing) and that something was wrong with him (more overgeneralizing).

To apply the cognitive approach, Jerry would recognize these thoughts, identify the errors they contain and replace them with constructive, realistic alternatives. His reasoning might go like this: "Wait! Am I being realistic here? Do I really know what Monica was thinking when she passed me? Usually when I see her she's friendly, so there's no reason to assume that she doesn't like me anymore. And there's certainly no reason to dwell on this little thing or conclude that I'm unpopular. Maybe she was preoccupied. Next time I see her I'm going to go up and talk to her."

Q: What else can I do to fight depression?

A: Check out the suggestions listed in the stress management section on pages 82–84. Some of those ideas also may help with depression. Reducing an overcrowded schedule may work; so may adding meaningful activities to an unchallenging schedule. Regular exercise, healthy eating and plenty of sleep are also recommended.

Depression is also often associated with social isolation. Although some solitude is good for you, too much time spent alone is demoralizing and can spawn irrational thinking. (Solitary confinement is used as the ultimate in prison punishment.) If, then, you can make one friend, or schedule even a single social activity, you may give yourself a vital boost. For tips on social skills, review the material in Chapter 1.

None of these measures is sure-fire. Besides, you may not feel up to them; you may be too depressed to act. If you can try them, though, you may experience relief from depression.

Q: What can I do to prevent mood swings?

A: Again, it depends on the severity. Some emotional variability comes with being human. You think diverse thoughts, you have ever-changing experiences and so naturally you have shifting moods. So for minor ups and downs, nothing special needs to be done.

For more frequent or pronounced emotional swings (perhaps an objective friend can help you recognize them), we recommend trying the cognitive approach explained above. All-or-nothing thinking, over-generalizations, unrealistic expectations and other flawed thoughts can send you on an emotional roller coaster. Substituting realistic thoughts can restore your emotional equilibrium.

On the subject of realistic expectations, it's particularly important to prepare yourself for changing fortunes. Life, after all, is a deliverer of mixed messages. In any given week, count on it that some people will be friendly and others cool, on some matters you'll shine and on others you'll screw up. Inevitably, good, bad and indifferent are all coming your way. If you learn to expect these fluctuations, you won't do emotional flip-flops when they happen.

As an additional suggestion, we encourage building routines or habits into your schedule. Practice consistency in your sleeping schedule, eating habits, exercise program and times of study and leisure. Don't hit the books for 10 hours and then blow off the next three days (while perhaps drinking too much). Don't binge today and starve yourself tomorrow. Consistent practices will cause you to view yourself evenly, and that in turn may stabilize your moods.

SELF-ESTEEM

Q: But I just don't like myself very much. Why should I?

A: How you feel about yourself takes into account your entire lifetime of experiences. Certainly your parents and siblings have done their share to mold your self-image. If they've harshly criticized you, then you may internalize their messages, converting their disapproval into self-disapproval. Teachers, peers and others have also left their mark on you. In addition, you've been your own judge through the years, evaluating yourself at reading, riding a bicycle, swimming or running, driving a car, more recently at fitting in at college, doing your coursework and finding new friends. All those countless times when you've thought "I did great" or "I'm lousy" are evidence you've used to decide what sort of person you are.

It's important to recognize, however, that self-esteem is not a uniform judgment. You may not generally feel competent at doing things but still feel that you're well liked and lovable, or maybe it's the other way around. And even if you don't feel particularly competent or popular, still surely there are many things about yourself that you give a passing grade. Perhaps you don't like your body but do think your smile is attractive; perhaps you don't think of yourself as a funny person but you have a good way with animals and small children. Everyone can find some points about themselves to like and to dislike.

Q: What can I do to improve self-esteem?

A: We do have some suggestions, but you'll need to be patient waiting for results. After all, your feelings about yourself have had two decades to take root. Here, then, are things you can try:

- Employ the cognitive approach described above to identify and replace self-belittling thoughts. For example, do you dwell on your faults and discount your strengths? Do you overgeneralize from a single setback and conclude that you're worthless? Do you disparage yourself for failing to be perfect? Such negative thinking erodes self-esteem. Watch out for these thoughts; you may find they come up often. Challenge them each time they appear, and in their place substitute fairer, more realistic self-appraisals.
- In order to acknowledge your strengths, take an inventory of your positive points. What do you like about yourself? What would others say they like about you? For example, let's say you're a responsible person. When you say you'll do something, it gets done, conscientiously and on time. You may be straightforward and honest as well—you don't play games. These are valuable qualities that can be the cornerstone of self-esteem, but most likely you haven't valued them enough. So write down on a piece of paper all your assets, large and small: "Responsible. Friendly. Sympathetic. Honest. . ." Study this list. From it you may start to appreciate some of the things that make you worthwhile.
- It may sound odd, but it also helps to catalog your negative points. So consider your shortcomings. In what ways are you deficient? How would others say you should improve? Be as honest as you can, neither exaggerating nor glossing over the truth, and write down what you find. Carrying out this exercise helps build esteem because it shows you can look at yourself honestly and unflinchingly. It feels good to know there's nothing so horrible about you that you can't admit it, nothing so dreadful that you can't still look yourself in the eye.
- Consider again the list of negatives and separate out the ones you can't change. For example, are you unhappy with your height? Your basic body type? Your sexual orientation? Your family's circumstances? A learning disability? These are the givens in your life, the cards you've been dealt. Though it's easier said than done, work on accepting these conditions. Reconcile yourself to your limitations. If you can live with them, not blaming yourself, cursing the fates nor

wishing you were somehow different, you'll have taken a big step toward self-acceptance.

- Now, take action on the things you want to change. To like who you are, rational thinking is not enough; you also have to behave in constructive ways. This doesn't mean you have to become an A+ student or captain of the football team (those people may not necessarily like themselves either). It does mean, however, that you have to be proud of your efforts. You have to develop skills, take care of basic responsibilities and not run away from important challenges. All in all, you have to respect what you do. It all sounds so simple— "Behave constructively"—yet surprisingly many students fail to grasp the principle. If you like what you do, you will like yourself; if you don't like your actions, you won't.

- So examine where you've been slacking off. Are you badly out of shape? Start jogging again. Is your room a mess? Try organizing the chaos. Have you neglected to write to your high school friends at another school? Drop them a note. Every time you behave constructively, even in small matters, you earn a dividend in self-esteem.

Q: But if I start building up self-esteem, won't I become conceited?

A: We doubt it. In fact, often it's the people who don't like themselves who are the conceited ones. They have an exaggerated sense of their own importance or abilities, or at least they try to convince you they're something special, because they're compensating for inner feelings of inadequacy. In contrast, people who have self-esteem are comfortable with their real selves, warts and all. Because they basically like who they are, they don't have to inflate their importance. So it's safe to work on building your self-esteem; you won't turn into an egotistical monster.

Q: I keep hearing this voice saying, "You're stupid, you can't do this, you're a jerk." Why do I do this to myself?

A: Our bet is that you learned it from someone in your past. If you listen carefully to the voice, you may recognize the words or intonation of a critical parent or sibling, or hear again the teasing you got at school. You're now saying to yourself what used to be said to you.

Oddly enough, you also may *want* to criticize yourself. Your harsh words may be intended to goad you to action ("Try harder, stupid!") They may be a backhanded way of declaring that you're really wonderful. (Thinking "I'm so dumb" when you get a B+ implies that you really consider yourself an A student.) Self-criticism can also be meant to inoculate you from outside criticism. Since you've already said the worst to yourself, you feel no one else's negative words can hurt you.

Despite such subtle motives, you still probably don't enjoy this critic inside your head. To rid yourself of it, we recommend the same cognitive strategy we outlined for eliminating other negative thinking patterns: Make yourself aware of the self- criticisms. Challenge unfair statements—talk back! Substitute fair self-assessments in their place.

It also may help to imagine being a parent someday. Do you want to criticize, find fault, always harp on the negative with your child? Or do you hope to be a supportive parent, patient and encouraging when your son or daughter takes on a challenge? We assume you agree the second way is better. The question now becomes why you'd be any less humane toward yourself than toward your child. Why do you mistreat the child inside of you—we all have one—when you know that method is wrong?

If you can, try to be a good parent to yourself. Like a child, you too will perform better and feel happier if you are told "Come on, you can do it" rather than "You can't do this, stupid."

IDENTITY

Q: I'm in a slump. I feel like I don't really know who I am.

A: That feeling, like low self-esteem, is common in people your age and can be another source of depression. According to Erik Erikson, the renowned psychoanalyst, identity concerns are characteristic of people from adolescence through the college years. Erikson explained that a sense of identity is complex, incorporating many dimensions—career direction, political and philosophical views, comfort with one's body, a sense of oneself sexually and in relationships.[5] Discovering yourself in all these areas and putting these "pieces" together is a slow and sometimes difficult process. It's natural at your age still to question who you are, and sometimes to feel rather uncomfortably confused.

Besides your youth, the college experience itself also can cause self-uncertainty. At college you are exposed to other students, professors and writers who call into question your ideas and beliefs. Your classmates come from differing backgrounds and have differing values and practices. You have more decisions to make than before, more responsibilities, more freedom. All in all, there's a lot going on that can shake your earlier convictions.

Although questions of identity are not unusual, some students have a more severe form of this problem—an identity disorder. These students have a basic deficiency in their sense of self. Without getting too technical, suffice it to say that they haven't psychologically developed in a normal fashion; they're out of touch with their own feelings and attitudes, wishes and needs, interests and values. This problem can be traced to early childhood, and it requires professional assistance.

Q: If I act inconsistently, does that mean *I've* got an identity disorder?

A: Probably not. All of us have various facets to our personalities. We might act silly with a friend, feel serious with an elder, express our emotional side with a loved one. Each situation and each individual may draw out subtly distinct aspects of our many-sided selves. As long as there's an overarching sense of "I" embracing these components, then there's nothing abnormal about this. There's still a basic organizing principle—a self—that contains the many parts. As the poet Walt Whitman wrote: "Do I contradict myself?/Very well then I contradict myself,/(I am large, I contain multitudes.)"

Q: How can I figure out or shape my identity?

A: There's no one foolproof method. Actually, the process of identity formation isn't fully conscious anyway; mostly it happens as a byproduct of life experience. However, most of the tips we've already suggested concerning depression, mood swings and self-esteem are also applicable to identity formation. We've separated these topics for purposes of discussion, but in actuality they are closely related. So if you're working on avoiding emotional slumps or on steadying your moods or on having a good opinion of yourself, you're also inevitably working on developing a sense of identity.

In addition to these efforts, we recommend pursuing creative interests. Writing, drawing or painting, taking up dance or doing any other creative activity can aid self-discovery. Relationships can also help you form your identity. Becoming close to a friend or a romantic partner helps you discover and develop aspects of yourself. Another idea is to keep a diary or journal. The process of writing down thoughts and capturing reactions to experiences helps you learn who you really are.

COUNSELING AND MEDICATIONS

Q: How do I know if I should see a counselor for one of these problems—depression, severe mood swings, low self-esteem or identity confusion?

A: One test is duration. If you've felt depressed for several weeks or more, or if you've had many episodes of depression during the past few years, then consult a counselor. The same holds true if your mood swings, self-esteem or identity problem has been troubling you for a long time.

A second test is lack of success resolving the problem through your own efforts. If you're getting nowhere on your own, then by all means turn to a professional.

And a third test is other people's concern about you. Depressed people are often unable to recognize their condition. Therefore if a friend, RA, parent or professor voices concern, we suggest taking the warning seriously and getting a professional opinion.

Q: I feel so depressed I can't believe I will ever get better, even with counseling.

A: You probably will, though. Most cases of pronounced depression eventually run their course—especially when they're professionally treated. The trouble is, time passes slowly and the future seems hopeless when you're depressed, so of course it's difficult to imagine feeling better. But try to remind yourself that depression is skewing your current thinking. You can eventually improve, even if that seems hard to believe right now.

Q: If I see a counselor about depression, will I be given medication?

A: In the great majority of cases the answer is no. The combination of support and insight that counseling provides is sufficient.

Sometimes, though, the "talking cure" may not be enough. Certain cases of depression—notably, major depressions—may not get better promptly without the aid of medication; the same goes for manic-depressive disorder. Often these conditions respond best to a combination of psychotherapy and a prescribed drug. However, you should know that a few professionals do question the advisability of drugs and whether they help or harm the process of counseling.

There are dozens of antidepressant medicines, with new ones introduced regularly. Adding to the confusion, each drug has both a chemical name and a brand name. Among the antidepressants, the most popular class has long been the tricyclics. Examples are amitriptyline (one brand name is Elavil), desipramine (Norpramin), doxepin (Sinequan) and imipramine (Tofranil). Another class of antidepressants, the MAO inhibitors, are prescribed for so-called "atypical" depressions (patients eat and sleep too much) or if the tricyclics don't work; examples are phenelzine (Nardil) and tranylcypromine (Parnate). A new, highly touted antidepressant is Prozac. Time will tell whether it's as helpful as some enthusiasts claim.

To stabilize extreme mood swings (manic-depressive disorder), the drug of choice is lithium, which has a similar chemical composition to table salt. Unlike the antidepressants listed above, lithium prevents you from getting either too high or too low. Usually people stay on lithium for many years or even a lifetime. It has to be closely monitored through periodic blood samples.

Antidepressants work by altering the levels of brain chemicals, called neurotransmitters. Though each drug is known to operate differently, the exact mechanism of action is not always clearly understood. When effective, antidepressants improve a person's mood within roughly 10 to 14 days.

Q: Won't I grow dependent on them if I take one of these drugs?

A: No, these drugs are not the type that lead to physical dependency. You may stay on them out of choice, but not because you become addicted.

Q: Does taking a drug mean I'm crazy?

A: Absolutely not. Medications are simply aids intended to help you feel better and think more clearly.

Q: What about side effects?

A: This is a serious issue. All drugs have potential side effects. A particular drug may cause you to gain weight, feel drowsy or have headaches or a dry mouth; it depends on the drug and your individual reaction. Therefore you and your counselor (or prescribing doctor) need to consider side effects carefully before you undertake drug treatment, balancing possible benefits against potential problems.

Sometimes side effects can be reduced or eliminated by changing the dosage, switching medications or using a combination of medications.

When taking a prescribed drug, you should never take any other prescribed or nonprescribed drugs, including alcohol, without your doctor's assurance that the combination is safe. Drugs tend to interact with each other in unpredictable and sometimes dangerous ways. The MAO inhibitors require dietary restrictions. It's unsafe with an MAO inhibitor to drink beer or wine or eat certain foods such as some meats and cheeses.

Q: What if the antidepressant my doctor gives me isn't working and I want to stop taking it?

A: Then talk to your doctor. There's no reason to take something that's ineffective or uncomfortable. You should take an active role in your drug therapy, asking questions, reporting your reactions and stating your preferences. However, don't go off the medicine or change the dosage without consulting with the doctor.

SUICIDE

Q: This girl down the hall swallowed a bottle of pills last year and had to be hospitalized. What would get her to the point of trying to kill herself?

A: We assume there was an immediate crisis in her life or a buildup of problems. Perhaps a boyfriend broke up with her, she had an unwanted pregnancy, her grades were dropping or her parents were getting a divorce. Along with the objectively serious situation, no doubt her reasoning abilities were impaired, too. Suicidal thinking, it's been found, involves a narrowing of options, a tunnel vision, so that suicide is seen as the only solution to ending psychological pain. The person regards his or her situation in either-or terms: "Either my problem resolves itself, or there's no reason to live."

For example, Andy, a political science major in his junior year, told his roommate about suicidal feelings after he failed a history midterm. His reasoning process had narrowed dangerously: "I have to get at least a B in this course to get into law school. I have to become a lawyer, since that's been my plan since I was little and that's what my parents and friends expect of me. If I botch up this course, all my plans will be ruined—I might as well end my life."

Another contributing cause to a suicide attempt, besides current problems and impaired reasoning, is the desperate wish to get help. Suicidal persons often don't know appropriate ways to signal their distress. They've learned, usually because of unhappy childhood experiences, that nobody responds when they're in pain. Suicide, then, affords a dramatic method to get attention—nobody can ignore their suffering now. Sometimes the desperation for help is mixed with feelings of rage or vengefulness. The person thinks, "When I die, you'll be sorry."

Another point we should stress is that college students who attempt suicide are often acting impulsively rather than carrying out a long-planned event. Typically they are reacting to an immediate disappointment—perhaps a fight with parents or a romantic breakup—which before long will fade in significance. That's why it's critical to take action when a classmate feels suicidal. If you can stop the person now, before long he or she probably will feel better and very much want to live.

Q: Lately I've been worried about a friend who seems very depressed. How can I tell if he's suicidal?

A: There are a number of warning signals. Look for the following:

- Hints about suicide or death: "You won't see me for long." "Maybe I'll kill myself" [even if said jokingly]. "I wish I were dead." "I'm going away for a long time."
- Withdrawal from friends, family and favorite activities.
- Signs of depression mentioned at the beginning of this chapter.
- Giving away of prized possessions.
- Alcohol and other drug use (they lower inhibitions and so greatly increase the likelihood of acting on a suicidal impulse).
- History of suicide in the family, or a recent suicide by a relative or friend.
- Self-destructive behavior—accidents, reckless driving, getting into trouble on campus or with the police.
- A dramatic falling off in grades, personal hygiene and responsibilities, as if the person is saying, "I don't care anymore."
- Recent severe stresses, such as romantic breakups, failing grades, parents' divorce or death of a parent.
- Previous suicide attempts.

Q: But people who talk about killing themselves don't really do it, right?

A: On the contrary, most suicide attempters reveal their intentions beforehand, although usually in disguised fashion. The sad part is, their warnings often are ignored. Since just talking about suicide doesn't get others to take them seriously, they feel desperate and carry out the threat.

Another myth about suicide is that you don't have to worry about people who've made a previous attempt—obviously they didn't really want to die. In fact, many people who take their own lives have made one or more previous attempts.

Q: If my friend is at risk of suicide, what should I do?

A: The first step is to sit down with him and ask what's wrong. Show by your patience and concern that you won't be brushed off with a curt "Nothing, I'm fine." Lead up to the topic of suicide and then, when you're both talking very frankly, ask the direct question, "Have you been thinking of killing yourself?" Don't be afraid to use these very words. Suicidal persons appreciate another's willingness to speak openly about suicidal feelings and intentions. By the way, there's no danger that you'll give your friend the idea of suicide simply by asking about it; if he's not feeling suicidal, your questioning won't drive him to it. If anything, your questions reduce the risk of suicide because he has a chance to talk out his concerns.

How you respond next depends on his answers. If he convincingly reassures you that your fears were groundless, then you don't have to take further action. But if he admits to having suicidal wishes, or if his answers are evasive or unconvincing—if you are left with any doubts at all—then you should promptly alert someone else, an RA, residence hall manager, dean or counselor. Most colleges have a residence hall manager and counselor available around the clock; your campus security office can help you locate them. The person you alert is trained to see that your friend is evaluated and helped.

The cardinal principle is to take your own fears and intuitions seriously. Don't dismiss suicidal signs you've observed and tell yourself, "No, it's not possible." And when you speak to your friend, don't dismiss doubts you have about his answers. Joking, evasive denials and ambiguous statements are not sufficient. Make sure he's said in so many words that he's definitely not planning to kill himself. Make sure you're 100% convinced. Otherwise, get help.

Q: My roommate asked if she could trust me to keep a secret, I said yes, and then she told me that she wants to kill herself. What should I do?

A: The value of human life far outweighs the importance of keeping a secret. Even after making the promise, you still need to inform someone in authority. Otherwise you'll be burdened by a terrible responsibility that no college student ought to shoulder. Your studies and peace of mind will be ruined, and you'll be afraid to leave your roommate's side. And if she does kill herself, you'll end up feeling terribly guilty.

For both your sakes, immediately tell someone in authority that she is thinking about suicide.

Q: Suppose after I tell a college authority it's decided that she continue to remain in our room with me?

A: Then you can relax. Her remaining in your room would mean that professionals have determined she's not at risk of killing herself. Of course, professionals are not infallible. It's conceivable that she might say or you might observe something next week or in several months that suggests she is feeling suicidal again, in which case once more you should alert someone in authority. Generally speaking, however, once you've contacted school officials, you should not feel obliged to continue watching over her, and you should not feel obliged to be her counselor. Once the professionals are involved, it's their job, not yours, to guarantee her safety.

It's likely your roommate may resent you for a while for reporting your fears. Ultimately, though, most students in her situation are grateful. They recognize the caring and concern that motivated you to get professional help.

Q: Jenny, who lives on my hall, threatened to cut her wrists last night. I'm the only one who knows. She begged me not to tell anyone, saying she's really okay now, and her parents would take her out of school if they found out. Should I leave well enough alone?

A: Again, the answer is no. Jenny's response is quite typical of suicidal people, who often resist any intervention and ask others to do the same. However, you're in no position to judge if Jenny really is in the clear. You should contact a school official immediately.

Q: I sometimes think about suicide. Does that mean I'm likely to go through with it someday?

A: Probably not. Practically every one of us has wondered about suicide. College students wonder more than most, since late adolescence and early adulthood are times of asking large questions about the meaning of life and one's own identity. But we need to draw a sharp distinction between thoughts and behaviors, between casual reflections and serious intentions. So long as you're not at all tempted to act on your thoughts, you are not in danger. This doesn't mean your suicidal thoughts are unimportant. They may be a sign of depression, as we mentioned earlier, and therefore, to be on the safe side, you may want to consult a counselor. However, so long as you know you wouldn't carry out a suicidal thought, then it's most unlikely that you'll do it.

The time to start worrying—and get help—is when your suicidal thoughts cross over into serious, hard-to-control urges, or when you find yourself thinking of ways to carry it out. Likewise if thoughts about suicide are persistent and won't go away, it's time to seek professional help.

Q: Two years ago I took an overdose, and I've been having strong suicidal urges again. I know I should seek counseling, but I don't see how that will help me get over the wish to kill myself.

A: Fortunately, almost nobody has a 100% wish to end his or her life. It's usually 60 : 40, or even 51 : 49. The fact that you've resisted recent suicidal impulses says loud and clear that a strong part of you clings to hope and wants to live. It's that life-affirming side of you that counseling can support and reinforce.

Counseling can help you see your situation in perspective. You can be assisted to widen your field of vision beyond your immediate problems. Counseling can give you empathic support during a lonely time, and encourage you to get support from others. Additionally, your counselor can teach you coping methods to resist suicidal impulses. For example, you may learn when you feel suicidal to call a friend, arrange for an immediate visit to your family or get someone to take you to the hospital.

Since inevitably you will continue to encounter both good and bad in life, the key to overcoming suicidal impulses is not to solve all your problems. Rather, the answer lies in a fundamental change inside of you. You must learn to make an inner pact, a binding decision, that in spite of problems you won't use suicide as a way out. You need to hold onto this decision even when the going gets tough. The decision won't come about all at once. It will take hard work in counseling before you're ready to give up the option of suicide once and for all.

FOR FURTHER READING:

A. Alvarez, *The Savage God: A Study of Suicide.* New York: Random House, 1970.

Jeffrey Berlant, Irl Extein, and Larry Kirstein, *Guide to the New Medicines of the Mind.* Summit, N.J.: PIA Press, 1988.

David Burns, *Feeling Good: The New Mood Therapy.* New York: Morrow, 1980.

DEALING WITH ANXIETY, INDECISION, ANGER AND STRESS

In this chapter, we take up a quartet of related problem areas. Anxiety, the first, is similar to fear. Both are unpleasant reactions felt in anticipation of danger, with both a psychological side (apprehension, uneasiness, worry), and a physical side (trembling, pounding heart, sweating). They are normally distinguished in that anxiety, unlike fear, tends to be brought on by something ill-defined, irrational or unrecognized. You know what frightens you but you don't necessarily know why you're anxious—and that can make you more anxious still.

Anxiety is an inescapable part of the human condition. It's not necessary to read existential philosophers or Sigmund Freud to know this; just observe your own rapid heartbeat whenever you make a speech in class, talk to someone you're attracted to or walk into an exam. But just because anxiety can't be eliminated doesn't mean it must reach crippling dimensions or cause intolerable suffering. You can learn to reduce disabling anxiety and deal with moderate anxiety. In the following pages, we describe the major anxiety concerns troubling college students—panic attacks, speech anxiety, phobias, obsessions and compulsions, nightmares and chronic worry—and we suggest ways to cope with them.

Our next three problem areas—indecisiveness, anger and stress— are also inevitabilities. It's almost inconceivable that you could make it through a single term, much less your whole college career, without feeling stuck sometimes on a decision, or furious with someone, or stressed out. It helps to think of these difficult occasions as opportunities to develop coping skills that will serve you throughout life. You can learn how to make decisions, handle anger and manage stress, and in these pages we make a number of suggestions with those aims in mind.

ANXIETY

Q: Several times recently my heart started to race and I began to tremble. I thought I was having some kind of attack and going to die. What's wrong with me?

A: It sounds as if you're having panic attacks—sudden episodes of intense anxiety. Panic attacks consist of dramatic, uncomfortable symptoms like shortness of breath, dizziness, racing heart, sweating, stomach distress and hot flashes or chills. They arise so suddenly, powerfully and inexplicably—you never know when they're coming—that you may be convinced you're going crazy, are losing control or are about to die. But panic attacks aren't a sign of insanity or losing all control, and they're not medically dangerous. They're basically an intense form of anxiety.

Q: What can I do to avoid ever having one again?

A: For starters, you shouldn't make that your goal. When you tell yourself "Never again," you make yourself worry about a recurrence, and the worry itself tends to bring one about. And if you do have another panic attack, your dread of it adds to its intensity. So don't fight against panic attacks; try not to fear your fear. Instead, here are some responses recommended by experts:

- Adopt an accepting attitude toward panic attacks. Tell yourself beforehand and during the attack itself that you can endure it: "I can handle this." Let anxiety come and run its course. (Panic attacks usually last only a few minutes).
- Oppose irrational, catastrophic thinking during attacks ("This is so weird!" "I'm going crazy!" "I'm out of control!") by giving yourself reminders of what is really happening: "These are only anxiety symptoms—nothing more." "I'm not in danger; I'm not losing control." "I'm completely safe here in my room." The more you can steady your thoughts, the calmer you'll feel.
- To grow more comfortable with panic-like symptoms such as a racing heart, you can deliberately induce these symptoms by running up stairs or breathing rapidly, or you can picture yourself having a

panic attack. Once your heart is beating rapidly or you're out of breath, the next step is to calm yourself with soothing, constructive thoughts like the ones given above. This exercise is a trial run giving you practice for coping with the real thing. (If these trials bother you, discontinue them.)

- Similarly, during the panic attack itself you can experiment with *increasing* your symptoms. Tell yourself to sweat more, to shake harder, to let your heart pound even faster. With this technique you not only accept anxiety, you invite it, which paradoxically reduces anxiety because you feel in control. How bad can these symptoms be if you welcome them?

- Learn to take slow, deep, regular breaths from the belly. Panic attacks are often associated with either excessive breathing (hyperventilation) or holding your breath. In contrast to these extremes, slow, deep, rhythmic breathing counteracts the physical symptoms of anxiety (midwives have known this for years). It also may help to say to yourself "Relax" each time you exhale.

- Train your attention on something outside of yourself: a chair, children playing outside the window, the person you're with, a popular song. With your mind otherwise engaged, you won't feed your panic by worrying about the symptoms.

- Get a medical checkup. Odds are your symptoms have a psychological rather than a physical basis, but occasionally panic-like symptoms are brought on by a medical condition, medication or withdrawal from medication, premenstrual syndrome, mitral valve prolapse (a heart disorder) or—rarely—hypoglycemia, (low blood sugar).

- Don't turn to alcohol for relief from anxiety. Not only do you risk developing an alcohol problem, but heavy drinking can cause a hypoglycemic reaction that 12 hours later produces panic symptoms. One student we know drank 10 beers every night to stave off panic attacks. To his surprise, once he stopped his drinking, the panic attacks eased up too.

- Experiment with eliminating coffee, tea and cola drinks. The caffeine they contain is a stimulant that can cause anxiety and even panic.

Q: Suppose nothing I try relieves my panic attacks?

A: That may happen. Panic attacks can be rooted in underlying psychological conflicts, irrational thought patterns or an inherited susceptibility. In these cases, the above remedies may not suffice.

If underlying conflicts or irrational thought patterns are the problem, psychological counseling may be needed (although you can work on your own to correct negative thinking, as we discuss later). In counseling, you may discover that you have a panic attack whenever there's a hint of anger—yours or someone else's—or perhaps whenever you feel attracted to someone from the same sex. Maybe you panic because you overreact to stressful situations—thinking "I'm going to fail," for example, when coursework piles up—or because you expect the worst from other people. Understanding such themes demystifies panic attacks. Instead of seeing the attacks as a curse visited on you for no reason, you realize they're a predictable reaction given what you fear and how you think. Understanding the meaning of the attacks may then lead to their disappearance.

We're not drug-happy, as we explained in Chapter 3, but if all else fails another recourse is drug therapy. Several of the common antidepressant medications appear to reduce and sometimes eliminate panic attacks. You need to work closely with your doctor to discuss possible side effects, interactions with other substances and other implications of drug treatment.

Q: Whenever I have to make a speech in class I get sweaty palms and a dry mouth, my heart goes a mile a minute and I want to run out the door. Does this happen to other people?

A: It certainly does. Of all human fears, stage fright, or performance anxiety, is the most common. Almost everyone feels a little uncomfortable standing in front of an audience, and many others besides yourself have a hellish time of it. Performance anxiety, which includes such situations as playing music in public, or even going to an interview, is one example of what professionals call social phobia, in which you're afraid to be observed by others because of possible embarrassment and humiliation. If we count shyness (see pages 12–13), social phobias are quite widespread.

Q: What can I do about speech anxiety?

A: To combat speech anxiety, or anything else you fear, first you must make up your mind to hang in there and confront what frightens you. No matter how anxious you are, resolve to speak in front of groups. This approach is called "exposure therapy," and it is based on the simple idea that avoiding a situation perpetuates fear, while facing the situation reduces fear. So look for opportunities to participate in groups or, better yet, to speak to them. Possibilities include participating in classroom discussions, enrolling in a public speaking class, becoming a teaching assistant who leads classroom discussions, or taking a Dale Carnegie class. At first with any of these activities you'll notice your heart pounding, but soon anxiety may taper off as you become familiar with speaking to groups.

A second general strategy to reduce speech anxiety—or again any other fear—is the cognitive approach explained above (see pages 50–52). The idea here is that you can reduce anxiety by challenging negative, irrational thinking and substituting constructive, realistic thinking. To do this, identify the negative statements you make to yourself both before and during a talk: the fears about fear ("Oh no, I'm getting scared again,") the catastrophic thoughts ("Everyone will be bored," "People will know I'm nervous," "I'm going to really screw up") the negative messages ("I can't do this—I have to leave"). In place of these anxiety-producing messages, substitute comforting, constructive statements: "Just relax, you're doing fine." "The anxiety is getting better already." "This isn't so bad." With the cognitive approach, you use your reasoning powers to restore perspective and you coach yourself to a more relaxed performance.

In addition to the main strategies of exposure therapy and the cognitive approach, the following tips may be helpful for speech anxiety:

- Practice your talk beforehand until you know it well. But don't memorize it, because then you'll panic if you forget the exact words.
- Stage dress rehearsals in front of a few supportive friends. If that's not possible, imagine an audience in front of you when you rehearse the speech.
- View your speech as a communication rather than a performance. Your purpose is not to wow your audience, it's to inform them. This mind-set takes the pressure off—you don't have to be a brilliant orator—and allows you to speak naturally.
- Similarly, concentrate during the talk on what you're trying to get across rather than on yourself. If you start paying attention to your voice or your hands, shift your focus back to the message you want to convey.
- Take slow, deep, regular breaths. Don't breathe too fast or stop breathing.
- Remind yourself that observers probably can't tell if you're anxious. Your symptoms of anxiety are much more obvious to you than to anyone else.

- Remind yourself too that anxiety peaks at the beginning of a talk and soon subsides. If you're fearful at the beginning, this is to be expected; it will soon get better. And actually, some initial anxiety is desirable. It means you're up for the task.
- Bring notes with you in case you get lost. But don't read your talk, if possible. Your audience will remain more interested if you talk to them, rather than read to them.
- Speak to one member of the audience at a time. Pick out several friendly faces in different parts of the audience, and direct yourself to them.
- Proceed slowly and easily. The tendency when you're anxious is to hit the fast forward button. Slowing yourself down to normal speed makes for a more effective talk and has the added benefit of calming your nerves.
- Although once again we hesitate to recommend this approach, as a last resort you can ask a doctor to prescribe a medication. A beta blocker such as propanolol reduces racing heart, sweating and other physical effects of speech anxiety or stage fright, and can be taken on an as-needed basis.

Q: I have a different kind of problem. I have to work with rats in my experimental psychology lab, and I'm afraid of them. What should I do?

A: What you've got is called a simple phobia. Simple phobias entail fear and avoidance of a particular situation or object. There are lots of simple phobias, many with fancy Latin-derived names: claustrophobia (fear of closed spaces), acrophobia (fear of heights), mysophobia (fear of dirt) and cynophobia (fear of dogs), to name only a few. Your particular problem has an official-sounding name, too: rodentophobia. (Agoraphobia, in which someone, usually a woman, is terrified of leaving the home, is related to the simple phobias but is more sweeping and crippling.)

To reduce a fear it's necessary to confront it, as we said before, but sometimes it helps to proceed gradually. With phobias, the recommended approach is called "systematic desensitization," in which you create a hierarchy of scary situations and then face them one by one, beginning with the least frightening situation. For example, you might start with the relatively nonthreatening task of staring at the caged animals from across the room. The goal is to be anxiety-free while doing this, so it's recommended that you relax yourself beforehand by using a relaxation technique (see below). After completing this step, next time you might try the slightly more scary step of walking closer to the cage, then next time walking up to it, then several steps later feeling a rat, and eventually placing one on your lap. It's essential with this method that you advance slowly through the hierarchy of situations, feeling comfortable and relaxed every step of the way.

The principle of systematic desensitization can be employed with many things that scare you. Just remember to start slowly, gain confidence and build up gradually to harder tasks.

Q: How can I stop having this fear that my father is going to die?

A: Unwanted thoughts that won't go away are called obsessions. The most common obsessive thoughts concern violence, forbidden acts and doubts about whether you've done something, such as locking the door. The commonsense reaction to obsessions is to try to stop them, which is called suppression. Suppression can be effective in the short term. During a test, for example, it makes sense to block out thoughts about dinner.

As a permanent solution for obsessions, though, suppression may not work. When you say to yourself, "Don't think about this," on some level you keep yourself aware of the thought, which paves the way for its return. As an experiment, concentrate for a few moments on *not* thinking about dogs. What happens? Chances are you can't help yourself from being dimly aware of something furry that barks.

Rather than forbidding the thought about your father dying, one recommended approach is simply to let the thought pop up when it will. Don't fight it, don't dread it, just allow it to happen. You can even try the paradoxical approach of *making* yourself have the thought; plan sessions of fifteen minutes or so for exactly that purpose. The idea is that permitting or even inviting an unwanted thought keeps it from tormenting you. By accepting the thought, you grow used to it, it can't frighten you, it can even start to bore you—and gradually it may fade away.

Also important is maintaining perspective on unwanted thoughts, seeing them for what they really are. Remind yourself that a thought is not an action, not a prediction. Your father suffers no harm because of what goes on privately in your head. If human beings were held accountable for all the strange, criminal and wayward thoughts that flit through their minds, every last one of us would be in jail. So tell yourself whenever the troubling thought occurs, "It's just a thought. Everyone has strange thoughts. Nothing has really happened to my father. It's okay."

Sometimes obsessions are a sign of psychological conflicts. Consciously you wish your father no harm, but perhaps unconsciously you are angrier at him than you realize. It may take some exploration to uncover such hidden sentiments.

In severe cases of obsessions a person is tormented by unwanted thoughts much of the time and to a disabling degree, interfering with schoolwork. These cases may have a biological basis and require medication. Certainly counseling should be sought.

Q: I know this is crazy, but I sometimes feel driven to do weird things. For example, whenever I enter a building I have to count to 100.

A: What you're describing is a compulsion, a repeated urge to perform a meaningless behavior. Obsessions and compulsions often occur together. For example, the obsessive thought "I'm dirty" may be accompanied by the compulsive ritual of constantly washing your hands. Like obsessions, compulsions are difficult to stop. If you prevent yourself from performing the action, your anxiety level rises. The only way to feel relief is to give in to the impulse.

While some obsessive thinking and compulsive behavior is adaptive and common, especially among bright people (like college students), 1% to 3% of the population suffer severely from these symptoms and have an obsessive-compulsive disorder.[1] This condition, you'll be relieved to know, does not mean you're going crazy. On the other hand, obsessive-compulsive disorder can be long-lasting and disabling.

Two treatments appear to be effective with compulsions. One is drug therapy; several of the newer antidepressant medications relieve obsessive-compulsive symptoms. The second is a behavior therapy technique called "response prevention," in which you deliberately place yourself where you normally perform the ritual, but restrain yourself from performing it. After a period of anxiety, preventing the compulsive behavior may gradually cause it to fade away.

To try response prevention on your own, you need to prevent yourself from counting when you enter a building. Your anxiety level will rise and you'll be sorely tempted to start counting; if you can, ride out these feelings. Later, go in again without counting, and then try it once more. If this is too difficult at first, try the gradual approach by first counting only to 70, then next time to 50, and so forth. Eventually, after enough trials, you may no longer associate the stimulus of the building with the response of counting, and your compulsion may end.

But let us not downplay the gravity of this problem. Compulsions are difficult to stop, and obsessions can be hard to control as well. Obsessive-compulsive disorder, if that's what you have, is a serious condition requiring professional assistance. If you have no success on your own dealing with compulsions or obsessions, you should consult a counselor.

Q: Every week or so I have a nightmare. Does that mean I have deep emotional problems?

A: Probably not. According to recent studies, college students average one nightmare every one or two weeks—the frequency subsides as you get older—and nightmares usually don't betoken psychological disturbance. One exception is if nightmares are the result of a traumatic event, like a severe accident, rape or childhood sexual or physical abuse. Nightmares then are a sign of what's called "post-traumatic stress disorder," and counseling is indicated. Counseling is also recommended if nightmares make you afraid or unable to sleep. Otherwise, bad dreams in and of themselves are probably nothing to worry about.

This is not to say you should dismiss your dreams. Dreams can reveal a lot about yourself; Freud called them the royal road to the unconscious. To understand dreams, your best bet is to write them down immediately and in detail if you woke up, rather than waiting to recall them in the morning (warning: you can lose sleep this way.) Then next day play with possible meanings, paying special attention to feelings (were you angry? scared?) and plot lines (were you trying to go somewhere? get away?). One dream in isolation may not make much sense, but over a series of dreams meanings may emerge.

Q: I'm a worrier. I worry about my grades, my girlfriend breaking up with me, you name it.

A: At least you're aware of your problem, which is one step toward solving it. Many worriers don't step back and observe themselves. They think worry is warranted under the circumstances, missing the fact that they always find something to worry about, whatever the circumstances.

Worry is an easy habit of mind to acquire. If you're at all imaginative, talented at fantasizing and inventing stories, then it's a simple mental exercise to imagine yourself in distress. Worry also serves psychological purposes. For one thing, it gives you the illusion of feeling prepared for the worst. By worrying about bad grades and a breakup, you feel as if you won't be badly hurt if these misfortunes happen. (You still will, though). Also, worry gives you the illusory sense of doing something positive to prevent bad outcomes. It's almost like praying. By worrying you feel that you're working for your happiness somehow; you're putting in effort.

Given these psychological payoffs, it's not easy to break the habit of worrying. However, one approach you can try is the paradoxical technique of deliberately worrying *more*. Make yourself worry, set aside time for it, exaggerate the disasters that can happen to you. Ultimately, the absurdity of so much wasted mental energy may get to you and you'll weary of the effort. Alternatively, you can employ the cognitive approach and give yourself a reality check when you worry: "Are my fears rational? Is there anything else I should do to prepare for this test or to strengthen my relationship? If not, then let me relax about these matters. Further worry is useless." You also may cut down on worry by reducing stress in your life, as we discuss later in this chapter.

INDECISIVENESS

Q: How can I learn to make a decision? I'm going crazy deciding between two majors that both appeal to me.

A: Making decisions is a skill that can be learned. Like any other skill, it improves with practice. Here are our recommended steps for decision making:

1. For important decisions, first gather information. For example, ask the opinions of other students and professors about each major; sample a few readings and attend classes in each. Keep doing this until you have a good—not absolute—understanding of both sides. Once you're at this point, don't prolong information-gathering on the grounds that you don't yet know everything; you'll never get to that point. When you have a good fund of information, go on to the next step.
2. Sit down by yourself to evaluate the information. To bring order to the process, it may help to put down on paper "pro" and "con" columns containing the positives and negatives you see for each choice. It's essential to form your own conclusions here—how do the choices seem to *you*?—rather than parroting other peoples'

views gathered during the first stage. Even if you feel stuck, try not to ask anyone else to evaluate the data for you. A true decision must be your own, based on your own judgment, and it may or may not coincide with what others would have you do.

3. During the evaluation, be prepared for mixed feelings, conflicting thoughts and competing motives, for pro and con columns that are closely matched. You may feel torn between what you "should" do and want to do, or between a safer route and a riskier, more exciting one. You also will feel torn because either choice you take means giving up the other. That's the nature of difficult decisions; they tug at you both ways. Don't wait for a feeling of 100% certainty or an overwhelming mass of evidence all on one side—that rarely happens. Just look for a leaning toward one side or the other.

4. Don't torture yourself asking what is the "right" decision, as if deciding were like a math problem where there's only one correct answer. Decisions involve judgment and feelings; they're not reducible to absolute right and wrong answers. By the same token, don't insist on knowing for certain how each choice may turn out in the future. You're not a fortune-teller; you don't have a crystal ball. You can only go with the information and evaluations you have available in the present.

5. Once you've gathered and weighed all the evidence, let yourself decide. Remember, your task is to make a *good* decision, not the "right" decision, not the sure-to-succeed decision.

6. After you've chosen, try not to second-guess yourself. Having made a tough, sensible, reasoned choice, now support yourself and give it a fair chance. If future events add new information that calls for a change of plans, you can always reconsider; few decisions in life are irrevocable. For now, respect your judgment and support the choice you've made.

Q: That's all very reasonable, but these steps aren't going to work for *me*. I can't even choose what clothes to wear in the morning. What's my problem?

A: It could be a number of things. Depressed students have difficulty making decisions. So do chronically anxious students, who think in catastrophic, "what-if" terms ("What if I change my major and then hate it?") and so resist taking any course of action. Also indecisive are students who have an identity disorder, which we discuss in Chapter 3 (see pages 56–57), and students with hidden psychological conflicts. If you really can't make even little decisions, or if there's a big decision that you feel incapable of making, then you may have one of these difficulties and should consider counseling.

ANGER

Q: I get angry a lot, sometimes outwardly but mostly inside. In my mind I'm always furious and telling somebody off. Why am I like this?

A: Anger is a basic emotion, like sadness and fear and joy, so it's no mystery that you feel it sometimes. Anger can be thought of as a source of energy with both constructive and destructive potential. When properly harnessed, it mobilizes you to correct wrongs and overcome frustrations, to fight for yourself when necessary. But when uncontrolled or misdirected or unrelieved, anger destroys relationships and injures mental and physical health. In recent years, studies have linked chronic anger to heart disease and early death.

Your proneness to anger may have any number of sources, more than we can list here. Certainly, sometimes angry feelings are justified. There's no shortage of selfishness and cruelty in the world, no lack of frustrations. But anger also can be a byproduct of flawed thinking or misinterpretation of events. For example, you may read people's minds and assume they mean you harm, or you may selectively focus on and exaggerate wrongs that they do. If you examine situations closely, you may find that you consistently assign people, whoever they are, to the same depriving or victimizing roles; you always see others in a way calculated to make you angry.

Anger can also grow out of a sense of powerlessness or inferiority. You feel at a disadvantage with someone, this is uncomfortable, and so your mind automatically shifts gears and you become angry. It can be satisfying, in a perverse sort of way, to feel righteously indignant. As still another possibility, you may be angry today because of hurts you were dealt as a child. The rage you originally felt toward your parents, siblings or childhood peers is now displaced onto classmates or professors.

Q: What can I do if I'm often angry?

A: For starters, we recommend being cautious about expressing it. Instead of making you less angry, openly releasing anger tends to make you angrier still—not to mention antagonizing the other party. A better approach if you have a legitimate grievance is to bring it up assertively (see pages 5–6). Focus on the issue of concern and what you want to happen in the future: "John, you forgot to give me the message when my friend called. Next time, please try to remember, okay?" Don't attack, accuse, bring up extraneous issues, threaten or raise your voice. You don't even have to stress that you're angry. Stick to the issue at hand, communicating as one reasonable, well-intentioned adult talking to another.

We also recommend a delay before expressing your concern. Folk wisdom tells you to count to 10 when you're angry; we say take several hours, a day or even longer to get perspective on the issue. Go off by yourself to think, or better yet talk the matter over with an objective friend. This is your chance to apply the cognitive approach of identifying irrational thoughts and replacing them with realistic alternatives: "John probably didn't deliberately forget to give me the message. That's an assumption on my part. He's forgetful, not mean, so I shouldn't get too worked up about this. And it's not that big a deal that he forgot." During this cooling off period you can think through how to deliver an assertive message, if that's what you decide to do.

Since disproportionate anger is often a sign of flawed thinking, poor self-esteem or painful early life experiences, you may not be able to lick this problem on your own. In that case you should consider consulting a counselor.

Q: Being angry makes me so uncomfortable. What can I do to prevent this feeling?

A: To deal with excessive anger, we recommend assertive communications and realistic thinking. But for appropriate anger, whether it's mild annoyance or full-blooded wrath, we have no solutions. You can't simply make feelings go away because you don't approve of them. You can't mold yourself into having only the "right" feelings. As long as you are human, you will have emotional reactions to experience—a succession of feelings will well up—and sometimes this means you'll be annoyed or even angry.

Let us expand on this point. Many people are intolerant of one kind of emotion or another. Those who pride themselves on niceness—perhaps you are one of them—are uncomfortable experiencing any anger. Those who think of themselves as tough tend to reject feelings of sadness, tenderness and fear. Self-sufficient personalities disown their dependent side; dependent personalities are out of touch with their longings for autonomy. All of these strategies are limiting, making people strangers to themselves and cardboard figures to others. When you deny yourself the full range of emotional responsiveness, you chop off part of what makes you human.

So, do work on curbing unrealistic angry thoughts and uncontrolled angry outbursts, if that's a problem. But experience and "own" your anger when you feel it. That way you know the real you and are genuine in relating to others.

STRESS

Q: What is stress?

A: Stress is the arousal of your mind and body in response to the demands of life. Taking tests, keeping up with reading lists and writing term papers cause stress, as do family problems, dating pressures, roommate conflicts and misunderstandings with friends. Stress is unavoidable, and, up to a point, healthy and desirable. Without sufficient stress life lacks zest. Over vacation, for example, you may find yourself feeling restless and unhappy for no apparent reason. The problem may be a lack of challenges to engage you.

Too much stress, however, and you suffer the consequences. That's because stress turns on your body's emergency response system. Your nervous and hormonal systems prepare for fight or flight—your heart, blood pressure and breathing rates speed up, muscles tense, digestion slows—as if you were a caveman threatened by a wild animal. But in today's world, where the challenges come from reading loads and roommates rather than saber-toothed tigers, your emergency response system may not turn off promptly. The stressors keep coming, you can't get rid of them by fighting or fleeing, and so you may remain mentally and physically aroused far longer than is healthy for you.

When stress becomes excessive, the goal is to reduce it to manageable levels. You can do this by cutting down on outside pressures, by inwardly responding to pressures in healthful ways and by learning to relax and develop healthy habits.

Q: How do I know if I'm under too much stress?

A: Look for the following signs:

- You always feel rushed, under time pressure.
- You can't slow down or relax.
- You feel a need to be perfect.

- You're irritable, moody, tense or anxious.
- You can't stop worrying.
- Your mind races; you're caught up in too many details to concentrate well.
- You turn minor matters into major concerns.
- You have difficulty sleeping.
- You have headaches, backaches, an upset stomach, hives or other physical problems.

Q: If I do have some of the signs of stress, what can I do about it?

A: The most straightforward approach is to lighten your load. Pare down external demands until you feel challenged but not overwhelmed. For example, you might drop a course now and pick it up in a later semester, or pass up an extracurricular activity or a standing social obligation. Even minor adjustments can make a difference. Say your roommate is adding to your stress by playing music late at night. Request that he stop the music after a certain hour—be assertive!—and you may start to feel less burdened. Or perhaps you can read assignments two times rather than your customary three, or spend less time than usual listening to your best friend's romantic woes.

For some students, though, cutting back is easier said than done. "I can't drop a thing," they say, explaining why it's absolutely unthinkable not to take 18 credits, visit a dozen friends, run for campus political office, compete on the varsity swim team and do 15 hours per week of volunteer work. If this is you, we suggest stepping back for a moment and examining your motives. Are all your activities truly indispensable? Or do you feel *driven* to do them, compelled by some psychological need?

Specifically, ask yourself these questions: Is your frenetic pace meant to compensate for feelings of inferiority, or emptiness? Are you worried about falling behind your overachieving classmates? Are you frightened to let anything go for fear of never having another chance? Are you afraid that dropping an activity will disappoint others—is it hard to say no? If some such motives are driving you to overextend yourself, you may want to talk it over with a counselor. Once you understand yourself better, perhaps you can slow yourself down to a good cruising speed.

Stress levels vary over the course of the term. Beginnings and endings—times of transition—tend to be especially stressful. At the beginning of the term, you may move into a new room, adjust to a new roommate, buy books, start classes, add and drop classes, seek out advisors—there are a thousand and one details to attend to. At the end, the pressure of final exams and term papers builds to a climax, you may fall behind on work and sleep, and meanwhile you're about to say goodbye to campus friends, return to your family and start a job over the break. Since these periods are inherently hectic, it's especially wise at these times to cut back on pressures in any way you can.

Q: Is it stressful to study too hard?

A: It can be. All work and no play is not a sound regimen; neither is all play and no work. A balanced schedule, like a balanced diet, is healthiest. Recently, one of us counseled an extraordinarily tense freshman who spent virtually all his waking hours in the library. He didn't see friends, he didn't date, he didn't play sports. Ordinarily he would never have gone to a counselor either, except that he hoped it would help him study. After a discussion in counseling, he agreed in the upcoming week to try an experiment. He would cut down on library time and instead visit friends, ask someone out and exercise at the gym. The results were dramatic. When he returned the following week, not only did he report enjoying these other activities, but he also felt less tense and had been able to concentrate at the library.

Q: I don't think I've taken on too many responsibilities, but I still feel rushed and tense. What now?

A: Let's move on to the second main strategy of stress management, the cognitive approach. To review this strategy: First you identify irrational thoughts and beliefs, then you challenge them and substitute realistic alternatives in their place. The cognitive approach can reduce your level of stress by helping you rethink the demands in your life.

For example, suppose you say to yourself, "I have to perform brilliantly, or else my professor won't respect me." Embedded in this one brief string of words is a pair of stress-inducing cognitive errors: all-or-nothing thinking (only brilliance is good enough), and over-assuming (your professor will think ill of you). To counter such flawed thinking, you would identify these errors and then reason as follows: "I don't know for sure what my professor thinks, but probably she'll respect me even if I hand in a flawed assignment. I don't have to be the class valedictorian. Working conscientiously is all I can ask of myself."

As another example, suppose before a job interview you keep saying to yourself, "I know I won't get it, and if I don't get this one I'll never get a good job." Such thinking contains a double dose of catastrophizing, and calls for a sharp rebuttal: "I don't know what will happen on the interview, but I'll give it my best shot. And if this job doesn't work out, another one surely will."

Employing the cognitive approach is like being your own counselor. You talk yourself into keeping perspective and thereby lower your level of stress. When this isn't enough, another option is to talk to someone else—a roommate, friend, parent or counselor. Another person can show you how you've lost perspective on your responsibilities, and it's amazing sometimes what a relief it is just to let out what's troubling you. Finding a sympathetic ear is perhaps the oldest stress reduction method of all, and it's still among the best.

Q: I'm always tense and I get headaches. Will relaxation exercises help?

A: Very possibly. Relaxation techniques are a third major strategy of stress management. Here are some suggestions that may help you relax:

- Practice deep, slow, regular breathing from the abdomen. Do this for 10 or 20 minutes alone in your room, or even for a moment or two in a classroom or at a party. You'll notice an immediate lowering of tension.
- Practice deep muscle relaxation. This involves systematically squeezing and then releasing large muscle groups in the body, one at a time: forehead muscles, jaw, neck, shoulders, each bicep, each forearm, each fist, chest, stomach and so forth. After you tense and then relax each muscle group, pay attention to the sensation. Not only will you feel thoroughly relaxed at the end of this exercise, but you'll learn to recognize tension in any part of your body.
- Alone in a quiet place, seat yourself in a comfortable position. Then, focus on a repeated word or phrase like "peace," "calm" or "let it be," silently reciting it each time you exhale. At the same time, gently let other thoughts, images and feelings drift out of awareness. This form of controlled meditation, practiced for 10- or 20-minute sessions, is described in detail in *The Relaxation Response*.[2]
- When you're distressed, imagine a pleasing scene: a beach, your parents' living room, a friend's face. This method is called relaxation through visualization.

- Relaxation can also be achieved with a warm bath, good book or music. Activities and hobbies are also excellent ways to relax and counter stress. Finally, sometimes you can attain peace of mind simply by "vegging out," doing nothing.

Q: Can an unbalanced diet add to my level of stress?

A: Anything unhealthy increases your stress level. Eating too much, too little, erratically or poorly (junk foods) is stressful. So is not getting enough sleep or keeping wildly irregular sleep habits.

Another contributor to stress is lack of physical exercise. Since stress arouses your nervous and endocrine systems for the exertion of fight or flight, regular exercise provides the physical release that restores your body to a relaxed state. The standard recommendation is at least four or five 20-minute sessions per week of aerobic exercise, such as jogging, swimming, basketball, rowing or biking. Build up to strenuous exercise gradually, and check with a physician if you have a medical condition that makes exercising hazardous.

Q: Sometimes I take a drink or two to relax. Is there any problem with that?

A: Drinking may help in the short run, but it won't change your situation or help you learn new coping skills. The same goes for tranquilizers prescribed by a doctor. Except in severe cases where a psychiatrist may recommend medication, we suggest you refrain from medicating away stress.

FOR FURTHER READING

Herbert Benson with Miriam Z. Klipper, *The Relaxation Response*. New York: Avon, 1975.

Edward A. Charlesworth and Ronald G. Nathan, *Stress Management*. New York: Ballantine, 1982.

John H. Greist, James W. Jefferson, and Isaac M. Marks, *Anxiety and Its Treatment*. New York: Warner, 1987.

Christopher J. McCullough and Robert Woods Mann, *Managing Your Anxiety*. New York: St. Martin's Press (Jeremy Tarcher), 1985.

R. Reid Wilson, *Don't Panic: Taking Control of Anxiety Attacks*. New York: Harper & Row, 1986.

COPING WITH
YOUR FAMILY

Students who go into counseling sometimes grow impatient when questioned about their families. "I came here to talk about my room-mate and study problems," they may say. "What's my family got to do with it?" The answer is that family issues have a long reach. After all, your parents and siblings were your first teachers. They influenced your basic opinions about yourself and the world; they helped create, for good or ill, your capacities for trust, love and independence. Even now, when events back home may seem remote, current family problems still work their influence. You don't slough off two decades of emotional involvement just because you've gone off to college.

Family concerns, then, are important not only in their own right. To understand problems at college, often you must understand what used to happen, and still happens, back home.

The material in this chapter is divided into three sections. First we address "normal" family concerns voiced by students from healthy families. Even good family relationships are strained sometimes, especially when students leave home for college. Next we consider the disruptive consequences of parental divorce and the death of a parent. Lastly, we focus on troubled family interactions and the effects of growing up in a dysfunctional household. Included here are the problems caused by critical or unloving parents, emotionally disturbed parents, alcoholic parents and family sexual abuse.

PROBLEMS OF A "NORMAL" FAMILY

Q: Over Christmas vacation I started fighting with my sister, snapping at my mother and running to my room in tears. I felt 14 years old all over again.

A: Your reaction is not atypical. Maturation is not a straight-ahead march from childhood to adulthood, where you advance step by step and leave behind old ways forever. Psychologically speaking, a 14-year-old still exists within you, and for that matter so does a 7-year-old and a 2-year-old. And there's no one like family to push the buttons that bring out these earlier yous. Your sister's whining, your mother's nagging, the noisy way your father chomps his food—these, for you, are old stimuli that trigger deeply ingrained responses.

Don't be surprised or too concerned if you misplace a few years of maturity when you go back home. Actually, you can even enjoy being a 14-year-old again and take a break from the sometimes confining role of college student. There's something comforting about being with people who still accept you even when your most obnoxious qualities surface.

But if you're really unhappy with yourself at home, make an effort to practice assertive communications (see pages 5–6). Expressing feelings and needs in plain language is one mark of the mature individual. Also, consider if there's anything your family can do to help you behave maturely. For example, request that they *ask* you to do chores rather than order you. If you point out ways they can treat you like an adult, maybe you'll find it easier to act like one.

Q: Why don't my parents see how much I've changed at college?

A: They're at a disadvantage if you live on campus. Not having a chance to observe you regularly, they remember you as you were back in high school. Also, there seems to be a conservative tendency in human nature to expect consistency from others. Since you've acted certain ways before, your parents naturally assume you'll continue acting those ways. Otherwise they'd feel as if they didn't really know you.

Assuming your parents have seen you accurately in the past, their perceptions of you should eventually catch up with reality. After you've spent a long vacation living again at home, they should come to recognize the ways in which you've grown.

Q: My parents say they want me to phone every Sunday night, but sometimes I can't get around to it, or I just don't feel like it.

A: Once a week doesn't seem unreasonable, especially if you're a freshman who's just moved away from home. Your parents understandably want to know that you're alive and hear about your doings. If the every-Sunday arrangement seems too inflexible, maybe you can work out a compromise where sometimes you'll write rather than call, or your calls may have to wait for a Monday or a Tuesday, when it's convenient for *you* to call.

Q: My mom calls me every day, sometimes twice. We've always been close, but I wonder sometimes if we're overdoing it.

A: There are two ways to look at this. The traditional thinking is that college is a time to separate from your family and turn your attention to peers. According to this theory, either you or your mother, or both of you, are finding it hard to let go, and that spells trouble for your personal development. But another way to interpret your closeness is as a blessing. Some students constantly fight with their parents, or hardly speak at all. If you and your mother are best friends, possibly you're just lucky.

So which is it? One test of your relationship is what your mother asks from you. Does she turn to you because she's lonely and unhappy, as if you're her spouse? Does she burden you with her problems, as if you're the parent? If in these ways she asks you to respond to her emotional needs, then the relationship as it stands is not healthy for you. You can't live your own life if you feel responsible for hers.

A second test concerns your involvement in college. Do you call your mother to discuss personal or academic problems instead of reaching out to make friends? Do you shy away from romantic opportunities? Relying on family for emotional fulfillment instead of having a full social life on campus is not in your best interests.

So, the issue is much more complicated than how often you speak on the telephone. You may want to explore any guilt or insecurity associated with becoming less involved with your mother. It also may help to raise the issue with her. She may have insights into your relationship and be sympathetic to your concerns.

Q: Every time my parents ask, I always say everything's "fine." Actually, I'm not doing very well in some classes, but I don't want them getting all bent out of shape. Is it wrong to lie to them?

A: In our opinion, you're entitled to keep some things to yourself, but it's a mistake to lie. Most lies will come out anyway; you can't hide your grades forever. And when your parents catch on to the truth, they'll become suspicious of you and question you even more in the future.

Do your parents pry into your affairs? Then point this out and ask them to let you bring up matters on your own. Tell them you'll keep them posted on what they need to know. Do your parents overreact to your problems? Then explain that their worry and anger make you reluctant to confide in them. Tell them you'll volunteer more if they respond calmly.

Such an honest face-to-face discussion will serve you far better in the long run than attempting a cover-up.

Q: I hate to admit this, but I wish my parents wouldn't come for Parents' Weekend. They speak with a thick accent and they always say and do the wrong thing in public. How can I control them around my friends?

A: Probably you can't. Parents say the darnedest things, and there's little you can do to stop them. If it's any consolation, you're not the only one who's embarrassed by your folks. Even young children, according to Freud, have an adoption fantasy that their real parents were royalty and were replaced by much inferior caretakers.

Will your friends really judge your parents so harshly? Probably not. What to you seems incredibly gauche behavior may just strike your friends as appealing and unpretentious. Besides, your friends will be too preoccupied with their own concerns on Parents' Weekend to give that much thought to your parents.

Here are a couple of tips about making the best of parents' visits to campus:

- Expect strong and possibly conflicting feelings. In addition to possible annoyance or embarrassment, you may experience an upsurge in homesickness; pride and excitement as you show off your college life; or keen disappointment because your parents don't seem equally excited. Expecting such reactions will prevent you from being overwhelmed by the feelings.
- It helps to plan beforehand. Work out the best time for them to come, and discuss what they will do during the visit, where you will

take them, when you will be together and when apart. This will help make your visit more comfortable.

Q: My parents are good people but they're really old-fashioned. I know it hurts them that I'm changing my religious views and attitudes about dating and sex. How should I deal with them?

A: This is a difficult question. Obviously, you don't want to alienate your parents. You also shouldn't take their opinions lightly. Many of their ideas which you now call old-fashioned may eventually, as you gain maturity, start to make sense. To paraphrase Mark Twain, parents can seem ignorant when you're young, but when you get older it's astonishing how much they've learned.

On the other hand, trying out new views is inevitable at college—that's why you go there. You have to do some independent thinking in order to grow up. And in a sense, you show gratitude to your parents when you do rethink your views. They sacrificed to get you an education, and now you are thanking them by figuring things out for yourself.

If you haven't already done so, try explaining what you believe in a frank discussion with your parents. Perhaps the differences between you are less wide than they think. For example, your parents may fear you've become an atheist when actually you're only questioning a few church teachings. They may have exaggerated notions about your sexual exploits and will feel reassured when they learn the truth. Talking openly with them may clear the air.

But some differences can't be explained away. When you and your parents have basic disagreements, our advice, in most cases, is to stick to your guns. Ultimately, you must decide about religion, dating and sex; you have to conduct your life as you see fit. Your parents may disapprove for now, but eventually they'll probably come around. In the long run, most parents accept the fact that their sons and daughters must follow their own natures.

We must qualify this advice in one particular circumstance, however. In some families, and particularly in some cultures, obedience to parents is a paramount virtue. To go against parental wishes, even in adulthood, is deemed wrong and causes enormous guilt. If you've been brought up this way, it will be extremely difficult to oppose your parents' views. In fact, doing so may be the wrong thing to do, since it runs counter to your own deepest values.

To help sort out your thoughts and feelings on this thorny issue, consider consulting a minister, sympathetic professor or counselor.

Q: My oldest sister is the brains in the family, my next sister is the athlete and the next one is creative. There's nothing left for me.

A: Talents and interests aren't like real estate. Your siblings can't claim exclusive ownership of them. No matter how impressive your sisters' accomplishments, you still should explore all your own potentials. You can be a scholar, jock or creative artist—or choose not to—even though your older sisters got there first. You can either follow in their footsteps or take a new path, whether or not you're as successful as they are.

If comparisons to your sisters deter you, it may help to examine and question family messages you have received. Have your parents implied that you shouldn't compete with your sisters, or that you shouldn't compete unless you're their equal? Have your sisters delivered one of these messages? Such family communications can be particularly powerful if you've never stopped to question them. Once you examine the messages, however, you may see that they are unreasonable. You have to follow your own bent regardless of such family expectations.

Some students who feel limited by comparisons to older siblings elect to attend a different college from them. There they feel free to fulfill themselves without being haunted by their siblings' past achievements.

Q: Everyone says I'm exactly like my father and nothing like my mother. Is that unusual?

A: No, it isn't. Quite often children superficially take after one parent much more than the other. These resemblances don't always respect gender lines. A son may be quiet and subdued like his reserved mother, his sister a scene-stealer à la her theatrical father.

Resemblances and differences become a problem only when they become rules of behavior, limiting who you can be. If you feel compelled to be everything your father is—say you must always be strong and in control like him—then you may deny other parts of yourself. The same holds true if you feel compelled to be totally *unlike* your mother; because, say, she gets violent, you never let yourself feel angry.

Similar to your father you may be, but look closely and you'll realize that you are your mother's child as well as your father's child. With genes and parenting from both of them, you can't escape either heritage. But look again and you'll see that you're more than the sum of their influences. Ultimately, you are an individual, complex and unique, not quite like them or anyone else.

Q: Nobody in my family has ever even finished high school. How will that affect me at college?

A: It can be rough being a first-generation college student. Your family can't prepare you for the college experience—you're a pioneer—and they won't fully understand it once you're there. They may unrealistically expect you to make A's easily or imagine the worst about the college social scene. They may even resent you for draining family resources or supposedly putting on college airs.

Since your parents may not be familiar with college life, we advise you to invite them to your school. You may have the opportunity to introduce them to friends and professors, and show them your classes and samples of your work. This way college becomes less alien to them and they can view your experience more realistically. At the same time, it may be helpful for you to find on-campus mentors such as upperclassmen, advisors or counselors. These persons can serve as role models and offer guidance about college that your family can't provide.

Q: I'm adopted and I've always gotten along really well with my parents. Lately, though, we seem to argue all the time.

A: All children, adopted or otherwise, go through rough patches with their parents. All have bitter moments of hating their parents and questioning their parents' love. These tensions may have nothing to do with being adopted; your adoption is but one factor among dozens that have shaped your relationship. If, however, you or your parents trace bad feelings to this one cause, then it can blow up into a big issue. Blaming problems on your adoption can turn adoption into a problem.

As an adoptee, naturally you'll have questions about your origins. What were your biological parents like? In what ways do you take after them? Why did they give you up? Should you try to contact them? You'll also wonder why your parents wanted to adopt you, and how they arranged to do it. These are normal questions for adopted persons, especially during the identity-questioning period from adolescence to early adulthood. Such questions do not in themselves signify trouble between you and your parents.

If the arguments continue, of course, you may want to address the problem with your parents or investigate what's wrong with a counselor.

YOUR PARENTS' DIVORCE

Q: I always thought my parents had the greatest marriage. Now I find out they're thinking about a divorce, and I feel devastated. What do I do?

A: It's not only young children who are shaken by news of parents' divorce. College students can feel the shock just as acutely. In fact, in some ways you are more vulnerable than younger children. They at least have the continuity of still living at home with a parent. But you have already left the home, which in a sense is one loss already, and now you must absorb a second loss. All of a sudden the family you left behind and still miss doesn't exist anymore.

With your parents divorcing, you'll need to prepare yourself for a difficult time ahead and a welter of powerful, disturbing feelings. Expect to be angry: "Why didn't they tell me about their problems?" "Why didn't he treat her better"—or "Why didn't she treat him better?" Expect confusion and uncertainty: "Will Dad move away?" "Will the house be sold?" "Is Mom having an affair?" Above all, expect a pervasive hurt, a wrenching sense of loss. One of the worst scenarios you can imagine has happened, and of course it has left you reeling.

To cope during this difficult time, we recommend the following:

- Get support from friends and other relatives. (Parents, for obvious reasons, may not be much support to you now).
- Be patient with yourself. Don't blame yourself for having strong emotional reactions or for being below par in your studies.
- Search for constructive activities and outlets, such as exercise, extracurricular activities, hobbies and volunteer work.
- Watch out for destructive activities and outlets, such as drugs and alcohol, compulsive eating and indiscriminate sexual activities.
- Consider going to your college's counseling center or to a private counselor for support and perspective.
- Be realistic about your capabilities. If you can continue with your current course load, great. But if you need to drop a course or even take a medical leave of absence, be open-minded about these options.

Q: My parents got divorced six months ago, and now my mother doesn't want me to have anything to do with my father. What should I do?

A: Your parents divorced each other, not you. You're still as much your father's child as your mother's child, and you shouldn't have to choose between the two. And you shouldn't stay away from your father based solely on your mother's say-so. Assuming you're no longer a minor, the decision to see him is one which you, at your stage of maturity, can and should make for yourself.

If you do choose to see him or even write or speak to him on the phone, you'll need to calm your mother and make your position clear. Tell her you are *not* taking his side. You are *not* betraying her. What you are doing is fulfilling your own need to maintain relations with both your parents.

Q: My father insists that I spend Christmas with him and my stepmother in London. My mother wants me to come home to San Francisco. Help!

A: A familiar problem, unfortunately. Divorced parents often play tug-of-war over their sons' and daughters' college vacations, just as they may play hot potato over who pays for college expenses. Sometimes it seems each side wants you home as much as possible while spending as little money on you as they can. The conflict partly concerns you—they genuinely want to see you—and partly it involves the two of them. Though legally parted, your parents still may feel emotionally attached and may be using you to get back at each other.

Like Solomon confronted with two women arguing over one baby, you obviously can't satisfy both your parents at once. Some sort of compromise needs to be worked out where you first visit one of them and later the other. In the meantime, explain to both sides the dilemma they are causing you. Tell them that their pressure frustrates you and casts the vacation as a duty rather than a pleasure. Explain that you want to visit both of them this vacation or the next; where you go first shouldn't be interpreted as choosing a favorite. With luck, they'll hear this message and allow you to work out vacation plans.

Q: My parents recently separated, and now they're not speaking to each other. Instead, they've been asking me to relay messages, and they pump me for information about each other. How much should I tell them?

A: Ideally, nothing. Whatever your parents need to say to one another, they should do so directly. Your interactions with each parent should be confined to matters that just concern you and that parent.

Q: But why can't I help them communicate and perhaps bring them together?

A: For one thing, you'll probably not do a very good job of it, positioned as you are in the midst of family dynamics. That's why there are marital counselors, trained professionals who are not emotionally involved with the family and who can view issues objectively. So if you really want to assist your parents, encourage them to consult a counselor.

There are also dangers in this arrangement for you. Ever since ancient days when messengers could be executed, being the deliverer of bad news has been a high-risk job. How will your mother or father treat you—and how will you feel about yourself—if you report something that hurts that parent? And how will they feel later if you decide instead to slant the news and withhold painful information? Being the middleman is a no-win proposition whichever way you play it.

Your best bet is to declare up-front that you won't pass along messages or give out information from one parent to the other. Explain that you want to be helpful, but not in that way.

Q: But if I don't cooperate with my parents, I feel guilty.

A: There are a couple of explanations for this feeling. Perhaps one or both parents has always placed undue responsibility on your shoulders. Now they are asking you to save the marriage or to take care of them, in effect to act as a substitute parent or spouse. If that's what's happening, you need to determine for yourself and clarify for them your appropriate role within the family. More about this later in the chapter.

The other explanation for guilt is that you feel responsible somehow for breaking them apart. You fear you've been too close to one parent, or have been a financial burden, or have disappointed them in grades or behavior or in not being lovable enough. Since you believe you've caused the separation, now you feel it's your job to patch things up.

If this is your thinking, you need to understand that children don't dissolve marriages; husbands and wives do. It wasn't you who stopped them from loving each other—you couldn't if you tried. And now you don't have the power, or the duty, to make them love each other again. The problems they are having are not your responsibility.

Q: My mother recently remarried and moved in with her new husband and his two daughters. Now I feel out of place when I visit her.

A: An understandable reaction. You have a new stepfather and stepsisters, and your mother has a new dwelling and new claims on her affection. With so much that's unfamiliar, it's no wonder you feel strange when you visit her.

Here are some thoughts about dealing with the situation:

- Be patient. It will take a good while and many visits before you come to know your stepfamily and get used to your mother's changed circumstances. Only gradually will you start to feel at home in this household.
- Although inner misgivings are inevitable, try to be open to these new people and the changes in your mother's life. An accepting attitude, a willingness to fit in, will greatly ease your adjustment.
- If possible, discuss with your stepfamily everyone's reactions to the recent events. It can be good to get feelings out in the open, and the discussions may bring you together and help instill a sense of family.
- It's possible after getting to know your stepfamily that you still won't feel comfortable with all of them or even like them. If so, accept your reactions but try to avoid open warfare.
- While you shouldn't begrudge your mother time with her new family, it's okay to ask to be alone with her. She's still your mother. Spending time with her will lessen your sense of loss and help you accept the changes.

Q: My parents divorced 10 years ago. Could that be connected to my current problems?

A: It's certainly possible. Judith Wallerstein has done research on the long-term effects of divorce on children. She found that many children experience difficulties—underachievement, worry, self-doubt and anger—years after the divorce. Sometimes the damage isn't apparent until the college years, when romantic and sexual relationships begin—and children become frightened of following in their parents' footsteps.

Divorce can be so devastating to children, Wallerstein found, because it delivers a series of blows. First there are the parental battles or coldness before the divorce, then comes the disruption caused by the divorce itself, and then the parents have a reduced capacity to parent after the divorce. In addition, children often feel rejected by one of the divorcing parents, especially the father if the children remain in the custody of the mother.

Not every divorce results in lasting damage for the children. However, if you are having problems in a relationship, are depressed, are an academic underachiever or have other inexplicable difficulties, there may be a connection to this decade-old divorce of your parents. Our advice is to consult a counselor.

DEATH IN THE FAMILY

Q: My father's dying of cancer and I don't feel a thing. Is it that I just don't care?

A: Your seemingly callous reaction is probably just numbness. We suspect it hasn't started to hit you yet that your father is dying.

Although there is no uniform, correct way to mourn or grieve, reactions to a loved one's death tend to follow a certain sequence. In the beginning you can expect to feel shock, numbness and a sense of disbelief. Later may come a period of intense suffering, a time of despair as the reality of the loss sinks in. In the next stage, depending on your style, you may cling to others or withdraw, and may obsessionally dwell on your father's memory or avoid ever thinking about him. You also may experience strong, seemingly inexplicable anger, and feel a profound sense of aloneness.

These reactions are all part of active mourning. Mourning can last as long as several years, although some of the pain endures for a lifetime. Mourning is a healing process, painful but necessary. When you've completed it, you can remember the dead person without being overwhelmed by your feelings, and you feel emotionally ready to get on with your life.

Q: I've never really been close to my father. Maybe that's why I'm reacting so calmly.

A: Maybe. Eventually, though, your distant relationship may actually intensify your suffering, not reduce it. Now he will never fulfill the promise of a father; now you and he will never become close. As these realizations gradually hit home, you may find yourself feeling bitter and profoundly sad, and perhaps blame yourself for your own role in shutting him out. It can be especially painful to let someone go when so much between you is left unsaid.

Maybe, however, you do still have some time. Are there things you want to say to him before he dies? If so, we encourage you to open up the dialogue. Confronting the death of your father requires confronting your relationship with him in life as well. We recommend seeing a counselor to sort out these issues and begin the necessary task of mourning.

Q: My mother is critically ill. Should I take time off from college?

A: It all depends. Certainly you should take time off if you feel unable to concentrate, unable to engage in college activities. You also should go home if being at college prevents you from attending to your parent and helping your family. On the other hand, a few students find that the best place for them to be during this crisis is at college. They can still visit home as needed but for their own sake and the family's sake they're better off remaining enrolled as a student.

If you do need to take time off, speak to a faculty advisor, dean or counselor about the options. Postponements, incompletes, waived assignments or a medical leave of absence may prove best in your particular case. For more information about taking time off for personal reasons see pages 42–43.

TROUBLED FAMILIES

Q: My younger brother has always been in and out of psychiatric hospitals, and now he's getting out of control again. What can I do to help my parents? They're going crazy with worry.

A: You're asking the "$64,000 question": What *can* you do? This same issue comes up when parents go through a divorce, a parent has a substance abuse problem, a single parent is lonely and needy or the family wage-earner loses his or her job. In each case, you have to decide whether or not to get involved, and if you do, what it is you can accomplish.

In making these decisions, it helps to review what you've tried and achieved in the past. Has it been useful during these crises to speak to your brother? Were you able to convince him to go to the hospital or to take his medication? Were you able to console and encourage your parents? If in such ways you've been helpful in the past, then maybe it makes sense to pitch in again.

But most likely your influence is limited here, as it usually is when college students get caught up in family tangles. Though almost grownup, you're still a child in this family, not a parent, only a lay person, not a professional; realistically there may be nothing you can do to help. You may even make matters worse. As a family member yourself, you can't be objective about disturbed family interactions and may unintentionally exacerbate the very problems you're trying to solve.

And then there's yourself to think of. Let's say to help your family you make sacrifices—frequent phone calls, personal anguish, weekends spent at home, withdrawal from college. In the end, you may forfeit your educational opportunity without benefiting your family, and that won't please any of you.

Q: My father says that either I become a pre-med major or he'll pull me out of school. In the past he's told me where I should go to college, who my friends should be and what jobs I should take. How do I deal with such a rigid parent?

A: Let's first place this in context. In the normal course of events, your parents would relax control as you got older. By the time you entered college, you'd mostly make your own decisions *and* your own mistakes. But some parents don't let this happen and continue managing their children's lives. Not only can this feel suffocating, but it makes it hard for you to know your own mind and enjoy your own triumphs. It deprives you of the opportunity to learn to take care of yourself.

So where does this leave you with your father? One issue to explore is the signals you send to him. For example, have you always ducked decisions in the past, inviting him to make them for you? In that case, explain that you are growing up and feel capable now of deciding on matters such as your own choice of a major. Have you typically reacted to his authority by shouting, crying, being sarcastic or sullenly withdrawing? Such immature tactics naturally inspire him to be authoritarian. A much better way to relate is to speak reasonably about the choice of majors, listening to his position while calmly presenting your own.

If better communicating doesn't do the trick, another possibility is to bring a knowledgeable third party to the discussion. Perhaps with someone like your mother, aunt, uncle or grandparent as a negotiator, you and your father may hear one another and work out a compromise.

If even this tactic fails to budge your father from his hard-line stance, you have a tough choice ahead. One option is to respect his authority and switch your major. This will maintain the peace at home, although at the considerable cost of abandoning your own wishes. The other option is to defy your father, try to finance college yourself and prepare for an angry, guilt-inducing rift within the family. This is a difficult judgment call, and you should consult with trusted friends or professionals before making it.

Q: No matter what I do or accomplish, my mother has always criticized me. I've never been good enough in her eyes—I'm stupid or lazy or selfish. How can I deal with such negative feedback?

A: Criticism from parents is not exactly headline news, of course. All parents criticize their sons and daughters sometimes, and the children almost always get through it. But when criticism passes a certain point and becomes verbal abuse—when the negative words are too harsh and persistent and reflect a basically unloving, disapproving attitude—the cumulative effect can be devastating. Verbal abuse can maim you emotionally.

Some children who grow up hearing excessive criticism react by trying everything to please their parents, always searching for the key to approval. Others give up the effort to please and sometimes deliberately invite criticism—it's the only parental attention they know. That's what one student, Vincent, did in high school, when he infuriated his critical, old-fashioned father by dyeing his hair purple, cutting classes and dropping hints about taking drugs. "Go ahead," Vincent's actions said. "Now you've really got a reason to yell at me."

As for your mother, you probably can't change her much. You can try, if you wish, to confront her when she laces into you, pointing out what she's doing and asking her to stop. You can ask her to praise you and acknowledge your successes as well as your faults. This straightforward, assertive approach is certainly worth a try.

Most likely, though, she will at best tone down her words, not adopt a new attitude. You can spend your whole life hoping she'll change, and feeling deflated each time she doesn't. Your chief, self-preserving task, then, is to come to terms with who she is. You need to face the reality of her limitations, face that whatever you do she'll never be loving and accepting. This truth may hurt, but false hopes will hurt more. Once you give up trying to win over your mother, you'll be free to look elsewhere—to friends, lovers and teachers—for the acceptance you rightfully desire.

With a critical, disapproving parent, you may have grown up submissive and overpleasing, or defiant and self-destructive. You also may be self-critical and self-disapproving, having taken your mother's harsh judgments to heart. If in some such way your mother's verbal abuse has proved damaging, we advise you to consult a counselor. Counseling can help you accept yourself as well as look into your parental and other relationships.

Q: My father never has been interested in me. Once or twice he's said he loves me, but in truth he just doesn't seem to care.

A: Sadly, what you describe is an oft-told story. Some parents, especially fathers, appear cold and remote within the family. They may show passion for their job or the dog or television football, but with spouses and children they turn off. Other parents are emotionally involved with certain family members but not with others, or up to certain stages of children's development but not afterward. Any way it happens, it hurts deeply to experience indifference or even cold rejection from a parent.

What's to be done about your father? As with the critical parent described above, you may want to experiment with how you relate to him. Possibly you're now as distant with him as he is with you, and so a friendlier approach is in order. If you try reaching out, maybe he'll respond. If you tell him about college or ask him about his job, maybe you'll spark some interest.

But again as with the critical parent, you need to have realistic expectations. Getting him to the point of chitchatting is a possibility, but more than that may be unlikely. He may never be warm, never show a real interest in you or allow himself to get very close. Learning to acknowledge this bitter fact can spare you further disappointments. The essential goal is to face his limitations squarely and give up hoping he'll miraculously take a genuine interest in you.

Lastly, take a close, honest look at yourself. Are you lacking in self-worth? Are you wary of getting close to others—or are you over-dependent, hanging on for dear life? Do you gravitate toward emotionally unavailable people, people like your father, and then vainly try to win them over? Consequences like these call for exploration in counseling. You can't transform your father, but at least you can do something about yourself and your other relationships.

Q: I never know what to expect from my mother. One minute she loves me, the next I'm the cause of her divorce. One minute she's bubbly and joking, and the next she's in tears.

A: Having an irrational, unpredictable parent can be just as damaging, in its own way, as having a verbally abusive or a cold parent. The tendency in such a home is to grow up insecure and apprehensive, always fearful about what's coming next. In reaction to your mother's erratic moods, you may have become a people pleaser, who does almost anything to head off an ugly scene. Another possibility is that you learned to shy away from people. You also may have developed a moodiness problem of your own.

Your mother's instability strongly suggests emotional disturbance. Even if you already suspected as much, this still can be hard to accept. Your mother brought you into the world, she and your father were your first teachers, and naturally part of you still wants to believe in her. We recommend speaking to a counselor to understand and come to terms with her difficulties. In counseling you can look at her objectively, and see how she distorted reality. You can also repair your self-image and relationships—both of which, unfortunately, have surely been casualties of your mother's disturbance.

In the meantime, we have a few thoughts about surviving visits home. When you see your mother, train yourself if you can to expect the unexpected. Her mood may shift at any moment, like a child's, and bearing that in mind will ease your distress when it happens. Remind yourself, too, that her emotional storms are not your doing, they're her nature, and therefore it's not your responsibility to pacify her and it's not your fault that she has an outburst. Finally, try to be as consistent, predictable and calm with her as you can. Since she is emotionally like a child, it may steady her a bit if you act around her almost like a patient parent or teacher.

Q: I think my father has an alcohol problem. What effect will that have on me?

A: Let's begin with your hedging opener, "I think." Does your father have an alcohol problem, or doesn't he? We make an issue out of this because adult children of alcoholics (ACOAs), like alcoholics themselves, often use denial. As an ACOA, you may have learned to deny your parent's alcohol problem—and deny your needs and feelings—because your family forbade you to speak plainly. You couldn't acknowledge the truth, so you learned to hide it from yourself. To help yourself, therefore, you need to break through the denial. Just as an alcoholic's first step toward recovery is admitting to alcoholism, your first step, as an ACOA, is to admit the truth about your family.

And what is that truth? Briefly put, your father, with his alcohol problem, probably hasn't provided you consistent caring and structure. Your mother, burdened by your father's problems, probably hasn't fully been up to parenting either. And you, therefore, probably have been short-changed. Raised in an alcoholic family, you may not have had a normal childhood.

Q: So how have I been affected?

A: Alcoholic families differ, and so do children's reactions within the family. However, we can generalize and say that you probably have trouble expressing or even recognizing needs and feelings. You probably have low self-esteem and judge yourself harshly. You probably have difficulty trusting others and forming relationships. You also are at risk of becoming an alcoholic yourself and of marrying an alcoholic.

In addition, there's a good chance you learned a role in order to survive in your family. Particularly common among college students is the "hero's" role. If you've learned to be a hero, you've made yourself achieve and are responsible. You're a top student, an officer of a club, a money-raiser for charities—an all-around model student. But behind the outer accomplishments lurks another reality. Inwardly you may feel insecure, terrified of being wrong and constantly in need of approval. No amount of success reassures you. Like a compulsive eater who never feels satisfied, you keep on proving yourself, but never feel secure.

The hero isn't the only role you may play. As an ACOA, you may be a "scapegoat," who's hostile, defiant and prone to alcoholism or addiction. Scapegoats get into trouble and therefore shift the family's focus of attention from the alcoholic onto themselves. You may be a "lost child," who's detached, lonely and shy. Lost children manage to avoid attracting attention altogether; no one worries about them, and no one attends to their needs. Or you may be a "mascot," who's humorous and cute, the family clown. Mascots follow the classic pattern of laughing on the outside and crying on the inside.

Whatever your own style, chances are you've adopted some fairly rigid ways of relating to people. It's as if you wear a mask. The roles you play helped you get by in your alcoholic family, but they're maladaptive when you try to relate to people outside your family.

Q: If I'm an ACOA, how can I change?

A: We recommend attending Adult Children of Alcoholics (ACOA) meetings either in your community or on campus. There you'll find others who have had similar experiences, and you'll have a chance to see your past realistically and explore current concerns. In the group you can experiment with taking off the mask and discover what genuine relating is like. Reading about growing up in an alcoholic home (two recommended books are listed at the end of the chapter) may help put your own experience in perspective. Finally, we advise you to consider counseling, which will let you probe family experiences and work on honest communications, healthy relationships and self-esteem.

Q: There's something I've never told anyone. For a couple of years when I was in elementary school, my teenage brother used to touch me and make me touch him sexually.

A: You're not alone, unfortunately. Studies tell us that in the United States 25% of girls and 10% of boys have been sexually abused, typically by someone known to them.[1] While sex play between same-age children is common and usually harmless, sexual acts imposed on a child by an older person can cause lasting harm, especially if the abuse continues over time. Many sexually abused children grow up with severe problems in self-esteem, relationships and sexuality. Some wind up abusing their own children or marrying an abuser.

You've never told anyone? Then we recommend consulting a counselor and telling him or her, or joining a support group for survivors of sexual abuse. With counseling or a support group, you can allay feelings of guilt or shame; tragically, many victims blame themselves for permitting the abuse or wanting the abuser's attention—as if a child bears responsibility for sex with an older person. You also can examine your complex feelings toward your brother and toward your parents, who failed to notice and protect you. You love these people but in different ways they all failed you, and that can be emotionally confusing, to say the least. These are difficult topics, but better to face them in counseling than let them fester inside of you.

Even in counseling, don't expect to resolve these issues right away. It can take months and even years to undo the pervasive harm that was caused long ago.

Q: I'm furious at my parents for all the psychological harm they did to me. Is that unhealthy?

A: Any counselor worthy of the name will tell you that it's good to know your feelings. So if you're furious with your parents, by all means admit it. Anger may be necessary and appropriate as you first face up to hurts from the past. Anger declares that you deserved better from your parents. It asserts that you are a worthwhile human being and shouldn't have been mistreated.

But anger is an emotion that should reach toward resolution. If you remain angry, you keep yourself in emotional turmoil. You can't fully get on with your life while looking back in anger; you have less energy for other enterprises. And if you wallow in anger, you also may see yourself as a victim, which holds you back too. At some point, you'll need to resolve your anger and put the past behind you in order to continue your development.

Your ultimate goal with damaging parents should be to let past injuries heal, like a mourner who lets a deceased person go. You need to accept who your parents are—even if you can never approve of what they did. Associated with acceptance comes a sense of perspective. You may begin to realize that your parents struggled with their own misfortunes, including perhaps inadequate parents of their own. Your parents hurt you, but perhaps they loved you too. They failed you, but perhaps they tried, in their own way, to do well by you.

Ultimately, acceptance and perspective will serve you better than anger.

FOR FURTHER READING

Ellen Bass and Laura Davis, *The Courage to Heal: A Guide for Women Survivors of Child Sexual Abuse*. New York: Harper & Row, 1988.

Susan Forward and Craig Buck, *Toxic Parents: Overcoming Their Hurtful Legacy and Reclaiming Your Life*. New York: Bantam, 1989.

Howard M. Halpern, *Cutting Loose: An Adult's Guide to Coming to Terms with Your Parents*. New York: Fireside (Simon & Schuster), 1990.

Judith S. Wallerstein and Sandra Blakeslee, *Second Chances: Men, Women, and Children a Decade After Divorce*. New York: Ticknor & Fields, 1989.

Sharon Wegscheider-Cruse, *Another Chance*. Cambridge, Mass.: Harvard University Press, 1981.

Janet G. Woititz, *Adult Children of Alcoholics*. Deerfield Beach, Fla.: Health Communications, Inc., 1983.

HOW TO
SURVIVE
FALLING IN
LOVE

If you're like most undergraduates, your mind is very much on romance while you're in college. Your studies are important, yes, but you also want to go out with others. You want a relationship.

None of this boy–meets–girl business is easy, however. Though you're surrounded by potential partners and many of them want an involvement too, college relationships can be tricky every step of the way. Here we discuss the insecurity-ridden beginning of the process—Why doesn't anyone ask me out?—right up to the nervous excitement of possible marriage. In between we take up such charged matters as fear of rejection, choice of partners, lovers' quarrels, jealousy and breaking up.

FIRST STEPS

Q: Guys always want to date my roommate but with me it's "Let's be friends." Why won't anyone ask *me* out?

A: The world of romance isn't strictly fair. There are some favored beings, like your roommate, who generate interest without even trying. Blessed with striking looks or whatever else it takes, they're always being pursued by an admirer or two (actually, this presents its own difficulties). But that's not the case for the average college student. The typical experience is more like yours, where you go through lean periods when it seems no one wants you, at least no one you really like.

Q: But what can I do to interest somebody?

A: We wish we could hand you a set of sure-fire rules, but in our experience romance begins unpredictably. There's no "right" way to go about attracting someone; all sorts of personalities, carrying on in all sorts of ways, manage to meet and pair off. So partly you just need to be patient. Your turn may come next week or next semester, or you may have to wait quite a while longer.

But while there aren't any absolute rules, we can offer a few modest suggestions. First, review the tips on relating presented on pages 14–15. These don't tell you exactly what to do, but they do suggest some social pitfalls to avoid. It's possible you're doing something basic to defeat yourself, and by correcting that you'll stop driving potential dates away.

Second, give some thought to the partners you've considered. Have you been open-minded about all the eligible people out there? This is not to say you can't be discriminating. You have a right, the same as anyone else, to like and be attracted to a romantic partner. But liking somebody doesn't require that he or she be gorgeous, or cool, or a certain height, or meet any such rigid standard. Liking somebody simply means that you *like* him or her. So check whether you've been focusing your search too narrowly, and, if so, try to open your eyes. Very possibly in your classes, dorm or club activities there are some promising sleepers you haven't given a fair chance.

Third, make sure you're sending off the right signals to people you like. Have you successfully shown your interest, either by letting them know or at the very least by managing to *be* with them? If not, you risk losing out because they assume you're not available. Have you presented yourself as more than friendship material? If instead you just pal around with people, they'll think of you that way, as a sidekick rather than a potential romantic lead.

Again, please don't misunderstand: We're not suggesting that you have to behave in a particular way. To interest someone, you don't have to flirt or play it cool or act like someone different than you are. The best romantic strategy of all is that timeworn cliché—Be yourself. But while being true to your own personality, do try to convey that you like the person and are receptive to something happening between you. That way you give yourself at least a fighting chance.

Q: Be myself, you say. How can I do that? When I'm with someone I like, I get all tongue-tied.

A: It can happen that way. Anxiety about pleasing can make anyone awkward and uptight. It's easy to be charming and natural with people you're not attracted to, but in the presence of someone special it's not unusual to be stiff and awkward like an actor with stage fright.

The best advice we can offer is: Hang in there. If you spend time with this person, you'll soon start feeling more comfortable and your true personality will emerge.

Q: My life seems empty without a relationship. Suppose I'm alone forever?

A: We sincerely doubt you'll be alone forever if you really want a relationship. But in the meantime, let's examine your reasoning. By imposing a condition on life—"I must have a relationship or else"—you guarantee yourself misery for as long as your condition isn't met. You so totally focus on what you don't have that you lose sight of what's already yours: friends, family, studies, activities. In short, you *think* your way into suffering.

And please note, thinking this way doesn't get you to your goal one day sooner. On the contrary, others will sense your great need and run the other way. Both men and women are attracted to self-sufficient individuals who also happen to like them, not to someone desperate who feels miserable and incomplete on his or her own. Friends too will grow tired of your I-want-a-relationship spiel. So your philosophy not only makes you unhappy, it's self-defeating. Desperation for a partner is likely to keep you without one.

Relationships are important, but not all-important. We urge you to give some thought to putting relationships in perspective.

Q: But what can I do if nobody at this college appeals to me? All the people here are geeks and losers.

A: All of them? You certainly are painting with a wide brush. Surely in an entire institution of higher education there must be one or two desirable persons lurking around somewhere.

Earlier we alluded to the problem of being too picky in choosing a partner. Let's look now at a few underlying causes. One reason you might reject almost everyone is because you lack self-esteem. Since inwardly you don't have a favorable opinion of yourself, you assume that anyone who would have you must be as unworthy as you are. This is the point of the famous Groucho Marx line: "I don't want to belong to any club that will accept me as a member."

Another possible motive is to spare yourself heartache. If you reject all possible partners first, no one can reject you. Your unreasonably high standards serve as a protective wall keeping out anyone who might hurt you.

Similarly, your pickiness may protect you from getting more involved than you'd like. If you had a relationship, you'd have to depend on someone, he or she would become dependent on you, you'd lose a measure of freedom—and that may not be what you really want. A good solution, then, is to dismiss all available partners and fantasize about partners you can't have. You might daydream about a person at other campuses, or professors, or even a classmate who seems unattainable. That way you can tell yourself that you'd like a relationship without running the risk of actually getting one.

These motives tend to be deep-seated and aren't easily laid aside. If you recognize one of them in yourself, you may want to consider consulting a counselor. Deficient self-esteem, excessive fear of rejection and fear of involvement are all worthy subjects for self-exploration. In the meantime, try to go beyond your first impressions and get to know some of your classmates better. Make a concerted effort to see individuals for the complex human beings they are rather than immediately reducing them to categories. If you can put aside your prejudices and fears, some of these "geeks and losers" may grow on you.

Q: How do I know if I should go out with someone?

A: Fortunately, at college you don't have to rush into anything. You can get to know someone casually, without having to make it an official dinner-and-a-movie date. So if someone has sparked your interest, arrange to chat in a study lounge or meet for ice cream at the snack bar. After a few informal get-togethers you should start having an idea whether you want to pursue this further.

Q: How do I approach someone I like? What's a good opening line?

A: How about "Hi"? The truth is that opening lines are vastly overrated. A person will either respond to you or not based on who you are, not the cleverness of your first words.

Q: But I can't just say hello. What should I talk about?

A: Once again, there are no rules. You can't prepare a dialogue or follow a script. Simply talk about things that interest you, listen to things that interest him or her and see how the conversation flows. The talk may be a bit strained at first because you like the person a lot and want to impress. Even so, you should get an idea early on about whether you and this person click. If you do, the conversation will proceed somehow and pursuing matters further will seem natural. If not, the problem isn't that you're saying the wrong things but that you and this person probably aren't right for each other.

In their anxiety to impress, some students ask someone out by turning in a kind of performance. They do a comedy routine or show off their sensitive natures or advertise their superior intelligence. Now if you're naturally funny or sensitive or brainy, that's great, but you don't have to stage a show. You can express yourself without having to calculate every line. Besides, a performance places so much attention on you—you're working so hard on your act—that you don't get to know the person you're so busy impressing. You can't find out about someone while consigning him or her to the audience.

Q: There's this friend I'm attracted to, but we've always dated other people. Do you think I should ask her out?

A: Tough question. Certainly you can make a case for taking a chance. Many couples originally get to know each other as friends, without the pressure of romance, and gradually develop an intimacy that leads to a relationship. On the other hand, you have a lot to lose if your gamble fails. She may not want to go out with you in that way, which will be awkward for both of you. And if she does agree to go out, you may not make it as lovers and you risk losing her as a friend.

Our advice in case you do ask her out is to move slowly. (This isn't bad advice for any couple, of course). Start seeing her if she's willing, but make it only one or two days a week, and don't hurry into sexual relations. Going slowly doesn't ensure that no one gets hurt; feelings are on the line from the moment you ask her out. But a slow pace does enable you to take stock of the relationship, and perhaps, if it isn't working, lets you salvage your friendship in time.

REJECTION

Q: I really like Sarah, but I just can't seem to ask her out. How can I get rid of my fear of rejection?

A: You can't, not entirely anyway, any more than you can rid yourself of fear of heights or of dangerous animals. Being afraid of rejection is a natural response, an outgrowth of the fundamentally social nature of human beings. All of us want to be accepted. Yet all of us have tasted rejection. So it's only natural when asking a person out to feel some trepidation.

The real issue here is not what you feel—of course you fear rejection—but what you do. You don't have to shy away because you're frightened, just as you don't have to slug somebody when you feel angry. You can still ask Sarah out, even though you're afraid. Good judgment, not feelings alone, should decide your course of action.

Although you can't eliminate fear, sometimes you can cut it down to size by performing the act that frightens you. If you ask Sarah out, it may be easier to ask out somebody else next time, even if Sarah says no. Or, you might go to a party and set a goal of asking three women to dance. The purpose is to show yourself that rejections aren't unbearable. You prove that you can endure a "no," and with this knowledge you now feel free to ask out anyone you wish.

Q: There's this guy I like. When I finally got up the nerve to speak to him, he blew me off. I felt mortified.

A: We didn't say rejection was fun. No matter how often it happens, getting turned down always stings a bit. But here are a few thoughts that may salve your wounds:

- If you're feeling bad after a rejection, visit or call a good friend, or your parents. When someone doesn't want you, it helps to be appreciated by people who do.
- Remind yourself that what you did was fine, and not at all humiliating. You have the right to approach anyone you want. When you do, inevitably you'll get rebuffed sometimes. But that doesn't cancel your right to have tried.
- In fact, you should give credit to yourself for asking. It takes courage to approach someone, and besides it's a smart thing to do, because now you know where you stand. Actually, words of self-praise are in order.

- Check for negative thoughts in reaction to the rejection, such as "Nobody will go out with me" or "I'm a loser." Such thoughts should be thoroughly repudiated: "What happened with this one guy doesn't prove others won't go out with me. I'm still attractive and desirable, whatever he thinks."
- Along the same lines, remind yourself that a single rejection communicates very little about you. You can't know when someone turns you down if it's because he only likes short blondes, he's interested in someone else, you remind him of his dreaded ex-girlfriend—or you scare him because you're too attractive! You can be turned down for any of a hundred reasons. (For men, obviously, the same holds true.) With this thought in mind, psychologist Judith Sills hammers home the comforting slogan, "It's nothing personal." Whenever someone rejects you, tell yourself that it bears on the other person, not you; it's nothing personal.
- Try to gauge the intensity of your reaction. Rejections do sting, as we say, but ideally they don't crush your self-esteem or threaten your sense of identity. If your reaction threatens to overwhelm you, then you have too much at stake here, and we recommend you take a step back and possibly explore the issue in counseling.

Q: How do you let someone down easy if you don't want to go out with him?

A: The kindest course is to be gentle but straightforward. Tell him you're flattered he asked, but you're not interested in a dating relationship. Perhaps then you can move on to a friendly conversation about other matters. He'll appreciate that you're willing to talk to him even if you don't want to go out.

When you turn someone down, you're not obligated to explain your reasons. All you have to say is "Thanks, but I don't want to," even if he presses you for an explanation. You also don't have to apologize or put yourself down with self-abasing comments like "I'm just too mixed up to be seeing someone right now." To explain your refusal, it's not a good idea to invent an off-campus boyfriend. This familiar white lie can come back to haunt you if later you want to date someone else on campus. It's also not recommended that you simply avoid your admirer until he gets the message. Running away from him spares you from having to say no, but it's crueler to him and implies that he couldn't withstand your rejection. It's better to simply tell him the truth.

Turning down someone is one of the more unpleasant chores in life, almost as bad, but not quite, as being turned down. But remember, everyone plays both roles sooner or later, and somehow everyone manages to get through them. Meanwhile, you can keep an awkward situation from getting any worse by stating your refusal tactfully but honestly.

Q: But suppose someone doesn't take no for an answer? This guy keeps showing up at my door, stopping me on campus and calling me. Does he have the right to do that?

A: Of course not. He has the right to ask initially, but you have the right to accept or decline. You don't have to go out with him, or even have a casual friendship, if you don't want to. And he should respect your wishes.

Have you clearly told him how you feel? Some people will interpret any kindness, hesitation or ambiguity as a sign that your defenses are weakening. At this stage, you need to be blunt. Tell him to leave you alone, and then have nothing further to do with him.

If he persists even after you've made your wishes clear, then he's harassing you. Speak to an RA, a dean or another college official about your problem.

PROBLEMS COUPLES FACE

Q: I'm not really sure how I feel about my boyfriend. How do you know when you're in love?

A: We can't give you a definitive answer, because love is such a multiform phenomenon. Certainly from your own experience you must know that people in love feel differently at different moments, at different stages of a relationship, and with different partners. There are quiet loves and stormy loves, tender loves and loves tinged with hate. To add to the confusion, the word "love" can take on various meanings. There's falling in love, that frenzied time-limited state when you are seized by an infatuation; there's ongoing romantic love, which is less intense but longer lasting and contains ingredients of affection, passion and commitment; and there's platonic love, which is caring without passion. When you say you love someone, you may mean any of these, or perhaps none of these definitions quite captures what you feel.

Having pointed out the complexity of your question, let us try to answer it with some questions of our own. Do you continue feeling as close to your boyfriend, or closer, as time goes by? Do you consider him a true friend, someone you can be intimate with? Do you feel physically attracted to him? Do you generally enjoy his company? Do you tend to think of yourself as "we" rather than "I"? Do you sense a deepening commitment developing between you?

If the answers to these questions are yes, then you are, by our standards, in love.

If the answers aren't clear-cut and you have reason to doubt your love, one step to consider is slowing down for a while or even taking time off from the relationship. From a distance you may be able to see things that appear muddled in the thick of day- to-day interactions. Of course, you'll need your boyfriend's understanding and agreement in order to do this. He may feel rejected by your request to slow things down, and you'll need to address his concerns.

Q: How can I know how my new boyfriend feels about me?

A: You can't know for a certainty, and what's more, he may not exactly know either. Lovers' feelings can be complex and changeable. Your boyfriend may cherish your vivacious personality but wish you were a different physical type, or love to be with you alone but feel uncomfortable when you drag him along to a party. He may pine for you on Thursday but hardly give you a thought on Friday. Asking him to pin down his feelings, especially at this early stage, may be asking for more clarity than is possible.

Another reason you can't be sure where you stand is because people are cautious, especially early in relationships, about expressing their true feelings. They don't want to frighten away or hurt their partners or get prematurely involved in a relationship, so instead of speaking directly they use what Judith Sills calls "coded communications." Any behavior can be a coded communication: a gift or a compliment, a promised phone call not made, a sexual come-on, a sexual refusal, lateness, teasing. What's frustrating is that codes are tough to crack; you can easily misinterpret what a partner's behavior is saying to you. If your boyfriend doesn't call, that may mean he doesn't care, but it also may mean he's afraid of appearing too eager, or he feels hurt and thinks it's your turn to call, or possibly he was tied up and couldn't get to the phone. You can't be sure what his not calling means, and so it's hard to infer from particular behaviors how he feels about you.

Eventually, your boyfriend's position will become clear. As you come to know him better, you'll have received a great many coded communications from him, you'll know how to decipher them, and meanwhile he'll probably start expressing himself directly. But for now, you have to live with ambiguity. You can have an idea about how he feels, but you can't know for a certainty.

Q: But shouldn't I be more direct and *ask* him how he feels?

A: You can, and with luck you'll get an honest answer and spare yourself either needless worries or false illusions. Assertive communications are often best. But bear in mind, again, that he may not yet know his answer or feel ready to deliver it. Pushing him for a response may frighten or annoy him without yielding a clear answer. At this early stage of your relationship, you may have to resign yourself to some indirectness and uncertainty.

Q: If my girlfriend and I argue, does that mean we're not suited for each other?

A: Not necessarily. There are couples who are happy together despite arguments, or even partly because of them. Arguing may be how they let off steam, liven things up, even show their affection.

On the other hand, arguments that are bitter may express serious incompatibility and leave lasting wounds. So if you and your girlfriend have gone beyond squabbling and are really at each other's throats, then you do have a problem.

Q: How can we stop arguing?

A: The first thing you need is your girlfriend's cooperation. Maybe it takes two to fight, but it also takes two to stop fighting. She has to agree with you to tackle this problem.

Assuming you have her cooperation, the goal then is to strive for improved communications. Please note that our advice here is different from that given to the question "How can I know how he feels about me?" While coded communications are par for the course early in a relationship, when you're deciding how you feel about each other, direct communications are a must later on, particularly concerning specific grievances. Arguments indicate that important issues aren't being addressed. You need to clarify what they are to put an end to the arguing.

Here, then, are some communications tips:

- Be assertive. Express your wishes and concerns directly and promptly, before you reach the exploding point: "What you just said really hurt my feelings. I think we should talk about it."
- Stick to the issue at hand without throwing in tangential complaints.
- Don't make personal attacks. For example, say "I wish you would spend more time with me" rather than "You're selfish for not spending time with me."
- Listen to your partner. Nothing escalates an argument faster than two people intent on lecturing each other. Saying "Yes, I see what you mean" can defuse tensions immediately.
- Similarly, try to avoid "It's your fault because. . . " and "It all started when you. . . " statements. These will elicit the knee-jerk reaction, "No, it's *your* fault" and "What do you mean—*you* started it," and you'll be off on a round of accusations and counteraccusations. Even if you think you're right—and what arguer doesn't?—the best way to avoid an argument is to acknowledge responsibility on both sides.
- Pay attention to your discussion style. What are your favorite tactics? For example, do you get very emotional, crying and yelling, and does that drive your partner crazy? Do you become hyperrational and lawyer-like—which can have the same effect? Do you threaten to break up when things get heated? Do you give the silent treatment afterward? Since whatever you're doing now is obviously not bringing you together, it's time to try something new. So experiment with a different approach and see if that brings better results.

Q: We've gotten nowhere in our efforts to stop arguing, so now we're thinking of going to a counselor. But which one of us should go?

A: Generally speaking, a couple's difficulties, like Caesar's Gaul, can be divided into three parts: his personal problems, her personal problems and their interactional problems. So in theory, the relationship could improve if either of you gets help alone, or if both of you go together. We recommend starting with an evaluation as a couple, and then discuss with the professional the merits of individual counseling and/or couples counseling.

Q: What should I do if my boyfriend always teases me and finds little ways to put me down?

A: This is a good question that will take some explaining to answer. When two people become romantically involved, they often slip into complimentary roles. For example, one of them may call the shots and be judgmental, while the other submits and looks for approval. One may be the giver of support and affection, while the other is the receiver. One may do most of the talking, while the other mostly listens. These roles tend to be a replay of early family interactions. Partners behave with their boyfriends and girlfriends as they remember their parents behaving, or as they used to behave as children.

While some of this role-playing is inevitable, obviously it can get out of hand. In your own case, it's no fun to be teased and put down, nor is it any consolation that maybe your boyfriend ridicules you because his father ridiculed his mother. Quite properly, you want to break out of the role he's assigned you.

The logical first step is to tell your boyfriend straight-out to stop what he's doing. Since his behavior may be well-ingrained, once won't be enough; you'll need to remind him often. Say "Please don't tease me" or "You're teasing me again" every time he does it. If he's at all sympathetic, he should soon start catching himself before he zaps you.

In addition, you need to weed out your own behaviors that may be setting you up for the victim's role. For example, do you habitually say "I'm sorry" or "I'm so stupid" or words to that effect? Do you make fun of yourself and belittle your own efforts? If in these ways you put yourself down, then it's not surprising that he follows your lead. Act with self-respect around your boyfriend, and perhaps then he'll treat you with respect.

If neither of these suggestions pans out and you're serious about your relationship, talk to a counselor about this problem, either alone or with your boyfriend.

Q: Should I tell my new girlfriend about personal problems?

A: That's a tricky one. We know it's tempting when you meet someone promising to let it all hang out. You feel close, you want her to know you, you want to prove your interest by entrusting her with secrets and vulnerabilities. The trouble is, you don't really know her yet. You can't know if she'll understand and accept the things you tell her, or if she'll judge you and think less of you. Today you may have a glorious feeling of being on the same wavelength. But next week you may think, "She's not who I thought, and I'm embarrassed I revealed so much to her about myself."

Our recommendation with self-disclosure is to risk smaller revelations first and save the most personal matters for later. Also, take turns disclosing, so both of you reveal yourselves at roughly the same pace. That way trust and understanding can develop, and you learn through experience that opening up is safe.

Q: My boyfriend loves to analyze my problems and explain what's wrong with me. It really annoys me. What should I tell him?

A: Tell him to cut it out. It's fine if he gives you support and understanding and offers occasional advice. You should do the same for him. But when he starts acting like your counselor, spouting lines like "You're an anal-retentive personality because of your relationship with your mother," then he's gone too far. For one thing, his psychologizing treats you like an inferior—it's demeaning. For another, your boyfriend is not a professional and can't possibly see you objectively because he's involved with you.

So ask Dr. Freud to turn in his therapist's badge and just stick to being your boyfriend. And for your own part, try not to relate to him in the subordinate role of patient. If you really need the assistance of a counselor, schedule an appointment with a professional.

Q: Eric is insanely jealous. If I just look at another man he's upset all night, and he doesn't want me to see my male friends anymore. What should I do?

A: First, ask yourself whether Eric has any reason for his insecurities. Do you flirt with your male friends? Do you often stare at men or talk about them in a jealousy-inducing way? Have you ever cheated on Eric? If any of the answers is yes, then to earn Eric's trust you first must change your own behavior.

But assuming he's jealous without cause, we advise you to try offering Eric a healthy diet of reassurance. All of us need reassurance from time to time; jealous people need it more than most. Reassure him that he's mistaken in his suspicions, and especially reassure him that you really care. With such reassurance, he may be less afraid of losing you and correspondingly less jealous.

At the same time, be truthful about the harm Eric's jealousy does to you and the relationship. He needs to be told plainly that suspicions and accusations are upsetting for you and distance you from him. Also, assert your own rights. You have a right to look at anyone you please (though preferably not seductively), you have a right to have male friends, and you have a right not to be grilled for your actions.

These efforts may not work. Jealousy can be fairly mild, in which case reason and reassurance have an effect, or it can be pathological, where nothing you say gets through. If Eric is pathologically jealous, you have two options: Convince him to get professional help, or consider leaving him for your own peace of mind.

Q: I'm the jealous type myself. Why do I feel this way and act like a jerk sometimes with my boyfriend?

A: Jealousy is rooted in insecurity. Maybe you simply need reassurance, or maybe you believe (perhaps unconsciously) that no one can love you, so you doubt your boyfriend's love and look for signs that he prefers someone else. Believe it or not, jealousy also can be caused by your own wandering eye. Employing the defense mechanism called projection, you attribute to your boyfriend what's really in your own mind: the wish to cheat.

Based on your question, you obviously have some perspective and motivation to change. This will help you work on this problem.

Q: My boyfriend transferred to another college and I only see him on Christmas and during summer vacations. Do you think it would be okay to start seeing some guys here on campus?

A: That depends. For one thing, you haven't indicated if you plan to tell him. Perhaps you think you can safely play around behind your boyfriend's back, but this is risky. He may pick up clues and figure out what's happening, or you may feel guilty and confess, and the upshot can be the end of your relationship. Besides, even if your boyfriend never catches on, what kind of relationship are you left with? If he can't trust you, how involved are you, really? Such are the dangers of sneaking around.

If everything's out in the open and you both agree to see other people, then you're certainly entitled to do so. Going out with others may even be desirable because you and your boyfriend aren't ready yet for a serious commitment. On the other hand, be aware that dating others puts your relationship at risk. You may like these new people more than you expect. And the men you meet on your campus, and the women he meets on his, have a strong geographical advantage over the partner who's not around.

Q: My boyfriend always wants to hang around with his friends. I say we love each other and should spend our time together. Who's right?

A: Probably both of you, up to a point. We agree with you that a healthy love relationship requires a certain amount of exclusive, just-you-and-me time. Unless you spend time together you can't come to know each other and develop genuine intimacy. But your boyfriend is also right in that too much time spent as a twosome can be stunting and stifling. To express and develop all aspects of your personalities, you each need to interact with other people. Otherwise you place more demands on one another than any one relationship can handle. Also, the richer your social experiences when you're apart, the more you have to share when you're together.

Let us add a few words about dependency. Many college students are still rather intimidated by people or frightened to be alone, and for these reasons they may attach themselves to a boyfriend or girlfriend, who alone makes them feel safe. They build their lives around this one person more out of fear than affection. Needless to say, this is not a sound basis for either healthy living or healthy relating. Dependency on a partner is no more beneficial than depending too much on Mom and Dad.

Q: My parents don't want me to go out with Robert anymore because he's not Korean. What should I do?

A: This is a concern we hear frequently, and from every conceivable group: Asian-Americans, African-Americans and whites, Christians and Jews, Greeks, Cubans and Indians, and so forth. Seemingly, it's an insoluble problem: Either you must give up your partner or forfeit your parents' approval, and neither is an acceptable outcome.

Yet before you despair, we suggest looking closely at your situation. First, ask yourself how much, and what, Robert really means to you. Is he truly special, someone you selected because of his particular qualities? Or is he rather a vehicle to assert your independence from your parents, an excuse to prove your autonomy? Did you, in fact, purposely choose a non-Korean boyfriend to force a confrontation with your parents? Don't answer these questions in haste, because motives can be difficult to discern. Time and reflection may be necessary to sort out your reasons for selecting Robert and to decide whether on balance you should stay with him.

Now let's consider your parents. Possibly they're adamant on this issue and won't listen to your side of things. But sometimes students are too quick to give up on dialogue with their parents. Have you tried to explain your feelings about Robert and also listened to their reservations? It's at least possible that after thorough discussions their stance may soften.

Q: My boyfriend sometimes hits me when he's angry. How can I make him stop?

A: Probably you can't. If he's done it more than once, his physical aggression may be a deep-seated reaction that you are powerless to prevent.

Q: But why would he act aggressively toward someone he loves?

A: Your boyfriend may act violently because he experienced violence in his own family. He also may not know constructive, assertive ways to cope with feelings of jealousy, anger, rejection or stress. Feeling powerless in these situations, he resorts to the only power he knows: brute force.

Q: What should I do?

A: In our opinion, if this has continued at all, you should seriously consider ending the relationship. No matter how much you may love your boyfriend, it's not good for body or soul to stay in an abusive relationship.

You may also want to consult a counselor to look into your need to stay with him. Is your self-esteem low and you feel you don't deserve better than an abusive boyfriend? Did you pick an abusive boyfriend because this is what you're familiar with in your own home? Do you seek out abusive people in other aspects of your life? With counseling you can investigate and work on these vital issues.

BREAKING UP

Q: My girlfriend just broke up with me. I can't study, I can't sit still, I can't think of anything but her. How will I get through this?

A: You will, but not without difficulty. Breaking up is a wrenching ordeal, particularly for college students. Because you're young, the experience may be shockingly new for you; you haven't learned yet that you can get through it. Making matters worse, if you both live on campus your "ex" is still around. You'll keep running into her, and everywhere you go will be a reminder of your loss.

In *How to Survive the Loss of a Love*, Melba Colgrove and her coauthors describe a three-stage process of mourning or grieving following a breakup. First you react with shock and disbelief, then you become angry and depressed, and finally you achieve understanding and acceptance. In our own experience, these stages progress unevenly, and no two people react quite the same. However, the basic point still holds: You have to mourn after a breakup, similar to mourning the death of a parent. You feel pain, it takes time, and there's no shortcut to healing.

In the meantime, here are a few suggestions:

- Get support from family and friends, persons who care about you. Though no one can replace your girlfriend (it's her company you want most), still it's consoling in times of grief to have people on your side. If you're concerned about burning out one or two friends, spread out your requests by using several sources of support.
- Expect to be shaken by this. Don't blame yourself for feeling sad or angry or for having trouble sleeping or concentrating: It's normal.
- At the same time, try to carry out your usual responsibilities and routines—going to class, studying, showing up at work, going to the gym, even doing the laundry. These mundane duties continue to be necessary, of course. More important, accomplishing them makes you feel purposeful and good about yourself, and that's what you need after a blow of this magnitude.
- Consider making an appointment at your college counseling center. Not only have you lost someone central in your life, but it wouldn't be surprising if you're questioning your self-worth, feeling depressed, even experiencing suicidal thoughts. A counselor can give you support and help you retain perspective during this difficult time.

Q: My ex-girlfriend and I haven't been speaking to each other for weeks, but I'd really like to see her just to talk. What do you think?

A: One of the cruel ironies about breaking up is that the person who used to be your main support is the same person who's now causing you pain. You've lost your best friend as well as your girlfriend. It's understandable, then, that you'd like to speak to her.

Perhaps, you hope, she'll be sympathetic and soothing. You also may want to find out if there's any possibility of reconciliation, and maybe you have questions about why she broke up with you.

But before you visit her, first you must make sure she agrees. If not, you have to respect her wishes; she has the right to avoid you if that's what she now wants. Avoidance doesn't mean she's lost all feelings for you. She may well feel strongly, but these feelings can be confusing and uncomfortable and make it hard for her to abide by her decision. Later, once passions have cooled on both sides, possibly the two of you can be friendly or even become friends.

Assuming she says yes, you still must decide if seeing her is in your best interests. Will a visit lift your spirits or cause sharper pain? Are you harboring false hopes about what will happen, setting yourself up for further disappointment? Unless you are confident about your own reactions and realistic about the meeting, the safest course is to stay away for a while.

Q: First my ex-boyfriend suddenly stops seeing me three weeks ago, telling me he's not ready for a relationship. Now he's going out with some bimbo on his hall. I'm furious, and I want to know what can I do about it.

A: Not much, we're afraid. It won't change anything if you badmouth either one of them, or act seductively, or play it cool. You can tell him off, if you wish, but that won't alter what's happened either. You've lost your influence over your ex- boyfriend, which is one of the bitter fruits of breaking up.

Your only constructive course of action is to continue with your own healing and get on with your life. If it's any consolation, you may want to remind yourself that the worst has now occurred, and you survived. This guy broke up with you, he started seeing someone else, and now there's nothing left he can do to you.

Q: I broke up with Frank about a month ago after a two-year relationship. Now someone new has been asking me out. If I start seeing him, will it just be on the rebound and prove a mistake?

A: You're asking an important question, but the only accurate answer, as with many questions, is "It all depends." Partly it depends on your current frame of mind. Are you still, as one would expect after only a month, preoccupied with losing Frank? Are you still very angry at him, still hurt, confused or sad? Are you feeling very vulnerable because of the breakup, as if one more blow would push you over the edge? If so, then you're not yet ready to throw yourself into a new romantic relationship.

Dating someone new also depends on how you feel about *him*, of course. Are you sure you really like this guy? Are you sure he's more than just a stand-in for Frank, more than a distraction to take your mind off your loss? Unless you really are drawn to someone new, the relationship will surely fizzle and cause one or both of you pain somewhere down the line.

Whether you should date someone new depends, then, on whether you feel emotionally available to him and he genuinely seems interesting to you. If these conditions hold, then we say go ahead, but take it slow.

Q: Since I broke up with Jeff I've been eating like a pig and have gained 15 pounds. What's going on here?

A: What's going on is that you're in pain and have turned, quite naturally, to a painkiller. Overeating can momentarily numb your suffering, as can abusing alcohol, taking drugs, compulsively spending money or having indiscriminate sex. But of course all these activities backfire; the remedy is worse than the disease. When you overeat and put on weight you simply compound the bad feelings due to the breakup.

By definition, compulsive behaviors—overeating is one—are difficult to resist. Considering your difficulties following the breakup, we urge you to consult a counselor. In the meantime, try to use healthy coping devices during this vulnerable time. Possibilities include friendships, physical exercise, studies, clubs, activities, creative outlets, journal writing, religious faith and volunteer work.

Q: Why am I still thinking about my ex-girlfriend three years after we broke up?

A: There's no precise timetable for getting over a loss. If you love someone deeply, some of those feelings last a lifetime. You still think about the person because she meant so much to you.

At the same time, you also may dwell on your past relationship because present relationships pale by comparison. Like nature, the heart abhors a vacuum, so of course you'd hark back to the last person who deeply mattered. Once you find someone new, thoughts about your ex-girlfriend won't vanish but should recede into the background.

Q: I hurt so bad when my last relationship ended two years ago. How can I know that my next relationship will succeed?

A: You can't. In fact, the odds are stacked against you. The majority of love relationships break off sooner or later, and when they do, usually one or both partners feels horrible about it.

Why then try again? Why expose yourself to probable future heartache? The best answer we can give is that anything worthwhile is achieved in spite of the risk. When you learned to ride a bicycle, you fell off sometimes and scraped your knee. When you started off at kindergarten—and years later at college—you dared to leave home and face the unknown of teachers and classmates. And so it is with romance. Achieving the goal of intimacy requires a determination to keep going even though there's the likelihood you'll get hurt somewhere along the way.

Meanwhile, consider the alternative. You can play it safe and steer clear of potential involvements. You don't have to date seriously or at all, and you won't get hurt that way. But if safety first is your motto, you'll lead a restricted existence, like an agoraphobic who's afraid to leave the house. You'll be secure, but confined.

Let us be clear. We're not saying that you must have a romantic partner to be happy or that life is empty without romance. With that kind of thinking, you become desperate for love, and that's not good for you. What we *are* saying is that it's a pity to narrow your experience deliberately. Why not participate fully and take your chances on romance, as does everyone else?

MARRIAGE

Q: I'm 20 years old and in college. Does that seem too young to marry my girlfriend?

A: Only in the late twentieth century would this question even be asked. Before that time, marriage was considered perfectly appropriate at your age, or younger; Shakespeare's Juliet was all of 13 when she pledged herself to Romeo. But nowadays we tend to think of persons your age, particularly if they're college students, as somewhere in a fuzzy middle zone: no longer quite adolescents, not yet fully adults. The usual assumption is that 20-year-old students aren't ready to marry.

Is that fair? Certainly you may be capable of loving and making a commitment, and in that sense you're ready to marry. On the other hand, you and your girlfriend do have several strikes against you. For one, neither of you is finished with emotional and intellectual development. As you continue to grow up, you may find yourselves growing apart. And then there are finances to consider. You and your girlfriend may need money from your parents while you're still in college, and that may affect your sense of yourselves as married. Right after college, it may be difficult for you to assume the financial responsibilities of marriage. Bear in mind, too, that as college students you face important unknowns, such as what jobs you will find after college and where you will be located. Getting married now puts constraints on the opportunities you can pursue.

Since marrying during college is fairly unusual and means going against the cultural grain, you also should examine your motives. Are you marrying to escape from domineering parents? Are you running away from the pressures of college social life? Are you marrying to defy your parents, marrying mainly because they're so opposed to it? Are you trying to compensate for an unhappy childhood? Are there other meanings marriage holds for you?

Such a consequential decision deserves as much examination as you can give it. We recommend that you and your girlfriend seek out objective third parties, and perhaps a counselor, to help you gain perspective on your decision.

FOR FURTHER READING

Melba Colgrove, Harold Bloomfield, and Peter McWilliams, *How to Survive the Loss of a Love*. New York: Bantam, 1976.

Erich Fromm, *The Art of Loving*. New York: Bantam, 1963.

Willard Gaylin, *Rediscovering Love*. New York: Penguin, 1986.

Stephen Gullo and Connie Church, *Loveshock: How to Recover from a Broken Heart and Love Again*. New York: Bantam, 1990.

Judith Sills, *A Fine Romance*. New York: Ballantine, 1987.

Philip Zimbardo, *Shyness*. Reading, Mass.: Addison-Wesley, 1990.

S E X

Rare is the college student who has no worries about sex. This may come as a surprise to you. College students love to talk about sex but not about their sexual anxieties, and therefore it's easy to assume that other students don't have any. Everyone else besides you must be confident, knowledgeable, certain about sexual matters—and, of course, totally "normal."

In reality, you're in good company if "doing what comes naturally" doesn't feel so very natural. One reason for this is inexperience. Many students entering college have had few or no sexual contacts, and even those with extensive sexual histories are still just learning about themselves and other people. Sex is not simply an inborn drive. Comfort with sexuality depends on sexual experience, life experience and personal growth. Sex gets better as you mature.

Another source of anxiety is questions about normality. Many students falsely believe that there are only a few normal feelings, normal fantasies, normal "moves," normal physical responses. Comparing themselves to these supposed norms, they then conclude there's something disturbingly wrong about themselves. While it is true that some sexual behavior *is* unhealthy, often students frighten themselves needlessly. In fact, some worry themselves into a sexual problem where none originally existed.

You will notice frequent references in this chapter to nonsexual issues. That's because self-esteem, assertiveness and ability to communicate, to name three such issues, have an enormous impact on sexuality. To work on sexual concerns, often it's not enough to learn new information about sex or try out new sexual behaviors. You also have to take a close look at what makes you tick and how you relate to others.

TOO LITTLE OR TOO MUCH?

Q: I'm a male college senior who's never had sexual intercourse. Am I the last inexperienced 21-year-old alive?

A: Not at all. According to a recent study, chastity is gaining in popularity. Fewer college students have had sexual intercourse today than in 1979.[1]

Actually, there are good reasons to delay having sexual intercourse, or any sexual experiences. Your religious convictions or family teachings may argue against premarital sex. You may feel sex is wrong unless you're in love. You simply may not feel ready; sexual closeness is more than you can handle emotionally at this time. And then there are health considerations. While we don't want you to be frightened of sex, the threat of AIDS and other sexually transmitted diseases (STDs) is compelling reason to think carefully before deciding to hop into bed with someone.

Abstaining from sex is a valid choice, whether you've had sex before or never have had a lover in your life. You can choose to have some sexual relations but draw the line at sexual intercourse, or choose to refrain from sexual activity altogether. What matters is that abstinence feels right to you.

Q: But that's my problem. Someone else may prefer abstinence, but I *want* to become sexually experienced. What's wrong with me?

A: Several possibilities come to mind. One is that you're approaching women the wrong way and scaring them off (see pages 14–15 for tips on social skills). A second possibility is that it's *you* who's scared. You may fear the sex act itself, because maybe you won't "perform properly" or you're ashamed of your body. Or you may fear getting shot down if you express interest in a woman, or fear the emotional closeness that sex brings.

If fear is holding you back, then you are working at cross-purposes, both approaching and avoiding sexual intimacy. See if you can identify what, if anything, is frightening you. Sometimes recognizing a fear reduces its hold over you. You may realize that the fear is irrational and shouldn't stop you from pursuing sexual experiences.

Some fears are stubborn and deep-seated. If you have trouble identifying or overcoming fears about sex, consider discussing the matter at your college's counseling center. You'd be surprised at how many students they see with problems like yours.

Q: If I'm still inexperienced at 21, haven't I fallen too far behind my classmates?

A: Sexual experience isn't a race. Though sexual maturity does take time, you'll eventually learn about lovemaking regardless of when you start.

Q: What about technique? Aren't there certain things I need to learn to become a good lover?

A: Sure there are. Possibly when you're ready to have sex you'll find an experienced partner to teach you. If not, you and your partner will have to learn together through trial-and-error (which isn't so bad either).

But in our opinion sexual techniques count for only a small fraction of lovemaking. Much more important is good communication. Good lovers let each other know what they want and don't want, communicating both in words and through their actions in bed. Good lovemaking also depends on a commitment to shared pleasure. Selfish people who are insensitive to their partners' pleasure aren't good lovers, and neither are self-denying people who disregard their own pleasure. Good lovers strive for a mutual experience in which both partners are givers and receivers.

Q: I've had sex with lots of guys. Does that make me a slut?

A: Let's begin with the matter of labels. Words like "slut" don't help you understand your situation. Their only function is to frighten and condemn. So drop the name-calling and let's take a calm, objective look at what may be going on.

The issue here isn't how many partners you've had, but the reasons for your behavior and your feelings about it. Some people sleep with many partners and feel genuinely fulfilled. They like the sex, they like the closeness, and afterward they don't feel guilty; they haven't violated their own moral standards. They also don't exploit their partners or feel exploited by them. For them, casual sex is a natural, healthy expression of tender and sexual feelings (although of course casual sex does increase their risk of contracting AIDS or other STDs).

But people have sex for all kinds of reasons, not all of them healthy. If you've had many partners, you need to ask yourself some tough questions:

- Do you go to bed because you are afraid to lose the guy, afraid he won't want you otherwise?
- Are you simply afraid to tell someone no?
- Are you having sex when what you really want, but can't ask for, is just to know the person—to get close to him?
- Do you use sex to escape painful feelings of loneliness, anxiety or depression, or to express anger, to get back at someone?
- Do you sometimes go to bed against your better judgment, even with men you don't really like?
- Do you go to bed because you are drunk or high?
- After lovemaking do you end up feeling hurt, or used, or guilty, or angry?
- Do you have sex to convince yourself that you're lovable? In other words, do you have sex to compensate for low self-esteem?

Please consider these questions carefully. (Men, this applies to you, too.) If the answer is yes to *any* of them, then you're not having sex for healthy reasons. At this point, a sensible response might be to hold off on sex until you can feel confident about your motives. And if you can't seem to stop yourself despite knowing casual sex is wrong for you, then we recommend taking up this issue with a counselor.

Q: My problem is that I'm dating a tease. She starts to get physical with me, and then when I want to have intercourse she makes me stop.

A: Slow down a minute. Just because a woman likes physical contact but draws the line at intercourse doesn't make her a tease. (There's that label business again.) Women have a right to say no at any point of lovemaking—men do too. Make sure you respect your partner's limits regarding sex. (More on this point later in connection with date rape and acquaintance rape.)

On the other hand, there *are* some people, men as well as women, who promise sex or romance and then back away when you get interested. They act seductively because turning you on feeds their self-esteem (in men this is called the "Don Juan" complex). It's not *you* they really want; they want you to want them. If you suspect your girlfriend of this kind of "teasing" (and it's often done unconsciously), directly ask her what she wants from you. Open questions may put an end to the game-playing, allowing you to find out exactly where you stand. If this approach doesn't clarify your relationship, you may want to reevaluate the relationship and move on to someone else.

Q: I've been seeing my boyfriend for a while and our relationship is somewhat physical, but I just don't want to go all the way. What worries me is that everyone else seems to be doing it. What do you think?

A: What matters is not what everyone else may or may not be doing but what feels right to you. If you don't want sex because of your personal values, the health risks or simply a sense of not being ready, then you are making a wise decision by setting a limit to your lovemaking. Just make sure that you and your partner are open with each other about your expectations in this area.

Q: This guy I just met says he wants to make love. I'd like to have sex with him, but how do I know when I'm ready?

A: The answer depends on your personal values and on what you want from sex. Assuming you want more than a casual experience, we suggest waiting at least until you sense the beginnings of a real relationship. For sexual intercourse—or any physical contact, for that matter—isn't only an experience, it's also a deepening of involvement. Sex draws you closer, implies that something is happening between you. But upon first meeting, people usually don't feel ready to take this step. Because sex is a plunge into involvement, one or the other party may get scared and run away before the relationship can get started.

If you have hopes for this new person, we suggest postponing lovemaking until your feelings and his feelings point toward a real relationship.

PROBLEMS COUPLES HAVE

Q: My boyfriend never wants to have sex anymore. I know infatuation dies after a few months, but this is ridiculous: We've become like brother and sister. What should we do?

A: Once again, we stress the importance of good communication, not just about sex but your entire relationship. Share your concern about your dormant sex life, and then ask what's going on with him. Have his romantic feelings died? Does he like someone else? Is he annoyed or angry at you? Is he so worried about school or the future that his mind isn't on romance? Does he feel *you* don't care about him or want to make love?

Partners often feel uncomfortable about speaking their minds. What they can't put into words, they may convey through sexual behavior. Hurt, anger, insecurity or lack of interest may come out in conflicting ways, through avoiding sex, demanding sex, acting physically cold or showing extra physical tenderness. You need, then, to talk openly with your partner and address the underlying problem, whatever it may be. If you can work out whatever's troubling him—and that's a big "if," of course—the sexual spark may return.

Q: Every time I get ready to have intercourse I lose my erection. Why is this happening to me?

A: It's possible you have a medical problem, and therefore your first step should be to consult a doctor. But if it's not physical, there may be a psychological cause; some thoughts, feelings or motives may be interfering with your sexual abilities. We realize this may not be a very comfortable notion for you. If you're like most young males, you want to be like those smooth characters portrayed in the movies—always ready to perform, under all conditions. Sorry, human beings don't work that way. If for some reason you are troubled, then you may not be able to have sex; your mind will make your penis go soft. This problem isn't rare, by the way. Perhaps half the male population has experienced at least temporary difficulties with erection, usually for nonmedical reasons.

Why might your mind turn off to sex? The cause could be stress (perhaps more than you realize) or depression; reduced "libido" is a classic sign of depression. You also could feel angry or distant toward your partner, in which case your impotence is sending a message that you haven't wanted to deliver directly.

Another possible culprit is worry about the sex act itself. When you fret about how good a lover you are or whether you can sustain an erection, your attention is on your worry rather than the pleasure of lovemaking. You're too preoccupied to be excited. The more you dwell on performing, the less likely you'll be able to perform.

Q: What can I do about this problem?

A: In this case, the wisest course is to seek help from a professional counselor. (And yes, these difficulties usually can be helped). In the meantime, we recommend doing what you can to take the pressure out of lovemaking. Specifically, choose a partner who is understanding and makes you feel comfortable. Don't act like a stud or pretend to more experience than you have; trying to live up to a "cool" image only increases the pressure. And let yourself enjoy *all* of lovemaking—kissing, touching, closeness—without putting undue emphasis on intercourse.

One method recommended by sex therapists is to postpone intercourse and slowly build up to it, as you learn to find sex pleasurable again. The idea is to advance toward more intimate sexual acts one comfortable step at a time. First, you and your partner might only caress. Later, you might freely explore each other's bodies, but without touching the genitals. Later still, you might incorporate genital contact, but without attempting intercourse. Finally, after a period of weeks or even months, you would feel ready to resume sexual intercourse. This approach depends on feeling comfortable at each step, and has the best chance of success if you're also seeing a professional.

One warning: Don't calm your fears through alcohol or other drugs. Getting high can depress sexual performance and leave you more discouraged than ever.

Q: What can I do if I come too quickly?

A: This is a common problem for young males, especially those who are sexually inexperienced. Since anxiety can be causing the problem, we again recommend taking the pressure off by choosing an understanding sexual partner and by not overemphasizing intercourse. Also, try not to upset yourself when you ejaculate—or come—quickly; if you do, so be it. To reduce sexual urgency, you may try masturbating before lovemaking, or try to have sex a second time after you've already come once.

You can also try this exercise while you masturbate: First stop stimulating yourself just before ejaculation, then start again when your excitement has subsided, then stop again, and so forth. Through this masturbation exercise, you learn to recognize your pre-ejaculation sensations, which helps you control your level of sexual arousal and so control when you ejaculate.

Q: What should the partner do? My ex-boyfriend kept losing his erection, and now my current boyfriend comes too soon. Is it my fault they're having problems?

A: No, it's not. You can't cause someone else to lose his erection or ejaculate prematurely. Besides, we discourage you from thinking in terms of fault anyway. An atmosphere of blame, whether self-blame or blaming your partner, heightens the tension and may make matters worse.

Your boyfriend's problem must be frustrating. As much as possible, though, try to convey support and understanding; encourage your boyfriend not to overreact to the problem. Search together for sexual satisfaction apart from intercourse through hugging and kissing, petting, masturbation, oral sex, whatever. Though his problem isn't your fault, your patience, flexibility and good humor may help him overcome it.

Q: I love my boyfriend, I'm attracted to him and in my limited experience he seems like a good lover. But I don't enjoy sex. Am I just frigid?

A: Again, we frown on using emotionally loaded labels like "frigid." More than likely, your problem has nothing to do with inherent sexual unresponsiveness, which is what frigidity implies. Consider four alternative explanations:

1. You were taught when you were young that sex, or at least premarital sex, is dirty and wrong, or you were taught to fear and loathe men. Your views since then may have changed; consciously you may be pro-sex and pro-male. But early teachings have an insidious staying power. To be true to your original teachers, you don't sexually let yourself go.
2. You lack sexual assertiveness. In bed, you devote yourself totally to pleasing your partner, discounting your own sexual needs and pleasures, not wanting to be "selfish." Naturally, sex isn't much fun.
3. You're not relaxed when making love; you're too worried about doing it right. Similar to men who have difficulty with an erection, you worry about being a good lover, having an orgasm, feeling the right feelings or possessing the right kind of body. Such worries, as we have seen, squelch sexual feelings.
4. You haven't discovered your full sexuality. You're not yet responding sexually because you haven't yet learned how. This is especially

likely if you don't masturbate and have little overall sexual experience.

Q: So if I'm not basically "frigid," what should I do about my problem?

A: For starters, you need to decide if premarital sex is right for you. If your beliefs run deeply against it, which may be why you don't feel pleasure, then the answer is to put off lovemaking until you're married and can feel really comfortable.

But let's suppose premarital sex feels right for you. In that case, certainly there are things you can try to work on the basic problem. You can, for instance, counteract negative thinking by repeating to yourself that sexual feeling is natural, that men are human. You can practice being sexually assertive, asking for what you want in bed and letting yourself be "selfish" and feel pleasure. You can try to reduce sexual pressure, perhaps by deemphasizing or postponing intercourse, or by encouraging yourself to relax while making love. And, if your religious and ethical beliefs permit, you can discover yourself sexually through masturbation.

But don't be alarmed if nothing much happens for a while. You may just be a slow sexual developer who takes years to reach full responsiveness. You'll probably get there, but it will take time and patience.

Q: I never have an orgasm when I'm with my boyfriend. What should I do?

A: Many women don't have orgasms with their partners, especially during intercourse. If your boyfriend doesn't stimulate your clitoris in the right way or for long enough, you can ask him to do this and show him how you'd like it done. If he's entering you before you're ready, speak up and let him know you want more foreplay.

Remember, though, that enjoying sex doesn't depend on having an orgasm. If lovemaking with your partner is enjoyable, then there really isn't a problem. Lovemaking is an expression of closeness and a shared experience of pleasure. It shouldn't be a goal- directed activity where success is measured by whether you climax.

Q: Sometimes sex is fantastic and sometimes it's just so-so. Is that normal?

A: Yes. However, you may raise your batting average of fantastic times if you and your partner openly communicate about what you like and want.

Q: My boyfriend always gets on top of me and has intercourse in the standard "missionary position." I'd like to try other ways to make love, and maybe have oral sex. How do I bring this up?

A: Your boyfriend may be sexually shy and inexperienced, or he may be a slave to sex-role expectations and feel unmanly unless he "mounts" a woman. We recommend simply telling him or showing him what you'd like to try. Make clear that you're not criticizing him; you just want to experiment. With luck, he'll be delighted to try something new now that he knows you approve.

Each of you should respect the other's limits, however. If there's something either one of you doesn't want to do—some people don't like oral sex, for example—then don't do it.

Q: Right after we make love my boyfriend turns over and goes to sleep. Why are guys like that?

A: Partly it's a question of biology. Males and females have some inborn differences in sexual responsiveness. Males are innately aroused more quickly than females, and after orgasm their sexual excitement subsides more quickly (and they can grow sleepy). Women can have multiple orgasms, while men for a while after ejaculation (the refractory period) can't have an erection or ejaculate again.

Other differences between the sexes depend at least partly on conditioning, or learning. Traditionally in our society, males are taught to be sexual pursuers and aggressors, who act and feel tough. Women are taught to let themselves be pursued, play a passive role in bed and express tender emotions. Males are taught to dissociate sex from love, while females learn to link the two. Males learn to value independence and competitive striving; females are taught to emphasize relatedness and cooperation.

But these are tendencies, not hard-and-fast rules. In recent years the feminist movement and other societal trends have blurred traditional sex roles, so that more women feel comfortable being assertive in and out of the bedroom, and more men are comfortable acknowledging tender emotions and dependency needs. We must also allow for individual differences. Even in the pre-feminist era, there were plenty of women and plenty of men who didn't conform to feminine and masculine stereotypes.

Now back to your boyfriend. Probably he turns his back on you partly for a biological reason—after ejaculation he *is* sleepy—and partly for the sociocultural reason that he isn't comfortable expressing tender, nonsexual feelings. Then again, his behavior isn't chiseled in stone. Have you tried asking him to stay awake? Perhaps in spite of biology and in spite of cultural expectations he'd be happy to cuddle with you if only you asked.

Q: My boyfriend is pretty awkward in bed, but I'm crazy about him anyway and frankly it's not a big problem. Is our relationship okay?

A: Satisfaction is entirely a personal matter. In our society we are bombarded with sexual images on TV, in the movies and in magazines, and it's easy to lose perspective about sex. But there are many important aspects to a relationship; sex isn't everything. If on balance your relationship truly pleases you, then you've answered your own question and you've got a good thing going.

MASTURBATION AND FANTASIES

Q: Shouldn't people stop masturbating by college?

A: They should? Many men and women masturbate their whole lives, even after they're married. Provided you have privacy—which isn't easy to find in college—and provided your religious and ethical beliefs permit, there's no reason why you have to stop masturbating.

Q: But suppose I masturbate too often?

A: What do you mean by "too often"? Do you masturbate instead of going to class, studying, spending time with friends? If so, then indeed you do it too often; we would say the same thing if you overdid physical exercise or snacking. The issue isn't how frequently you masturbate but whether it interferes with important activities in your life.

Masturbation won't hurt you physically or mentally. It won't prevent you from making love with a partner. (Many lovers incorporate masturbation into their lovemaking.) And guys, masturbation won't use up your sperm or leave you physically weakened.

In our experience, many college males who are ashamed of masturbation come from law-and-order, authoritarian or perfectionist households. They've been taught rigid standards of right and wrong, and masturbation is a natural for the "wrong" column. If you are one of these men, you have two options. You can cease and desist, which is hard to do but possible. Alternatively, you can reevaluate your attitude that masturbation is wrong or bad. It may help to know that over 90% of your peers do in fact masturbate. If you have trouble coming to terms with masturbation, you may want to work out negative feelings by talking to a counselor.

Q: Sometimes I have odd sexual daydreams, like making a woman my slave. Should I be worried?

A: Probably not. All of us have diverse sexual wishes that come out in fantasies and dreams. Heterosexual men, it's been found, may have occasional fantasies about sexual dominance, making love to two women, women making love together, even sex with other men—and lots more besides. Heterosexual women may have occasional fantasies about being viewed naked, having sex with young boys or with other women, even being forced to have sex—and, again, many other themes.

The point to remember is that fantasies and dreams fall into a separate category from actions and behavior. Just because something excites you in imagination doesn't mean at all that you'd actually want to do it. (No one *really* wants to be raped.) As long as you can enjoy sex without acting out harmful fantasies—as long as you don't hurt yourself or someone else in reality—then your fantasies are probably nothing to worry about. It's only when your fantasies are disturbing to you, perhaps because they're violent, or you feel compelled to act out harmful fantasies in reality that you would be wise to seek some assistance.

Q: What does it mean if I think about other people when I'm having intercourse with my boyfriend?

A: Here again we are talking about fantasies. Most people do have occasional wandering thoughts during lovemaking. It's not uncommon to think of other places, other acts or other persons.

On the other hand, the essential pleasure of sex is to be with a separate individual and briefly unite. If during lovemaking you mostly feel apart from your boyfriend, then something may be amiss. Possibly you don't feel sexually or romantically drawn to him, in which case you need to ask yourself why you stay in the relationship. Maybe you mentally withdraw because something about emotional closeness or the sex act itself makes you uncomfortable. You don't fully want to be doing what you're doing, and that's why your attention wanders to other people.

One commonsense tactic worth a try is focusing on the here-and-now during lovemaking. Concentrate on touching and being touched, on what you hear and see and smell, right at the moment. Whenever your attention wanders, gently bring yourself back to the here-and-now, and to your partner. This simple exercise may enable you to share the immediate experience with your partner.

Q: Sometimes I've passed by windows and peeked inside at women who are undressing. What's wrong with me?

A: Your problem is called voyeurism. It's one of the "paraphilias," a group of sexual problems that includes exhibitionism (publicly exposing your genitals), sadism (getting sexual pleasure from hurting your partner), masochism (getting sexual pleasure from your own suffering) and fetishism (getting pleasure from objects or nonsexual body parts).

All of these themes are common and of no concern, so long as they remain just fantasies. There's no harm in imagining a woman taking her clothes off; most heterosexual men do. There's also nothing wrong if you and a partner consent to act out a fantasy where no one actually gets hurt. But that's not what's happening in your case. You are peeking at women without their permission. You are violating their rights and also breaking the law.

Why are you doing this? Shyness and a sense of inadequacy may play a part. It seems safer to sneak a look at women than to approach them and risk rejection. At any rate, don't wait to get caught before you seek assistance. We urge you to go into counseling without delay.

PROTECTION

Q: My boyfriend and I are ready to start making love. What's the best protection to use?

A: At the very least, use latex condoms ("rubbers") and for extra protection combine the condoms with a contraceptive jelly, cream or foam containing nonoxynol-9, a spermicide (it kills sperm). Condoms and spermicides, though not foolproof, provide some measure of contraception (birth control), and are your best bet other than abstinence against the threat of AIDS and other sexually transmitted diseases (STDs). The only exception to condom and spermicide use would be if you and your partner are totally monogamous (more about this later), and you're both certain, through lab tests, that you don't carry the AIDS virus or have another STD.

Condoms are available without prescription at drugstores and most likely at your college's health service. Thin rubber sheaths placed over the erect penis before intercourse, they collect sperm and prevent it from entering the vagina. They must be applied at the *beginning* of foreplay so that no sperm or pre-ejaculation fluid (pre-come) enters the vagina, and a new one is necessary every time you have intercourse. Because of their role in protecting against AIDS and other STDS, many colleges have promoted their use, giving away free condoms and publicizing them at health fairs. At Wellesley College a student group, AIDS Alert, sold condom jewelry to raise AIDS awareness and increase students' comfort with condoms.

Condoms are equally necessary for gay male couples and heterosexual couples.

Q: What other forms of protection should I consider in addition to condoms?

A: First, let us emphasize that *whatever* other method you use to prevent pregnancy, there is no substitute for condoms and spermicides in preventing the spread of AIDS and STDs. Condoms alone are 90% effective in preventing pregnancy.[2] Other methods can be used in addition to condoms and spermicide as an extra form of contraception. For every method, it is essential that a woman follow a doctor's instructions and/or read the product's instructions carefully.

The most popular contraceptive method for college women is the *pill*. Prescribed by a doctor, the pill prevents ovulation, the monthly release of an egg from the ovary for possible fertilization. Birth control pills are more than 99.9% effective in preventing pregnancy, if used properly. The trouble is that some women forget to take them every day; missing even a single day renders them ineffective. Another question is the pill's effects on health. Some studies indicate that the pill reduces a woman's chances of developing ovarian cancer and cancer of the lining of the uterus, but increases the chances of a heart attack or stroke later in life.

Diaphragms are placed in the vagina and prevent the man's sperm from reaching the uterus. They are used in conjunction with a cream or jelly spermicide. Prescribed and fitted by a doctor, diaphragms have no dangerous side effects and are effective in preventing pregnancy if used properly. However, with typical use, diaphragms and spermicides are only 81% effective. They require insertion before intercourse and must be left in for several hours after intercourse.

Similar to diaphragms are *cervical caps*. Fitted onto the cervix with suction, cervical caps prevent sperm from entering the vagina and are used in conjunction with a spermicide. Available by prescription, they must be inserted every time before intercourse and require time to learn to use correctly. They have no serious side effects and with typical use are 87% effective.

Intrauterine devices, or *IUDs*, are placed by a specialist into the uterus, where they prevent the egg from implanting. They are 95% effective in preventing pregnancy and require no further action after being inserted. Because they are quite expensive and they possibly increase the risk of pelvic inflammatory disease—sexually transmitted infections that can cause infertility or even be life-threatening—IUDs are not recommended for college-age women.

Several other contraceptive methods are available at drugstores without a prescription. The *sponge* is a relatively new device consisting of a sponge that contains spermicidal chemicals. Like the diaphragm and cervical cap, it must be inserted into the vagina before intercourse and left in for several hours afterwards. With typical use, the sponge is 80–90% effective in preventing pregnancy. *Foams*, *creams* and *jellies* also contain spermicides and are placed in the vagina before inter-course. Typically only 82% effective in preventing pregnancy, these methods are better used in combination with condoms.

Another method is based on *fertility awareness*. The woman learns to observe bodily signs of fertility, and she and her partner then abstain from intercourse around these times (during ovulation) or use an alternative method of contraception. This method requires special training and both partners must cooperate for it to work; it is not recommended for college students, who because of stress may ovulate at different times of the month. Incidentally, checking calendar dates to calculate times of ovulation—the "rhythm" method—is considered unreliable, especially if the woman has irregular periods.

Finally, we should mention *withdrawal*, where the man withdraws his penis from the vagina just before ejaculating. This method is unreliable because the man may not withdraw in time, and even before ejaculation a small amount of semen-containing fluid may be released into the vagina.

This brief summary of birth control methods in no way exhausts the issues involved with each method. Before making any decisions about protection, we urge you to speak to your doctor or to a specialist at your college's health service or birth control clinic. Also, make sure you discuss the matter with your partner, if you have one. After all, if there's a pregnancy or a sexually transmitted disease, both of you will be affected.

Q: But what if my partner doesn't like us to use condoms?

A: He or she isn't the only one. According to recent studies, the majority of college students fail to use condoms on a consistent basis.[3] They may know about AIDS and other STDs, but their knowledge isn't translated into safe behavior.

The reasons your partner may feel this way are many. He or she may think that:

- "Nothing can happen if we only take an occasional risk." But this simply isn't true. As one student said, "It's like playing Russian Roulette with your dick."[4] Just one time of unprotected sex may infect you with the AIDS virus or another sexually transmitted disease.
- "People our age don't get infected." Again, this is wrong. True, you personally may not know any classmates who have AIDS; warnings and educational programs may seem like crying wolf when AIDS itself seems invisible on campus. But the reason you don't know anyone is because AIDS takes years to develop after infection with the HIV virus. There are plenty of college students who've been infected with HIV. Some time in the future, these young, healthy people—including, chances are, someone you know—will develop AIDS. What's more, other sexually transmitted diseases—especially chlamydia and genital warts, or human papilloma virus (HPV)—are skyrocketing on college campuses; the risk of contracting either chlamydia or genital warts is one in ten.[5] Among other consequences, chlamydia can cause sterility, and genital warts have been linked to cancer.
- "Straight people won't get AIDS." This is no safeguard. Not only is the AIDS epidemic growing, but there's a higher rate of increase among heterosexuals than homosexuals. While experts are still sorting out the facts about AIDS, certainly there is a risk of transmission of AIDS by unprotected sexual intercourse between men and women. And the other STDs don't care about your sexual orientation either.
- "We don't have to use condoms because we're monogamous." Being monogamous only protects you if neither of you is infected, which you can't know unless you're both tested for the AIDS virus and for

other STDs. Further, monogamy implies a long-term, years-long relationship in which neither of you has another partner, and this is rare for college students. An article in the student paper at Columbia University rightly observes, "Most students have multiple sexual partners during their time on campus. Having unprotected intercourse with one person at a time does not guarantee safety."[6]

- "I don't want to ruin the mood by discussing protection and putting on a condom." To this argument we say: Don't wait until the last minute to discuss protection. Talk about condoms well before intercourse becomes a possibility, so you don't have to stage a debate in the heat of passion. As for putting on a condom, with practice it becomes an easy procedure, part of the lovemaking.
- "Sex doesn't feel as good with condoms." We can't argue with what you feel. However, consider that the problem may be more in your attitude than in loss of sensation. With an open mind, it's certainly possible to use a condom and enjoy full sexual pleasure.

Q: But if my partner still doesn't like us to use condoms, what should I do?

A: Here are some suggestions:

- Take seriously what you know about the transmission and dangers of AIDS and STDs. Even before confronting your partner (or partners), pledge to yourself that a condom, and preferably a spermicide too, will be used every single time you have sex. Be firm in your resolve that these protections will be used from the beginning to the end of all sex acts, without exception.
- Next, discuss protection with your partner before you make love. Be assertive; insist that a condom and spermicide be used. Stick to your position if he or she raises objections or downplays the importance of these protections.
- When in bed, back up your agreement with consistently assertive behavior. If your partner gets all hot and bothered and wants to race into lovemaking, call a time-out (we know it's hard) and insist on protection. If he or she promises that protection isn't needed, simply say you won't have sex otherwise. If your partner refuses, then leave or tell him or her to leave. The bottom line is, *you have to take responsibility for your own health; you can't leave it up to your partner.*
- Avoid drinking or taking drugs before you have sex. Getting high impairs judgment and increases the chances you'll forget about

protection. In many cases of unprotected sexual intercourse, one or both partners have been drinking or taking drugs.

Q: But suppose I have trouble bringing up the topic of protection?

A: This can be a problem. You may be a shy person, embarrassed to talk about sex, or an unassertive person, who lets your partner call the shots. You may fear your partner will reject you if you insist on condom use. You may like to think of sex as something that just happens, a spontaneous act of passion, rather than a purposeful activity requiring planning for protection.

Consider, though, that we're talking here about your health and *your life*. Whatever your hesitations, you can't afford to remain silent about protection. So if it's hard for you to speak up about condoms and such, rehearse beforehand what you want to say. Remember that this serious topic can be addressed with humor; the discussion doesn't have to be grim. Ask a close friend to let you role-play the situation. If necessary, consult a counselor to build up your assertive skills. One way or another, you need to overcome your inhibitions and communicate assertively to protect yourself.

Q: Even though I know how to protect myself, I'm still frightened about getting AIDS. Is that irrational?

A: It depends. If you have the wrong idea about AIDS transmission, then yes, your fear is partly irrational. Despite campus educational programs, some students are still convinced that the AIDS virus (HIV) can be transmitted through tears, saliva, food, casual contact with an infected person, or through association with a gay or lesbian classmate! But the AIDS virus can only be transmitted when: 1) the semen or female genital secretions of an infected person, either straight or gay, enters your body during sex; 2) an infected person's blood is transmitted to you during sharing of needles for intravenous drug use; 3) an infected person's blood is transmitted to you during a blood transfusion (thanks to blood testing, this is very rare); or 4) an infected person's blood is transferred from his or her open wound to your wound (again, this is rare). You cannot get AIDS in any other way.

Fear of AIDS also can get out of hand if you mix up AIDS with other issues. Consider this case. Ever since Steve had a single homosexual experience one year earlier, he had been terrified about contracting AIDS. The fear had no medical basis—he and his partner had used condoms and he'd recently tested negatively for HIV—but Steve resisted reassurance. He was obsessed with AIDS because it represented the punishment he felt he deserved for acting on homosexual impulses.

Although fear of AIDS can have an irrational basis, obviously it's not crazy to be afraid of a disease that can kill you. If AIDS makes you wary, perhaps it's just as well. That way you'll take the proper precautions.

Q: How else should I protect myself against AIDS and STDs if I want to be sexually active?

A: The first rule bears repeating: Use latex condoms and spermicides containing nonoxynol-9 whenever you have sex. In addition, here are other precautions:

- Get tested if you have any reason to suspect you've been exposed to an STD infection. Not only are STDs dangerous in their own right, but they may facilitate the transmission of the AIDS virus.
- Some common symptoms of STDs are: discharge or bleeding from the vagina, discharge from the penis, burning sensation while urinating, painful sores, a rash or blisters on or near genitals, small pink growths on genitals, genital itching, unexplained fevers and weight loss.
- Some STDs don't cause these symptoms, however; chlamydia, the most prevalent STD on campus, often has no symptoms and goes undetected. Therefore even without symptoms you should get tested if you've been sexually active, particularly if you're not conscientious about using protection.
- Choose your partner or partners carefully. Ask about his or her past and current sexual partners, history of STDs and history of needle use.
- Think it over if you tend to have many partners. The more partners you have, the greater the risk of contracting the AIDS virus or another STD.
- Be cautious about engaging in anal sex, where there is a higher risk that condoms will break.
- For a couple of reasons, don't mix sex with alcohol and drugs. Not only do alcohol and drugs impair your judgment and lead to risky behavior, but they can damage your immune system and make you more susceptible to AIDS.

- For more information on AIDS and STDs, contact the organizations listed at the end of this book.

UNWANTED PREGNANCY

Q: I just found out I'm pregnant. I don't want to have an abortion, but if I keep the baby my life is ruined. What do I do?

A: We recognize how overwhelming all this must now seem. This is a decision you weren't expecting, and now that it's here you don't have much time to make it. You have to consider many factors in making your decision, factors which may pull at you in different directions.

What are these factors? There may be your religious and ethical values for or against abortion. There is your relationship, close or casual, with the man involved. There are the probable reactions of family and friends, assuming you choose to tell them. If you lean toward having the child, there is the dramatic change in your immediate life (college probably must be postponed), and possibly a reassessment of your career plans and future goals. If you opt for adoption, there is the guilt you may feel, and perhaps a surprising disappointment at missing out now on being a mother. With an abortion, you also must promptly arrange for the procedure, find a way to pay for it and prepare yourself for the experience.

As complicated and distressing as all this can be, bear in mind that the decision is hardest at the beginning, when the shock of being pregnant clouds your thinking. After the shock subsides, you'll be better able to decide what to do. Although unwanted pregnancy isn't a small matter, remember that thousands of college women have faced, and come through, the same predicament.

To help you cope, get support and guidance from others you trust, especially from your parents if they're likely to be supportive. (Some parents are initially upset but soon calm down and are tremendously helpful.) If at all possible, include the man in the process. Not only does he share responsibility, but he has feelings of his own concerning the pregnancy and the possibility of an abortion. The college health service can also help; if you decide on an abortion, they can refer you to a clinic. Finally, we recommend counseling sessions both before and after you make a decision to help you sort out complex feelings and get on with your life.

HOMOSEXUALITY

Q: I'm terrified that I may be gay. How do I know?

A: Before you jump to conclusions, let's first talk about the fear itself. Some college-age people have "homosexual panic"—massive anxiety about being lesbian or gay. Often they come to the college counseling center convinced that their lives are ruined, dreading what their parents will think. Sometimes they feel suicidal.

As it happens, some of these terrified students don't turn out to be gay or lesbian after all. Despite their fears, they have prematurely and incorrectly labeled their sexual orientation. So if you want to find out about your sexuality, the first step is to put aside the doomsday outlook and objectively examine the evidence.

Q: But how could I be wrong about my sexuality?

A: It's possible, especially if you have naive notions about hetero-sexuality. Heterosexuality signifies that you're predominantly attracted sexually and romantically to the opposite sex. It does not necessarily mean that you find big breasts a turn-on if you are male or large penises if you are female, or that you're excited by the thought of oral sex or any other sex act, or that you are horny all the time, or in short that you feel what your friends say they feel. But you may not realize this. Since your inner experience doesn't match the supposed norms, you may decide there's something wrong with you and you must be homosexual. This hasty conclusion is especially likely if you're not yet sure of what you feel. If like many undergraduates you're still discovering your sexual interests, you may take your uncertainty as a sign of being gay or a lesbian.

You can also be wrong about your sexual orientation because of comparing yourself to societal sex role stereotypes. You may be a male who doesn't like football and beer or have large muscles, who's shy and sensitive. You may be an assertive, large-framed female, and not particularly interested now in finding the right man, getting married and having a family. Male or female, you may not be popular with the opposite sex or go out on dates. None of these facts proves anything about your sexuality, but again you may not know this. Since you fail to fit the conventional image of masculinity or femininity, you foist a "gay" or "lesbian" label on yourself that may not apply.

The truth, of course, is that heterosexuals have diverse sexual interests and come in all shapes and personality types. You don't have to get turned on by what turns on your classmates in order to be straight; you just have to be excited by the opposite sex. Neither do you have to be a stereotypical macho male or a stereotypical cute and dainty female.

Of course, gays and lesbians too are diverse. Despite the stereotypes of the limp-wristed, effeminate gay male and the "butch" lesbian, the majority of gay men and lesbians aren't like that and can't be identified unless they choose to reveal their sexual preference.

Q: Are there other reasons why I might think I'm gay when I'm not?

A: Certainly. For one thing, you may have conflicts about heterosexual relationships. You may be frightened, for example, of rejection by the opposite sex, or of not being able to perform well in bed. You may not want to become emotionally close to somebody, not want to deal with the demands and intimacy of a commitment. If for such reasons heterosexual relationships scare you off, you may mistakenly decide that you're gay or lesbian.

Another explanation is a low self-esteem. You're awful, you're "abnormal," you're homosexual—in our society, unfortunately, these judgments are sometimes used interchangeably. Accusing yourself of being gay or lesbian provides a terrific excuse to beat yourself up.

Identity problems can also mislead you. If you are generally confused about who you are, then it can happen that you'll question a major component of your identity: your sexual orientation. The real issue here isn't whether you're straight or gay, but whether you have a deficient sense of self.

In sum, there are many reasons why you may mistake your sexual orientation. Just as children call each other "queer" as an all-purpose insult, you may brand yourself "gay" or "lesbian," as an all-purpose explanation for your problems.

Q: But what if I really do feel sexually attracted to members of my own sex? At times when my roommate Laura walks around our room undressed, I know I've felt excited.

A: It happens sometimes. At college, you share a room with someone your own age. You see one another naked; you may talk about erotic experiences and fantasies; you become emotionally close. Given this degree of intimacy and the strength of your late adolescent hormones, it's not surprising if occasionally you feel something sexual toward Laura—or, for that matter, toward friends, acquaintances and professors. In the supercharged collegiate atmosphere, expect to have stray sexual thoughts about lots of people, male and female.

But a few isolated instances of attraction don't determine your sexuality. You need a lot more evidence pointing in one direction or the other before you can reach a conclusion.

Q: During junior high school I had some sexual contact with another male student. Does that make me a homosexual?

A: Again, not necessarily. Sexual experimentation with the same sex is not rare among young people. Neither is it new. The Kinsey Report, conducted in the 1940s, found that 37% of American males and 13% of females had had a same-sex experience to the point of orgasm at least once since adolescence. Many of these individuals were not basically homosexual.

Q: Then I'm confused. How do I find out if I'm heterosexual, homosexual or bisexual?

A: It is the overall *pattern* of your sexual and romantic interests that decides. Are your arousing fantasies *primarily* about persons from the opposite sex? Is it *usually* someone from the opposite sex who turns you on, whose company causes your heart to pound? Has this been the *predominant* trend? If so, then you're probably heterosexual. If, though, the majority of your sexual and romantic feelings are directed toward the same sex, then you may well have a homosexual orientation. And if you are aroused equally by both males and females, then your sexual orientation may be bisexual.

Some college students recall being aware of their homosexuality from a very young age, although they didn't have a name for it or fully understand their feelings. Many heterosexuals "know" their sexuality just as early. But as noted earlier, other college students are still unsure at age 18 or 21, still trying to discover what they feel, and for whom. If you're one of these undecideds, you may be tempted to end uncertainty by assigning yourself an identity—heterosexual, homosexual or bisexual. But in our view, it makes sense to forgo labels until you've sorted out your feelings and desires. There'll be plenty of time later, once you're certain of your sexual leanings, to declare your orientation.

Q: Couldn't I be mistaken the other way and think I'm a heterosexual when I'm not?

A: Absolutely. If you are truly homosexual but ashamed of it, you may not admit to yourself what you really feel. You may explain away homosexual experiences ("I was drunk") or your lack of heterosexual desire ("I haven't met the right person;" "I'm not interested in a relationship right now"). You may tell yourself that attraction for the same sex is just a phase, something you'll outgrow, or a weakness, something you can work on.

Denying your homosexuality makes you a stranger to yourself and prevents you from making informed choices about sex and relationships. That's why, again, you need to be honest with yourself and certain of your feelings before you declare your sexual orientation.

Q: Isn't there something psychologically wrong with me if I'm gay or a lesbian?

A: No more so than if you were straight. After years of debate, the American Psychological Association and the American Psychiatric Association now view homosexuality as a valid expression of human sexuality, not a psychological disturbance. What's more, some studies have found that homosexuals are no more likely than heterosexuals to have psychological abnormalities.[7]

While homosexuality itself isn't a psychological problem, it can cause you psychological distress. One reason is society's "homophobia"—its fear and intolerance of homosexuality. Even on a college campus, where overt gay-bashing is relatively rare, homophobia does exist. Through innuendos, hostile looks and small rejections, some heterosexual classmates will treat you as different and inferior. These incidents hurt. You may feel depressed or embittered when you confront homophobia at your college.

Being gay or lesbian can also cause internal conflict. If you internalize society's rejection of homosexuality, you become homophobic yourself. You fear and hate your own desires, in effect fear and hate yourself. If this happens, you then have something psychologically "wrong" with you, as you suspected, but it's self-rejection rather than sexual orientation that's the problem.

Q: Why am I homosexual?

A: This is a debatable question. There is some scientific evidence, at least for males, pointing to a biological predisposition to homosexuality.[8] Another theory suggests, again for males, that distant fathers and overprotective mothers tend to produce homosexuals; by no means, however, does every gay male come from such a family. According to a third theory, homosexuality is something you learn based on what happens to you. Say you're positively reinforced for homosexual behaviors; someone from the same sex accepts you and gives you sexual pleasure. Meanwhile perhaps you're rejected by the opposite sex, or teased by heterosexual peers. You then may learn from this carrot-and-stick reward system to become a gay male or a lesbian.

Though each theory has plausibility, most experts think homosexuality is caused by a combination of factors. In any event, no one can say for certain what factors account for your own sexual orientation. Certainly there's no point blaming your parents, let alone yourself. Why you get turned on when you do is a puzzle still well beyond the reach of modern science.

Q: If I'm homosexual, can I change?

A: Probably not. Sexual orientation is too integral a part of the personality to be reversed. Over the years, mental health professionals have tried behavior therapy, psychoanalysis and other forms of treatment to change homosexuality, but most therapists today see these efforts as a waste of time. As some gays have puckishly observed, changing homosexuality is no more realistic than "curing" heterosexuality.

Counseling can be helpful for some gay men and lesbians, however, by reducing their guilt, self-hatred and fear. With counseling, you can go from cursing your sexuality to accepting it, and you can decide how, if at all, you want to act on your impulses.

Q: But considering my upbringing and society's homophobia, how can I ever learn to be comfortable with being homosexual?

A: Like any other large goal, this one takes time and effort. Here are some suggestions:

- Talk to other gay, lesbian or questioning students. If you don't know anyone personally, attend discussion groups sponsored by your college's gay/lesbian organization (most colleges have one) or the counseling center. Through conferring with other students or reading the existing literature you will feel less strange and alone.

- Identify your reasons for rejecting homosexuality. Are you concerned about family attitudes? Friends' opinions? Religious teachings? Prospects for future happiness? A fear of being "abnormal"? Upon reflection, you may find that these reasons just don't hold up. Consider that your heterosexual friends and your parents may prove understanding if you come out. Organized religion is not unanimously opposed to homosexuality; some members of the clergy are openly homosexual themselves. Though homosexuality may in some ways change or complicate your life, you can be just as happy, or as unhappy, whether you're gay or straight. And homosexuality does not imply abnormality; it is an alternative sexual orientation. Challenging irrational assumptions about homosexuality in this fashion may quell your fears.
- Assess your overall level of self-acceptance. Are you generally self-condemning, and is that part of the reason you condemn your sexuality? On pages 54–55 we offer suggestions for building self-esteem that may help you come to terms with being gay or lesbian.
- To gain perspective on homosexuality, consider discussing your concerns with an accepting minister, priest or rabbi, or a professional at your college's counseling center.
- Never lose sight of the fact that you, not your sexual desires, are in charge of your life. You can choose to express homosexual yearnings, or you can choose not to. If you do have homosexual relations, you can choose whether to come out, and to whom, and whether to involve yourself with gay political causes or the gay social scene. You can also choose, if you want, to live as a heterosexual and even someday get married and have children. Though for most homosexuals this probably would not be a good decision, some do choose to and are able to live this way. You are not a slave to homosexuality. Knowing that you're in control of your actions, you need not fear and loathe your passions.

Q: I'm gay, I feel good about it and I've been thinking about coming out. Do you think that's a good idea?

A: We can't give a blanket answer. Telling your best friend privately and confidentially may be relatively safe, provided this person is trustworthy and accepting. But announcing your sexuality to a wide audience or to relative strangers is a much riskier proposition.

Some in the gay/lesbian community advise against coming out publicly during the college years. In their view, other students may reject you because fitting in and being "normal" is so valued in college,and meanwhile you can better handle rejection after college, when you're more mature and may have a stronger support system. Keep in mind, too, that you can't take it back once you let the cat out of the bag. Once you've identified yourself as gay or lesbian, you'll have to live with the consequences for the rest of your college career.

That's the cautious view. According to another school of thought, hiding your sexuality makes it seem there's something secret and shameful about you, and so you demean yourself. Others don't get to know the real you, which leaves you feeling alienated, possibly depressed. Further, college is not really such a bad time to come out. You're not threatened at college by loss of job or housing, and by and large your classmates are a tolerant bunch, as accepting or more so than the people you'll encounter later in life.

As you can see, you can build a good case either way. You need to think carefully before deciding this issue. Here are some things to consider about coming out:[9]

- Do it only if you're ready and are sure it's right for you. If you feel pressured into coming out, are unsure about your sexuality or are uncomfortable being gay or lesbian, then you're probably not ready.
- Do it in the spirit of enhancing mutual understanding. Don't come out because you're angry, or want attention.
- Don't come out to someone who can't handle the news. Don't come out to someone who's sure to reject you.

Q: When I did tell my roommate Cindy about being a lesbian, I thought she'd be understanding. Instead she hardly said anything and she's started acting weird around me. What should I do now?

A: Let's be optimistic for a moment. Possibly Cindy just needs time to digest the news, and soon she'll accept you as before. However, it's also possible that she's backing away because she's afraid that you want her to be your counselor, that you plan to bring female lovers into the room or that you are coming on to her. If those are her reasons, having another talk may allow you to correct her misconceptions. Conceivably, too, Cindy has her own conflicts about lesbianism, conflicts your disclosure has stirred up. Maybe she now needs a chance to open up to you.

If none of these explanations fits, then Cindy may remain estranged from you whatever you do. Perhaps it's a small consolation, but you can tell yourself then that the friendship wasn't worth much anyway if it couldn't survive a dose of honesty.

Q: I want to tell my parents, but I'm scared. How do most parents take it when their children come out?

A: Every parent is different, of course, but there are some general trends. At first, you can expect shock and denial. Don't be surprised if they try to talk you out of being gay or lesbian and insist you see a therapist, or if they are guilt- ridden and focus on themselves: "Where did we go wrong?" Later on, after the initial impact has subsided, their reaction can be predicted from their usual behavior. If they've been supportive and caring up to now, chances are they'll continue that way in the future. If support and caring aren't their style, then they may never accept your homosexuality. They may even refuse to discuss it again, as if it didn't exist.

You'll need to be patient with your parents. This is a big pill for them to swallow, and it may take months or even years for them to grow comfortable with this new image of you. Giving them reading material may help them make the adjustment. (See the suggestions at the end of this chapter.)

With some parents you can predict disastrous results. If your parents will probably stop speaking to you or will stop paying for your college education, you may want to avoid the issue or at least wait until graduation before you break the news.

Q: What do I do if someone attacks me because I'm gay? There have been some ugly incidents of gay-bashing on my campus.

A: Harassment of gays and lesbians is no less serious than harassment of women, blacks or Jews. Any incidents that may have occurred are undoubtedly a violation of your college's code of conduct and carry disciplinary penalties. We recommend reporting any harassment to college authorities. If you are ever assaulted, the proper step would be to report the incident to the police. On the other hand, with subtle forms of harassment it may be futile to lodge a complaint. Minor incidents such as hostile looks and snide comments you may just have to let go.

Colleges are moving—some would say too slowly—to eliminate bias against gays and lesbians. Many colleges have written policies banning discrimination on the basis of sexual orientation. You should become familiar with the policies on your own campus.

FOR FURTHER READING

Boston Women's Health Collective, *The New Our Bodies, Ourselves*, 3rd ed. New York: Simon & Schuster, 1984.

James W. Chesebro, *GaySpeak: Gay Male and Lesbian Communication*. New York: Pilgrim Press, 1981.

Don Clark, *Loving Someone Gay*. Millbrae, Calif.: Celestial Arts, 1977.

Sue Johanson, *Talk Sex*. New York: Penguin, 1988.

Eric W. Johanson, *Love and Sex in Plain Language*. Toronto: Bantam, 1988.

Gary F. Kelly, *Learning about Sex: The Contemporary Guide for Young Adults*, third edition. New York: Barron's, 1987.

SEXUAL HARASSMENT AND RAPE

Tragically, many students are uncertain about the limits of acceptable sexual behavior. In order to protect yourself from sexual harassment, even rape, you must have a clear understanding of what these offenses are. In this chapter we clarify the meaning of rape and harassment, list ways you can protect yourself and discuss the aftermath of rape: how victims react, cope and can recover.

Q: My English professor invited me into his office to talk about my term paper. While we talked, he put his arm around my shoulder and I felt uncomfortable. Was this wrong for him to do?

A: It's not clear. Your professor's gesture may have been innocent, but maybe it wasn't. But regardless of his intentions we recommend trusting your feelings of discomfort. Don't meet him again alone in his office.

Professors have influence over students. They command respect, they assign grades, they write letters of reference. The vast majority of professors, use their influence constructively. But occasionally a professor (usually a male) exploits his influence to get sexual favors from students. This is sexual harassment, and it should be reported to the appropriate authorities on campus—the dean of students, the campus security office, or the affirmative action office.

Sexual harassment may be perpetrated by students or staff members as well as by professors. It can take various forms: unnecessary touching and fondling, sexual comments, leering at your body, or lewd phone calls or letters. If something like this happens to you, you may talk to the person who is harassing you and strongly denounce the behavior, you can just avoid the person, or you can notify him or her in writing that you will contact university authorities—possibly by sending a copy of the letter—if the harassment continues.

Sometimes a student is harassed anonymously through phone calls or letters. If this happens to you, notify the local police, your campus security office, the dean of students or the affirmative action office.

Don't let yourself be victimized. Take action.

Q: Do I really have to worry about rape at college?

A: Unfortunately, you do. As many as 15–25% of college women are victims of rape. Understand, however, that the greatest danger comes from persons you know—dates and acquaintances—rather than strangers, and that rape can occur because of threats, intimidation, pressure and persistence as well as physical force.

The popular image of rape—a stranger jumping out from behind the bushes and attacking you with a knife or a gun—may happen infrequently in your college community. But date and acquaintance rape are threats on every campus.

Q: What you're describing sounds unfortunate but it's not what I'd call rape.

A: Rape is defined as sexual penetration performed against someone's will or without the person's consent. When this happens, it's rape, even if the rapist knows the victim and doesn't use violence.

Q: That 15–25% figure sounds scary.

A: We don't intend to scare you; we want to *alert* you. If you take proper precautions, you can greatly reduce your risk. Here are some safety measures you should remember:

- Know your rights. You have the right to say no if someone asks you out. If you do go out, you have the right not to have physical relations; no one but you should decide who touches your body. If you do choose to have physical relations, you have the right to set limits; you don't have to have sexual intercourse. It also doesn't matter if a man is sexually aroused, says he loves you, has spent money on you, or even has regularly slept with you before. You have the right in *every* instance to say no to sex.

- Whether you're alone or with a new date or male acquaintance, avoid secluded places where you can't call for help. Stick to public places, with lots of other people around. If you're alone at night and need to return to your room, call your college's escort service to have somebody accompany you. Make sure your roommate is within earshot if you invite a new male friend to your dorm room, and take along a friend on visits to fraternities.
- Pay attention to uncomfortable feelings you have with a man. If a casual friend seats himself too close to you at the cafeteria or a new date has "wandering hands" during a slow dance, you'll have uneasy feelings about it. Trust your instincts and either tell him to stop, or leave.
- Decide for yourself before meeting a date if and under what circumstances you want to have physical relations, and if so, how far you want to go. Determining your limits beforehand makes you less vulnerable to pressure during the date.
- If physical contact becomes a possibility, clearly express what you want before anything begins. And be consistent in your messages. Psychologist Diana Pace gives an example: "Don't engage in petting, then say you don't want to go any further, then return to petting."[1]
- Make your intentions known before either of you has taken a drink. Better yet, don't drink at all if physical relations are a possibility. Staying sober is the surest way to retain good judgment and clearly communicate your intentions.
- If you are uncomfortable at any time during petting, confront your date directly. Clearly stating "I don't want you to do that!" may stop him in his tracks.
- If you feel in danger or are attacked, leave at once. Don't reason with the person or hope he'll "come to his senses."

Q: After a party last week, this guy who's sort of a friend invited me into his bedroom. I thought he just wanted to talk, but instead he forced me to have sex. I'm very upset about the whole thing, but I really don't want to report it. Do you think I should?

A: A tough decision. We can understand why you might hesitate to report a rape. You may feel guilty or responsible for what happened (even though it's not your fault). You may not want to accuse your attacker publicly, or you may fear that he'll retaliate somehow and hurt you. You may want to avoid the ordeal of being questioned by police and lawyers. You may worry that your friends or parents will disapprove of you, or even want you to leave college when they find out what happened.

Given these considerations, we obviously can't tell you just to go ahead and do it. It's not a routine matter to report a rape. However, consider that this man has committed a crime, and unless he is caught, he may rape someone else. So please give careful thought to reporting the incident, or at least discuss doing so with a professional counselor.

Q: If I were to report a rape to the campus authorities, what would happen next?

A: If you reported the rape right away, you would be encouraged to go to the emergency room to be physically examined and treated. The doctors would check for possible internal injuries, test you for sexually transmitted diseases and evaluate the possibility of pregnancy. They would also gather physical evidence—semen samples, hair, etc.—which would be used if you chose to report the crime to the police. Probably, a rape crisis counselor would be called in to provide emotional support and information.

The decision to notify the police would be yours. If you went ahead, the police would ask for specific details about the rape and might ask you to identify your attacker. Being accompanied by a friend or rape crisis counselor would help during this potentially difficult process. If there were enough evidence and you chose to pursue it, the case might then be brought to trial. There you would face your attacker in open court, tell your story, listen to contradictory evidence, and undergo cross- examination by a defense attorney who might argue that you consented to have sex. "Shield laws" are meant to protect you, although there's the possibility that you'd be questioned about your prior sexual history and that your identity would be revealed in the media. All of this would be emotionally trying, of course, but reporting a rape can be an important and empowering experience as well.

You also could choose to report the crime to your college's disciplinary system by notifying the dean of students or the affirmative action office. This route might be less disturbing than hiring a lawyer and pressing legal charges, and sometimes charges that would not stand up in court do result in college disciplinary sanctions against the attacker. Of course, the college's sanctions against the attacker are also probably less severe than legal penalties.

Q: Since I was raped by another student, I don't want my boyfriend to touch me and I've been having nightmares. Is this normal?

A: Yes, it is. After a rape, certain reactions can be expected. Initially, the tendency is to experience emotional shock and confused thinking. Later a return to normal life is usually possible, but typically there are psychological aftereffects such as fear, anger, depression and sleep difficulties. You may feel ashamed and humiliated, or dirty and defiled, or guilty, as if you were to blame. Other common reactions include social withdrawal, mistrust of men and a lack of interest in, or even revulsion to, having sex. So the responses you describe are perfectly understandable.

But everyone is different. A few women cope rather well considering the trauma they've endured. Other women *appear* to be doing fine. They go on with their lives as if nothing had happened, only to have the pain and emotional distress reemerge at a later time. Sometimes they come into counseling with puzzling symptoms, which are then traced back to the rape they suffered years earlier.

Q: Aren't I partly to blame for the rape, since I invited the guy into my room?

A: No, you aren't. True, your judgment may have been off, if for example you didn't know him well or he'd been drinking. But that doesn't mean you invited the rape. Other men in the same situation wouldn't have raped you. There's only one person to blame in a rape: the rapist.

Q: I was raped some time ago and thought that I had dealt with it, but I've been having a rough time since then. What should I do?

A: Get help! Many colleges and universities have special counselors trained to handle sexual assaults, sometimes on staff at the counseling center. These professionals can help you understand medical, legal and psychological issues associated with rape. If help is not available on campus, utilize the medical, legal, and counseling resources available in the college community. Talking to a trusted friend, family member or clergyman can also help.

Rape is a traumatic experience, a severe psychological shock. The passage of time helps, but time alone is usually not enough. You need to talk through the experience with a professional for healing to take place.

Q: My girlfriend was raped by her ex-boyfriend over two years ago. It gets hard to take sometimes when she acts as if I'm like him, an abuser too. I've always tried to treat her with respect. What should I do?

A: First, make sure you're sizing up the situation accurately. Are you really as respectful of your girlfriend as you say? There are many shadings of abuse that fall short of physical abuse or even blatant verbal abuse. Insidious language and subtle actions are quite enough to make somebody feel pain.

That having been said, let us emphasize that you shouldn't let yourself be unjustly accused. Certainly try to be understanding about your girlfriend's rape, and be open to what she says about you and your relationship. But at the same time, inform her that it hurts to be unfairly cast as an abuser, and point out examples where she is misreading your intentions. Another option is for you and your girlfriend to go together for counseling.

Q: My best friend was raped last week. How do I help her?

A: Let her talk to you about it. The opportunity to air her feelings to a trusted friend can be a great comfort. At the same time, don't force her to talk about the rape if she doesn't want to. Be accepting of her moods and feelings, and make sure she knows you're not judging or blaming her and don't think less of her.

Finally, strongly encourage her to seek counseling. As a friend you have a lot to offer, but both of you need to understand that you can't take on a professional's role during this crisis.

Q: I'm a male student. What about me? Can I be raped too?

A: It's possible. Occasionally a man rapes another man, or a woman uses threats or intimidation to force sex on a man. When this occurs, the male victim may have problems, just as female victims do, and he may be even more reluctant than a woman to report the crime for fear of being laughed at or viewed as weak.

However, in the overwhelming majority of college rape cases, a man assaults a woman. So as a male you're not at great risk.

Q: How likely am I as a male to be *accused* of rape? I know someone who was charged with date rape and he seemed like a regular guy to me. If *this* guy's been accused of rape, the same thing could happen to me.

A: You sound worried that you'll be falsely accused of rape, but this is unlikely. It's rare that a woman would report a rape frivolously, and in almost all cases she won't mistake the identity of the rapist because she already knows him fairly well. Of course, you should get legal counsel immediately if you're ever accused of rape.

Of much greater danger to you than false accusations is the possibility that you will actually rape someone. This may sound absurd if you think of all rapists as psychotics or psychopaths, as people fundamentally different from you. But many males who commit date or acquaintance rape aren't disturbed or usually considered malicious. Otherwise "normal," they may force a woman into sex because they misinterpret what she wants, they think it's the man's role to overcome the woman's resistance, they feel peer pressure to "score," or their judgment is clouded by alcohol or other drugs. Afterward they may be shocked to discover that what they've done isn't simply a bit of harmless fun or a regrettable incident. In fact, they've committed rape.

To avoid this grievous mistake, you need to take the following precautions:

- Communicate with your date *beforehand* if the evening promises to turn sexual. Make sure you explicitly discuss the extent of lovemaking both of you want to have.
- Respect a woman's limits. Don't bully, cajole, force or threaten her into going farther than she wants.
- Don't interpret "no" as "yes." For that matter, don't take silence, "I don't know," "maybe" or "I'm not ready" as consent either. And don't assume that sexy clothes, a flirtatious smile, a touch, or even a kiss is an invitation to sex. Make sure she's expressly told you her wishes regarding sex.
- Be cautious with alcohol. Having as few as two drinks can impair judgment and the ability to communicate sexual decisions. So discuss sexual intentions before you and your partner take a drink. Otherwise if you have sex you may not have obtained informed consent, and possibly she'll feel she was raped.

FOR FURTHER READING

Susan Brownmiller, *Against Our Will: Men, Women and Rape*. New York: Bantam Books, 1976.

Linda E. Ledry, *Recovering from Rape*. New York: Henry Holt and Co., 1986.

Andrea Parrot, *Coping with Date and Acquaintance Rape*. New York: The Rosen Publishing Group, 1988.

Robin Warshaw, *I Never Called It Rape*. New York: Harper & Row, 1988.

ALCOHOL AND
OTHER DRUGS

At college, you're going to hear competing points of view about alcohol and other drugs. College officials and some fellow students will argue against them, bombarding you with information about the health hazards of alcohol and drug abuse. They'll stress the legal angle, too: Underage persons (which usually means under 21) cannot legally buy or be served alcoholic beverages; driving under the influence of alcohol is illegal (and also dangerous); and so-called "street drugs"—marijuana, cocaine and the rest—are of course illegal too.

But these aren't the only voices you will hear on the subject. In private, some classmates will casually dismiss all the fuss about alcohol and drugs and urge you to experiment, to have fun, to get trashed. Some of them may make it seem that either you drink heavily and take drugs or else forget about fitting in. Usually they won't even bother making their case; they'll just assume you intend to "party."

In the end, it's left squarely up to you at college to decide what to do about alcohol and drugs. No one can force you to take these substances, but no one can shield you from them either. How you react when a mystery punch is served at a party or a joint is passed in a dormitory room depends on your ability to be your own person, to consider all the arguments and then think and act for yourself. The material in this chapter is intended to help you make sensible decisions.

Q: When I'm out on a date with a new guy, I like to have a few drinks to relax. Any problems with this?

A: Could be. Alcohol loosens sexual inhibitions, which is one reason people like it. But alcohol also impairs judgment and decision making and can lead to disastrous sexual experiences. As a woman, the danger is that you'll have sex you didn't really consent to, and next morning you'll be tormented by guilt and shame. The corresponding danger for a man is initiating sex without the woman's consent: committing rape. (See Chapter 8.)

Mixing dating and alcohol also can lead to ignoring safer sex and contraception techniques. So, if you do plan to have sex, get intoxicated on the lovemaking, not on the booze.

Q: I get buzzed faster than my boyfriend. Is that common?

A: Yes. Serve a woman and man the same amount of alcohol, and typically it's the woman who feels it more quickly. Previously it was thought this difference is because women are usually smaller than men, and it's known that smaller people need less alcohol to get drunk than larger people. However, recent studies have found that women compared to men have less of an enzyme that breaks down alcohol in the stomach. And so if you and your boyfriend each take two drinks, you will be affected more, even if you're the same size.

Q: I hold my liquor better than my friends. Does that mean I can safely drink more than they can?

A: Not really. True, high tolerance protects you from some of the immediate penalties of drinking, such as blackouts and vomiting. But being able to drink large amounts without paying the price makes it easier for you to drink to excess and develop a drinking problem or even alcoholism. Given your high tolerance, you need to keep close tabs on your drinking.

Q: Everyone around here drinks, and I want to drink too. But I'd like to try to do it sensibly.

A: First of all, it's not true that everyone does it. Contrary to popular belief, 30–40% of college students drink rarely or not at all. Some stop drinking when they realize they're developing or already have a problem; others never get started at all. It really *is* okay not to drink.

But if you do plan to drink sometimes, here's a "survival kit" for staying out of trouble with alcohol:

- Avoid drinking games. They usually make you drink more than you intended.
- If you don't know what you're drinking, don't drink it! Avoid unmarked mystery punches. They may disguise huge amounts of alcohol.
- Remember that beer and wine are alcohol, too. A can of beer or a glass of wine has as much alcohol as one shot of hard liquor. So monitor your trips to the keg.
- Plan beforehand how much you'll drink; set a limit you're comfortable with. Then keep track of your drinking so you stick to your limit. Although we can't specify exactly how many drinks is too many, remember that the liver can eliminate roughly one drink per hour. If you take five drinks in the first hour, you still have four drinks in your system an hour later, three after two hours, and so forth. One rule you may want to experiment with is never to have more than one drink in your system, (i.e., one drink per hour).
- To keep to your goal, pace yourself; drink slowly. Another tip is to alternate alcoholic drinks with nonalcoholic drinks such as soda or water. And be sure that your mixed drink isn't too strong; if necessary, dilute it with soda or water. Remember, too, that a "double" mixed drink is equivalent to two drinks.
- When you've had enough, stop! If someone insists that you have another, be assertive and decline. If saying no seems difficult, cultivate drink refusal skills: change the subject, say "I'll get one later" or "I've got a test tomorrow," or make any other excuse that lets you turn down an unwanted drink.
- Never drink and drive. Tragically, on every campus some college students have ended up dead because they've gotten into a car after they've been drinking. Even small amounts of alcohol impair your ability to maneuver a vehicle. If you drink away from campus, make sure to go back with a "designated driver" who doesn't drink at all that night.
- If because of drinking you or someone you know appears to be in bad physical or emotional shape, head immediately to a hospital emergency room or the college health service. Do it even if you're unsure. You just may save a life.
- Don't be afraid to ask for help. If you think you or someone else has a problem, get a professional opinion.

Q: If there's a party on the weekend I have maybe a six-pack of beer at most. Is that too much to drink?

A: Possibly. We can appreciate that you'd like to know an exact limit, but there is no magic number. "Too much" is whatever amount causes a problem, either immediately (an acute physical reaction) or over the long term (chronic difficulties).

Alcohol can be dangerous. Don't be fooled because it is legal (for those over 21) and comes in liquid form. Alcohol is a drug, in particular a depressant that slows down the central nervous system. As with any drug, you can overdose or even die from a single episode of excessive drinking.

Q: How do I know if I have a drinking problem?

A: Look for any of the following:

- Medical problems: accidents and injuries, nausea and vomiting, hangovers, blackouts (you can't remember the next day what happened while you were drinking), or passing out (you became unconscious).
- Academic problems: missed classes due to hangovers; low or even failing grades due to drinking; procrastination on assignments.
- Sexual problems: sexual activities that you regret later, including taking advantage of someone or being taken advantage of sexually; failure to use birth control; impotence in males.
- Inability to drink moderately or to cut down on drinking; concern from others about your drinking; drinking alone.
- Drinking to feel confident; drinking to stop feeling anxious, depressed, bored or lonely.
- Having arguments and fights, or causing property damage; social isolation; drinking while driving.

Q: I've had a few of those things happen to me. Are you saying I've got a drinking problem?

A: At the very least, you have misused alcohol, even if you do not yet have a full-fledged drinking problem. But possibly you *do* have a drinking problem, especially if you checked off several symptoms and they happen often. It's even possible that you're addicted to alcohol. Though a professional can help you make these judgments, the bottom line is that you need to take a serious look at your drinking.

Q: You mean I could be an alcoholic?

A: Yes. Most alcoholics are not how we picture them, as falling-down drunks lying in the gutter. Most look surprisingly normal and live surprisingly normal lives. Some of them, in fact, are your classmates; approximately 10% of college-age people qualify as alcoholics.

Who is an alcoholic? Basically, he or she is someone who is dependent on alcohol and has lost control over its use. But don't get caught up in the question of whether or not you're an alcoholic. The more important question is whether you ever *misuse alcohol.* And if some of the items we've noted apply to you, the answer is yes.

Q: I stopped drinking three months ago because I realized I was turning into an alcoholic. How long will it take before I've got this problem licked?

A: Unfortunately, you may never be permanently in the clear. We can't know whether you really are an alcoholic. But if you truly are—and the same would go for dependency on other drugs—then you face an ongoing battle. What's more, stopping usage is only the first step. To work on this problem you also must address the thoughts, emotions and behaviors that are so much a part of alcoholism.

Perhaps 15% of alcoholism has to do with drinking itself. The remaining 85% concerns poor coping skills, difficulties getting along with people, depression and anxiety, low self-esteem and a host of other personal issues. To maximize the chances of never abusing alcohol again, you have to work on these *personality* issues. And that takes far more than three months' time, more than simply abstaining from alcohol—and very possibly more than you can do all by yourself.

Q: Where can I get help?

A: Many campuses have substance abuse specialists in the counseling center or health service; some campuses even have entire offices devoted to students' alcohol and drug problems. These specialists may provide substance abuse counseling, or they may refer you to counselors in the community. If your campus lacks these resources, look in the telephone book for off-campus specialists. See also the hotline numbers listed at the back of this volume.

Other resources that often are recommended in combination with counseling are Alcoholics Anonymous (AA) for alcohol problems and

Narcotics Anonymous (NA) for other drug problems. Listed in the phone book, and perhaps even found on your own campus, AA and NA offer group meetings providing information and support.

Since these meetings will be new and perhaps anxiety-provoking for you, we recommend going at first with an AA or NA member or a friend, and trying at least half a dozen meetings before making up your mind about continuing. You don't have to talk if you don't want to; just listening to other people's experiences can be an eye-opener. Also, since there are meetings catering to different groups—young people, smokers, nonsmokers, gays—you may want to look around for the meeting where you feel most comfortable. You also may want to check out some new groups whose philosophies differ from those of AA and NA, such as Rational Recovery and Women for Sobriety.

If you can't stop drinking even with the help of counseling and support groups, then you may need an extended stay in a hospital or rehabilitation facility, or at least an intensive outpatient program. There's no shame in taking this step, and it may be the only way to solve your problem. Consult a specialist if you think this option is warranted.

Q: I smoke marijuana to relax after I study, but now a friend wants me to try cocaine. That's really asking for trouble, right?

A: Yes it is—but marijuana can be trouble, too. Occasionally, pot causes students to become acutely anxious, disoriented or paranoid. Some long-term users become unmotivated in their studies; a few develop an outright addiction. Studies also suggest that long-term use may cause physical damage to lungs and other organs.[1] It also lowers male sex hormones and causes changes in the menstrual cycle and possible birth defects.[2] So, it's a myth that marijuana is harmless.

As for cocaine, or crack, a derivative of cocaine that is smoked, you are right about its dangers. Cocaine is a stimulant that people take to get a rush and a sense of self-confidence and well-being. But these effects are short-lived and are typically followed by a "crash"—a period of extreme depression. Cocaine can cause grave physical damage: heart attacks, strokes, and coma or death from an overdose. One student we know who experimented with cocaine landed in the hospital emergency room with an acute cardiac arrhythmia, or irregular heartbeat. (He never tried it again.) Perhaps cocaine's greatest danger is its extreme addictiveness; once you get started, you may find it very difficult to stop.

While we're on the topic of drugs, we should also touch briefly on some of the others. Psychedelic drugs or hallucinogens (LSD ["acid"], mushrooms, mescaline) can create vivid perceptual effects and flights of imagination. However, they carry the considerable risk of a "bad trip"—acute panic and paranoid feelings—and they can even lead to a psychotic reaction requiring hospitalization. Amphetamines ("speed") are stimulants, like cocaine, which may boost energy and alertness and therefore are sometimes used for late-night studying. But amphetamines also may cause anxiety, rage, dependency, even seizures and death; they, too, are sometimes responsible for a psychotic reaction.

MDMA ("ecstasy"), chemically similar to amphetamines,was originally touted as safe and enlightening, half mind expander and half truth serum. Later evidence, though, points to its irreversible effects on the brain and its addictive potential. Narcotics, such as heroin, have a strong addictive potential. In addition, because they are generally injected, you run the risk of contracting AIDS or hepatitis from a contaminated needle. Finally, anabolic steroids have been illegally taken by some campus athletes to build up muscle tissue and enhance performance. We now know that steroids can cause serious emotional disorders and lasting bodily damage, even death.

Heard enough? Well, there's more. In addition to these drugs' health risks, there are the risks of criminal penalties and college disciplinary sanctions. Drugs are *illegal*. In one recent, well publicized case, a drug raid on campus resulted in the arrest of more than half a dozen students and the seizure of three fraternity houses. What's more, you can never be sure with street drugs exactly what you are getting. The marijuana you smoke may be tainted with paraquat, a herbicide, and what you think is LSD may actually be PCP ("angel dust"), which can lead to wild, violent behavior. The Food and Drug Administration does not provide quality control on illegal drugs.

Q: I've heard all about the dangers of drugs, but I've taken them and have never had any problems.

A: There may not be any warning signs. Since cocaine, amphetamines, LSD and other street drugs can be dangerous even if taken only once, you may think based on past experiences that you're fine with these substances and still have a disastrous experience next time around. For example, one student we know took LSD with a group of her friends. Twice before she'd experimented with LSD without any trouble, but this time she suddenly went berserk, started shouting incoherently, and tried to climb out the tenth floor window. Her terrified friends barely succeeded in restraining her until the police arrived to take her to the hospital.

As for signs of an ongoing problem, we suggest you consult the checklist for alcohol-related problems on page 168 because this list also applies for drugs. If because of drugs you have some of the problems listed there—medical, academic or sexual problems, problematic patterns of use, poor motives for usage or self-destructive behavior—then yes, you've got a problem with drugs.

Q: What do I say if my friends insist that I try cocaine? I know they'll tell me I should experience it and judge for myself, or else I'm being narrow-minded.

A: Would you swallow cyanide to be open-minded? If you believe cocaine's bad for you, tell them you *have* judged for yourself—and you don't want to do it.

With drinking and street drugs, peer pressure has to be expected. There will always be friends who urge you to experiment, and in some circles the thing to do will be to "party," to get wasted, to get as drunk or high as you can. Despite this, most classmates really will respect you for refusing to take drugs or abuse alcohol. They may even respect you more for staying true to your convictions rather than caving in to pressure.

But if your friends aren't understanding and won't take no for an answer—or if you can't say no and make it stick—perhaps you should plan to see them when drinking or drugs won't be involved, or even, if necessary, reconsider your choice of friends. Look around, and you'll find plenty of other students who will respect your point of view, and plenty more who aren't drug takers either. Certain campuses, such as Rutgers University, Dartmouth College and the University of Michigan, have even set up substance-free living areas where you can live in a totally alcohol- and drug-free residence.

Q: Sometimes I pop a few pills and then have a couple of beers. Is it okay if I take moderate amounts of each?

A: Don't do it. Mixing alcohol and drugs, or mixing any combination of drugs together, can be dangerous. This holds true even if one of the drugs is prescribed by a doctor. Combining alcohol and a tranquilizer, for example, can cause extreme side effects, even death.

Consult a qualified professional about drug interaction effects if you have any inclination to mix substances.

Q: I think my best friend, Bob, is drinking too much. I want to speak to him but I'm afraid of saying the wrong thing. What should I do?

A: By all means do speak up. A real friend is honest about these things, even at the risk of upsetting the other person. We suggest you start by pointing out that you care, and that's why you want to talk to him. Then express your concern about his drinking, citing specific facts and events to back up your case rather than saying generally, "You have a drinking problem." While giving evidence, speak in the first person and convey your personal feelings about what he's doing. Bob can dismiss your judgments and opinions, but it's harder for him to argue with the facts and your feelings.

Here, in abbreviated form, is the kind of the message you might deliver: "Bob, I want to talk to you about your drinking because I care about you, and I'm concerned. When you got drunk Friday night at the party, you came on to Ellen and started pawing at her. And then the next day you didn't remember doing it. I have to tell you I was embarrassed for you and angry. And you also didn't remember those hostile things you said to John at the department cocktail party. It scares me when I see how you act when you drink."

The next step is to specify what you think Bob should do. Since he obviously has a problem, ask him to reevaluate his drinking, cut back or stop his use altogether, or go into counseling.

Q: I've tried that before, but Bob blew up at me and said I was exaggerating everything. Now what?

A: His reaction isn't unusual. Substance abusers often get angry when they're confronted, partly to discourage the confrontation. Typically, too, they use the defensive maneuver of denial, refusing to acknowledge the extent of their problem. ("I can stop drinking whenever I want." "I only drink on weekends." "Lots of people drink more than me." "My low grades have nothing to do with my drinking.") As a general rule, the worse their problem is, the stronger the anger and the denial. These reactions are not necessarily intentional or conscious; they are part of the whole substance abuse picture. Recognizing that anger and denial are characteristic of abusers may ease your frustration in dealing with Bob.

Since he reacted as he did, your next step should be to consult a professional. One option the professional may recommend is simply to back off for the time being. Bob may not be ready to face his problem, which would make further efforts futile. But at least on some level he heard your concern; your words may help him look honestly at his problem at some future time. Another option the professional may suggest is to ask someone else—a friend, family member, professor or member of the clergy—to speak to Bob and reinforce your message.

The professional also may propose that several of you confront him together, a technique called an "intervention." Interventions can be dramatically effective. They also are trying and emotionally upsetting for all concerned, and for this reason the professional may need to coach you through the process.

Q: Marcia got drunk last night and was really hung over this morning. I told her professor she couldn't take the test today because she was sick. Did I do the right thing?

A: What you did is called "enabling"—sparing the person the negative consequences of substance abuse. Though you meant well, enabling makes matters worse because Marcia can keep on abusing alcohol without facing the music. Other examples of enabling would be typing her papers because she's too hung over to finish them herself, or lending her money because she's spent her own on alcohol or drugs.

If you really want to help Marcia, don't bail her out.

Q: But I'm really worried about Marcia. I lose sleep over her problem. Can't I help somehow?

A: You can help, as we've indicated, by avoiding enabling behaviors, confronting Marcia about her problem, speaking to a counselor about her, and possibly persuading others to join you in confronting her, either individually or through an intervention. But beyond these measures, we urge you not to get too wrapped up in Marcia's problem. It's better for both of you if you maintain a certain detachment or distance.

If it's hard to achieve the proper amount of detachment, or if you're slipping into the role of enabler, check out the support group called Al-Anon. A companion group to Alcoholics Anonymous, Al-Anon is designed for the friends and family members of alcohol abusers. Similarly, Nar-Anon is the companion group to Narcotics Anonymous.

Q: My problem's not at school, but at home. My father has been a problem drinker on and off ever since I was a child. Now he's "on" again. How do I handle him?

A: The same basic options apply: You can confront him with the events you've observed and your personal feelings about these events; you can urge other family members, either individually or in a group, to join you in confronting him; or you can leave him alone and wait until the time is right. The same basic cautions apply, too. You should expect anger and denial; you need to watch out for your own enabling behavior; and you should try to maintain some objectivity.

Of course, it's doubly hard to be dispassionate and rational when the substance abuser is your own parent. Growing up in an alcoholic family leaves scars, as we discuss on pages 101–103, and his drinking again can be traumatic for you. Therefore we strongly advise consulting a professional about this turn of events. Though it may not seem this way, the issue isn't so much helping him (though that would be desirable) as addressing the effects of his drinking on you.

In addition, consider attending Adult Children of Alcoholics (ACOA) meetings. These meetings can provide support and give you perspective on alcoholic families. Also, be aware that having an alcoholic or drug-addicted parent puts you at risk, too. To play it safe, you should drink less than your friends or not drink at all.

Q: I don't feel comfortable on this campus with all the drinking and drugs around here. Should I just switch to another school?

A: You can try that, but before you make this move take a close look around you. Are you sure you've given your college a fair shake? On any campus the drinkers and drug takers tend to make a lot of noise, drowning out the nonusers and occasional drinkers who quietly go about their business. Maybe if you search harder you'll find the sort of people and events you prefer.

Have you also considered making a difference on your campus? Almost every college has a committee of students, faculty and administrators responsible for programs and policy regarding substance abuse. Opportunities for action may also exist through the student government, the campus health service or peer counseling programs. Not only can you improve your campus, but you'll meet like-minded students.

TOBACCO

Q: I've tried to stop smoking cigarettes, but without any luck. What do you recommend?

A: Stopping smoking is hard; nicotine is highly addictive. But given the grave health risks of lung cancer and heart disease, you're wise to keep trying. Experts recommend several steps to stop smoking:

- Hide or give away ashtrays, matches and all other paraphernalia associated with smoking.
- If you miss having something in your mouth, switch to sugarless gum. As a substitute for handling cigarettes, toy with a pen, coin or some other object.
- Identify high-risk situations where you're most tempted to smoke. Different for each individual, these situations may be parties, dates, a particular store where cigarettes are sold, exam periods—or times of loneliness, anger, boredom or anxiety. Then if you can, avoid these situations. For example, it makes sense not to visit friends in a room where everyone is smoking, or to steer clear of the store where you've always purchased cigarettes in the past.
- When avoiding a high-risk situation is impossible, use coping skills to deal with temptation. These might include taking deep breaths to relax, reaching for a stick of gum, assertively refusing when someone offers you a smoke, and inwardly coaching yourself to keep to your pledge.
- If you've had a slip and smoked one or two cigarettes, don't make this an excuse to abandon your resolve. Take immediate steps to prevent a full-fledged relapse: Leave the scene immediately, call a friend, and renew your commitment to stop smoking.
- Don't get discouraged after a slip and interpret it as proof of failure, evidence that you can't stop smoking. Instead, treat a slip as a learning experience that teaches you traps to avoid in the future.
- During your campaign to stop smoking, it may help to have support from friends or family. A formal smoking cessation program may help too, although quitting the habit must be accomplished through your own effort.
- Don't be discouraged if you've tried to stop before but couldn't make it stick. Very few people are able to stop smoking permanently on their first attempt. Most who successfully beat the habit do so after a series of sincere efforts.

Q: I chew tobacco. How safe is that compared to smoking?

A: Nicotine is an addictive drug, whether you smoke it or chew it. Even more importantly, the chewing of tobacco can lead to deterioration of teeth and gums and has been associated with cancers of the tongue, mouth, throat and larynx. In short, chewing is no way to avoid the dangers of tobacco use.

FOR FURTHER READING

James Cocores, *The 800-Cocaine Book of Drug and Alcohol Recovery.* New York: Villard, 1990.

Mark S. Gold, *800-Cocaine.* Toronto: Bantam, 1984.

Alan G. Marlatt and Judith R. Gordon, *Relapse Prevention: Maintenance Strategies in the Treatment of Addictive Behavior.* New York: Guilford Press, 1985.

Gayle Rossellini and Mark Worden, *Strong Choices, Weak Choices.* San Francisco: Harper & Row (Hazelden Educational Materials), 1988.

Richard Seymour and David E. Smith, *Drugfree: A Unique, Positive Approach to Staying Off Alcohol and Other Drugs.* New York: Facts On File, 1987.

EATING
DISORDERS

Not that long ago, a book like this might have made no mention of eating disorders. Anorexia nervosa, after all, was considered rare until fairly recently, and bulimia had not even been identified until the late 1970s. Now all that has changed. Today eating disorders have become topics of concern in society at large, and they are major problems on the college campus, particularly bulimia. In addition, many college students who aren't anorexic or bulimic are troubled nonetheless about body image, overeating and dieting. In this chapter we provide a perspective on these worrisome topics and offer suggestions for healthy eating.

BODY IMAGE

Q: I weigh what the charts say I should for my height. But I still feel fat and I hate my body.

A: In our society, unfortunately, it's exceedingly difficult for women to escape concerns about body image. Women, who naturally have more body fat than men, often see themselves as fat even if they're actually a little underweight. And if they don't feel fat, they worry about their wide hips, flat chest, large breasts, short legs or excessive body hair. Men worry too. In the privacy of counselors' offices, many male students confess that they feel too short, scrawny, pudgy or ugly, that their hairline is receding or their penis is too small.

Society is partly responsible for instilling these ubiquitous feelings of inferiority. In movies, television and magazines, stunning, lean women and men are held up as an ideal that few of us can match. But it's hard to imagine any culture not celebrating the human form, and even if society's attitudes were different, the college years are so

179

marked by self-consciousness anyway that some insecurity about appearance seems inevitable. At your age, it's normal to inspect yourself in the mirror. It's not surprising if in some respects you don't like what you see.

Q: Is it superficial to care about my looks?

A: Not really. Wanting to look good is a natural human motive. Feeling attractive is an expression of healthy self-esteem.

However, being *obsessed* with your appearance is something else. Excessive preoccupation with looks may be a sign of psychological problems—low self-esteem, shallow relationships—that call for counseling.

Q: How can I learn to accept my appearance?

A: First, make the most of what you've got. Exercise regularly and eat properly to give yourself a healthy look. Stand up straight, carry yourself with pride and learn to smile. Wear flattering clothing and hair styles, choose attractive glasses, or switch, if you prefer, to contact lenses. If you have a skin problem, consider consulting a dermatologist. Another option if you're severely unhappy with your looks is to have your nose fixed, body hair removed or other imperfections corrected. Though quite expensive and not to be undertaken lightly, these procedures are sometimes helpful in improving self-image.

But external changes can only take you so far. Since you can't remold your basic bone structure, the key to accepting your appearance is to view yourself acceptingly. To do this we recommend applying the cognitive approach of rooting out flawed thinking and substituting constructive thoughts. Check, then, whether you are:

Dwelling on the negative—focusing only on your supposed weak spots. Try instead to see yourself as others see you, as a totality, an overall physical and personal presence ("Sure, my rear end is a little big, but overall I'm pretty attractive").

Overassuming—taking for granted that someone is turned off by your face or body. If so, remind yourself that tastes vary, that some people prefer your features and body type, and you can't know for certain how any one person will react to you.

Thinking in all-or-nothing terms—concluding that you're fat when you're really just a little plump, or ugly when you're actually average.

If so, work on accurate self-assessments: "I'm a few pounds overweight, but I'm not really fat."

Catastrophizing—thinking that it's disastrous to look the way you do, that with your appearance you might as well join a nunnery, or a monastery. Instead, place your concerns in perspective. "I'm not the most gorgeous woman on campus, but I'm sure some people find me attractive, and I've got a lot going for me besides my looks."

Your feelings about your face and body are a reflection of your deepest attitudes about yourself. There are physically striking college students who think they're ugly, just as there are rather plain students who feel attractive, and the difference is that the latter basically like themselves while the former don't. In fact, one sign of progress in counseling is when students start feeling comfortable with their appearance. It's also worth noting that your opinions about your looks have an influence on other people, as psychiatrist Willard Gaylin has observed: "Think of yourself as ugly and eventually you will be so considered. Think of yourself as beautiful and it is extraordinary to what degree people will treat you as a beauty."[1]

For help in accepting your appearance, see if your campus has a women's group—males, look for a men's group—where you can talk about these issues. To work on poor self-esteem that causes you to dislike your appearance, also consider consulting a counselor.

DIETING

Q: I'm now 30 pounds overweight. Why do I do this to myself?

A: At one time, this would have been a perfectly valid question. It was taken as a given back then that overweight people did it to themselves. They gained weight because they overate, they overate because they had problems, and that was that.

Without a doubt, some people do overeat for one reason or another. Some are truly compulsive eaters, who consume food continually, without pleasure. Reasons that have been linked to overeating include depression, stress, loneliness, anger and fear of intimate relationships. Another possibility is eating in response to external cues ("I'm watching TV—it's time to eat") instead of heeding internal signals of hunger.

However, some experts feel that most overweight people don't actually overeat. Rather, overweight people may be heavy because they're genetically programmed to be that way. Their bodies are quicker than normal to convert calories into fat, and therefore their natural "setpoint"—the weight they gravitate toward—is higher than normal. In short, psychological problems or even bad eating habits may have very little to do with your problem. You may eat a normal diet and still put on the pounds.

Whatever the reason you are overweight, you shouldn't condemn yourself for it. You may decide to work on your weight problem, but don't fault yourself for having one.

Q: So how can I lose weight? Should I go on a crash diet?

A: The natural tendency is to do just that. Liquid diets and crash weight loss programs are all the rage these days. What often happens, however, is that weight lost during the program is added back soon afterwards—and sometimes more for good measure. With crash diets you may repeatedly lose and then regain weight, in what is called the "yo-yo" syndrome. Not only is this discouraging and embarrassing, but an up-and-down weight cycle has been linked to heart disease.

Crash diets may fail for several reasons. First, they slow down your metabolism (remember, the body tries to protect its fat stores and remain at its setpoint). At the end of the diet, the combination of a still slowed metabolism and a return to normal eating may jack up your weight in a hurry. Second, crash diets don't teach proper eating habits. You learn how to avoid food while dieting; you don't learn how to deal with food when the diet ends. Third, crash diets—or brief fasts—create a feeling of deprivation. You can only stint yourself for so long. Sooner or later, the urge to eat becomes irresistible, and then the tendency is to go overboard and truly gorge yourself. Finally, often people go on diets when they're not really ready. If you do want to lose weight, you must be prepared to work hard over a long period and make basic changes in your lifestyle.

Fortunately, crash diets are not your only hope. While you can't change your genetically determined setpoint, you can learn healthy eating and living habits that *may* result in weight loss. Experts advise doing the following:

- Think in terms of permanent changes in eating habits, not temporary sacrifices. Changes in eating should be incorporated into your way of life. Make a commitment to carry out these changes. If you're not prepared to make this commitment, then it's probably pointless to try to lose weight.

- Set realistic goals. Plan small eating changes rather than drastic revisions, and, if you're determined to lose weight, try to lose one or two pounds per week rather than huge amounts all at once. With realistic goals you're less likely to get discouraged and give up.
- Be realistic about your body type. If you'll never be svelte, try to accept that. Set your sights on a realistic final weight given your body type. Better yet, don't focus on a particular weight goal at all but on new eating and living habits. Aim instead to be healthier than you are now.
- Assess whether you overeat as a response to particular feelings, such as loneliness, anger, depression, even joy. If so, try to find substitute coping responses (call a friend, take a walk, chew sugarless gum) when these emotions arise.
- Concentrate on the types of food you eat rather than total calories. Fats in your diet are trouble because they put fat on you (and can lead to heart disease), and simple sugars are undesirable because they raise your insulin level and make you hungry again soon. On the other hand, low-cholesterol, low-sodium and high-fiber foods are considered healthy. So cut down or eliminate red meats, butter, mayonnaise, whole-milk dairy products, candy bars, ice cream, cookies, pies and potato chips. In their place, eat pasta, poultry, fish, bread, skim milk, fruits, vegetables, cereal, unbuttered popcorn, bagels and pretzels. For more information about a nutritionally balanced, healthy and possibly weight-reducing diet, consult a nutritionist—your college's health service may have one—and read about nutrition.
- Don't eliminate treats from your diet—eating should still be fun— but choose them wisely. Frozen yogurt and pretzels will satisfy a need without sabotaging your goals. If life seems meaningless without hamburgers and pizza, then have them sometimes but cut back on the frequency and size of your portions.
- Exercise regularly. At least three or four times per week for 20–30 minutes or more, engage in an activity that raises your heart rate. Exercise burns up calories both during the workout and for hours afterward, while your metabolism rate is still raised. Exercise also instills confidence and a sense of well-being, which can inspire you to eat well. However, if you are bullimic or anorexic, consult with a doctor before starting an exercise program.
- In devising an exercise program, make sure the workouts aren't boring, too strenuous or too time-consuming. Like eating, exercise ought to be fun, a treat rather than a chore. Experiment to see which activities you prefer—tennis, racquetball, running, fast walking,

basketball, dance, swimming, biking. Varying activities and doing them with a friend may also help keep you interested. Also, build exercise into your schedule; make it a habit. Rather than asking "Should I or shouldn't I?" make your way to the gym automatically. If you have any medical concerns, check with a physician before starting an exercise program.

- Expect slipups. One day, you'll eat more than you should; sooner or later, you'll fail to exercise. When this happens, get right back on course. Don't tell yourself after a slipup, "I can't do this, I quit."

- At the same time, if possible, control the damage after a slipup. If you've already had half a pint of ice cream or a bag of potato chips, stop right there and don't go back for seconds. Dieters sometimes defeat themselves through "all-or- nothing" thinking: "Either I follow my eating plan to the letter, or I've failed miserably." "I've blown it already, so the rest of the day (or week) is shot." Such rigid reasoning, of course, justifies turning a slipup into a major setback, an unplanned snack into a full-scale binge or series of binges. Instead, say to yourself, "Okay, I went too far, but I can stop now."

- Consider attending Overeaters Anonymous sessions, which you can find in your community and possibly at your college. Similar to Alcoholics Anonymous, OA offers social support that can help you stick to your eating goals.

Q: I'm proud of myself for losing 20 pounds. So why am I so unhappy?

A: There are a number of reasons why you might feel unsatisfied. Perhaps you had unrealistic expectations about the consequences of losing weight. You assumed that once you became thin you'd be beautiful, irresistible, the object of everyone's attention. Now you are discovering that life's not that simple. You can be thin yet still feel unattractive, reach your ideal weight yet still be lonely or depressed.

Another possibility is that you've always been hesitant about dating, romance and sex. Now that you're thin there are no more excuses to stay on the sidelines, and you're frightened. Or maybe you're anxious about keeping the weight off. You've reached your target weight, but how in the world will you stay there?

Becoming thinner requires a psychological adjustment. It's stressful to make such a major change, even a positive change. After a while you may grow comfortable at your new weight and reap the emotional benefits of being slim. If, however, you remain unsettled, you should consider discussing your concerns at your college's counseling center.

BULIMIA

Q: My roommate always sneaks into the bathroom after we go to dinner and gets sick. And sometimes I notice a cake or a quart of ice cream missing from the refrigerator. Could she be bulimic?

A: Very possibly. Bulimia, technically known as bulimia nervosa, is the binge-purge syndrome. It strikes women most often, but some men, especially wrestlers and rowers, are at risk too. During binges bulimics consume huge amounts of calories, often gorging on "forbidden" foods like those you mentioned, cake and ice cream. Afterward they purge themselves, often in the bathroom, by means of self-induced vomiting, or by using laxatives or diuretics (which induce urination). They may also diet, fast or exercise strenuously. Some bulimics purge after normal meals as well as after binges. Because often they feel ashamed of their problem, many bulimics binge and purge on the sly.

It's hard to be sure about your roommate, though. Not only haven't you directly observed her bingeing or purging, but you can't necessarily tell by looking at her whether she's bulimic. Unlike anorexics, most bulimics are approximately their normal weight.

Other signs you might look for are frequent fluctuations in her weight, expressions of concern about eating and weight, and indications that she feels out of control or depressed. You can also keep an eye out for calluses on her knuckles, frequent sore throats and rotted teeth—all consequences of frequent self-induced vomiting.

Q: If I'm not sure she's bulimic, should I do anything?

A: Definitely. Although you don't want to overreact, you should take action. Bulimia is a serious condition associated with both psychological problems (depression, mood swings, low self-esteem) and serious medical consequences (erosion of tooth enamel, digestive tract disorder, urinary tract infection, and even heart attack). It is far too serious to ignore.

Here, then, are the steps we suggest you follow:

1. Approach her with your concerns. Tell her exactly what you've observed (the bathroom visits, food missing from the refrigerator) and say you are concerned. Ask her what's wrong.

2. Avoid making accusations, threats or judgments. Convey an attitude of concern.
3. Give her a chance to explain herself. Be a good listener.
4. Your next move depends on her response. When you've heard her out, it's possible she'll convince you that your fears were unfounded, in which case you needn't do anything further. Another possibility is that she'll admit to a problem. Ask her then to consult a college counselor, physician or nurse, and make sure she follows through.

But the third and most likely possibility is that she'll respond with some unconvincing statement like "There's nothing wrong with me." While of course there may be nothing wrong, this reaction also may be denial—a refusal to admit to a problem—and it's typical for persons with eating disorders (as well as for substance abusers). If this is her reaction, you may want to bide your time for a while and give her an opportunity to face up to the truth. Possibly after your conversation sinks in she may come back later and say, "You were right, I do have a problem. I need help."

If she continues to deny difficulties and you continue to have concerns about her, then you should eventually speak to an RA or residence manager. Don't let the matter drop without contacting someone in authority. Bulimia, like suicide and substance abuse, is too serious for you to stand by and do nothing.

Q: Is it my family's fault that I'm bulimic?

A: That's a difficult question to answer. Certainly, how you were raised may predispose you to bulimia—as it can predispose you to many conditions. Recent studies show that some bulimics and anorexics have abusive or alcoholic parents, or have a father or brother who was very critical about their weight.

Another common family picture, even more for anorexics than bulimics, is that of a seemingly stable, successful, normal upper-middle-class household. Behind the scenes these picture-perfect families aren't what they seem, however. The parents are controlling and demanding of their daughter, who consequently stifles her own needs and feelings and instead tries to be perfect and pleasing. An eating disorder results when she also stifles her nutritional needs, and tries to be "perfect" about weight too—perfectly thin, that is. In other words, food and body weight become bound up with parents' expectations and her own sense of identity.

But not everybody from such families develops an eating disorder, nor does everyone who has an eating disorder come from such families. Your upbringing, if it was troubled, is only part of the story.

Q: Then why else might I be bulimic?

A: There could be a number of reasons. One contributing factor may be biological—a deficiency in a hormone that turns off appetite after eating.[2] Another factor may be underlying depression, which may or may not be related to your family background. Then there's the societal pressure to be slim. Although dancers, models and actresses feel this pressure most intensely, all women are affected (as are some men). Societal pressure can lead to erratic eating habits, which is how bingeing may start, and it can also make purging seem tempting as a quick-and-easy method of weight control.

Another factor behind purging may be the influence of friends and classmates. Many students start vomiting or using laxatives by following the example of a peer. "That's cool," one woman student remembers thinking, when a high school friend taught her to vomit after eating. Purging can be like drinking and taking drugs. Everyone seems to do it, it seems harmless—until you end up with a habit over which you've lost control.

Q: If I think I'm bulimic, how can I stop myself?

A: Let's start by putting first things first: You should get professional help. Once caught in a web of binge eating and purging, you will find it very difficult to extricate yourself without assistance. Both your college's counseling center and health service have dealt with many students who share your problem. These offices can offer individual counseling, medical monitoring if necessary, and a referral to an off-campus eating disorders clinic if that's called for.

Many colleges also have on-campus groups for students who have eating disorders. In a group, you can overcome your sense of shame, give and receive support, identify feelings, and share experiences. See also the organizations listed at the end of this volume.

In conjunction with professional assistance and support groups, here are measures you can try on your own:

- Remind yourself that purging doesn't keep your weight down. Despite its appeal as a weight control method, the truth is that vomiting doesn't actually rid your body of calories or result in weight loss. Using laxatives or diuretics doesn't work either.

- Avoid crash diets and spartan eating programs. When you deprive yourself of normal amounts of food or forbid yourself from ever having treats, you create a rebound effect in which eventually you're sure to overeat. Sensible, moderate eating habits, by contrast, make binges less likely.
- In the same vein, don't eat too little to make up for eating too much. After a binge, return to your normal eating routine rather than compensating for the binge by starving yourself.
- Try, if you can, to resist purging no matter how much you've eaten. We realize this is impossible for many bulimics; the impulse to purge may be simply too strong to resist. However, if you can avoid or cut down on purging, you may positively influence your eating habits. That's because purging reinforces overeating. It lets you binge without paying the price of calorie intake—or so it erroneously seems. Abstaining from purging gives you an incentive to eat sensibly, and may be the first step in overcoming bulimia.
- Set realistic goals with your bingeing, purging and eating habits. If you're bingeing and purging twice a day now and can't stop, shoot at first for once daily, then once every two days, and so forth. If you're trying to eat sensibly, introduce realistic changes into your diet, changes that you're likely to keep.
- Chart your progress. Accurately record in a notebook binges, purges and all your food intake. Treat any reduction at all in your symptoms, any increase in sensible eating habits, as a step in the right direction.
- Don't let setbacks discourage you. If several good days are followed by a relapse, get back to your goals rather than giving up in despair. It's the overall trend of progress that counts, not occasional lapses.
- In addition to charting your eating behavior, keep a written record describing the situations when you binge and your feelings and thoughts at the time. A journal entry might look as follows: "Oct. 11, 10 P.M. Johnny didn't call. I was hurt and angry. Ate 2 bags of potato chips." Through this exercise, you may discover a pattern of binges following anger, loneliness, insecurity, or any strong emotion at all. This exercise helps you tune into these internal states and recognize when you're at risk of overeating.
- As a second part of this same exercise, write about the times you successfully cope with strong emotions. For example: "Oct. 13, 9 P.M. Johnny didn't call again. Angry, of course. Called Susan and read for a while. Didn't stuff my face!"

- Learn to identify self-defeating and irrational beliefs. (This is the cognitive approach again.) Psychologist Randolph Lee lists several irrational thoughts typical of college students with eating disorders: "I am either fat or I am thin." "My weight is the best measure of my self-worth." "I must be perfect or no one will like me." "Others' expectations for me are more important than my own."[3] When you recognize such thoughts, replace them with realistic substitutes, such as "I may be five pounds overweight, but I'm hardly what you'd call fat," and "I'm still attractive, whatever the scale says."
- Try practicing assertive behavior. Many bulimics attempt to please under all circumstances, afraid to express their own needs. This passive strategy results in feelings of frustration, with food then seen as the only outlet. So stand up for your needs and you won't have to retreat to the refrigerator.
- Work at accepting yourself as you are. This includes accepting your body, too, as we discuss at the beginning of this chapter.

ANOREXIA

Q: A friend of mine is very thin and keeps on getting thinner. How can I tell if she's anorexic?

A: Weight loss alone doesn't qualify her as having anorexia nervosa, just as occasional bingeing and purging, though still a problem, doesn't make someone a full-fledged bulimic. An anorexic is someone, usually a woman, who starves herself and often exercises compulsively until she's seriously underweight. Anorexics have an intense fear of gaining weight, see themselves as fat despite their emaciation (in a sense, they're delusional on this point), and have skipped their menstrual period at least three times consecutively. A professional would be needed to make the diagnosis.

Q: How does anorexia compare with bulimia?

A: In certain respects they are similar. Both anorexics and bulimics are obsessed with diet and weight and are afraid of becoming fat (actually, anorexics already feel fat). Both endanger their health; anorexics may do serious damage to their digestive system, muscles, bones and major organs, including causing heart arrhythmia that can lead to death. Both may come from controlling, perfectionist families. And women who are anorexics sometimes go on to become bulimics.

But the two conditions also have significant differences. Unlike bulimia, anorexia is usually not a secret. The skin-and-bones young woman who may jog for miles around campus is a sight for everyone to witness. Also unlike bulimia, anorexia usually doesn't involve shame and secrecy. The anorexic doesn't view her eating disorder as a problem, and seldom goes into treatment of her own accord. To her way of thinking, reducing food intake is logical and necessary because she needs to lose weight. On the personal level, the anorexic tends to be perfectionist, stubborn and not very social, unlike the usually pleasing—too pleasing—bulimic. Lastly, anorexia is rarer than bulimia. Though estimates vary, maybe one in several hundred women is anorexic, while perhaps one in 20 is bulimic.[4]

Q: What should I do about a friend who may be anorexic?

A: Speak to her about it, following the same procedure we outlined for bulimia. Because of the anorexic's characteristic denial, which is typically stronger even than the bulimic's, she is likely to discount your concerns. But converting her to your way of thinking isn't the goal. The key is to find out if she's in treatment or at least has been evaluated by a professional. If not, then discuss your concerns with an RA or residence hall manager, who can follow through to have her evaluated.

FOR FURTHER READING

Marlene Boskind-White and William C. White, *Bulimarexia: The Binge/Purge Cycle*. New York: W.W. Norton, 1983.

Paul Haskew and Cynthia H. Adams, *When Food is a Four-Letter Word*. Englewood Cliffs, N.J.: Prentice-Hall, 1984.

Jane Brody, *Jane Brody's Nutrition Book*. New York: W.W. Norton, 1981.

Hilde Bruch, *The Golden Cage: The Enigma of Anorexia Nervosa*. New York: Vintage, 1979.

Susie Orbach, *Fat is a Feminist Issue II*. New York: Berkley, 1982.

IS COUNSELING
FOR YOU?

Sprinkled throughout this book we've suggested you "consult a counselor." But what happens when you see a counselor or a psychotherapist? How is talking supposed to help? Who is the best kind of counselor for you? In this chapter we take up these and other questions that may be puzzling you about the counseling process.

Q: I've been thinking of going into counseling. But what is it, exactly?

A: Counseling is a general term for professional guidance to help a person (the client or patient) solve problems. The counseling practiced at your college's counseling center is specifically geared toward the conflicts and problems of college students—fitting in, depression, anxiety, relationships, substance abuse—the issues discussed in this book.

Q: What happens at the counseling center?

A: Usually you can either call in or stop by the office to schedule an appointment. On the day of your appointment, the receptionist may ask you to fill out some confidential forms providing information for your counselor. You then are directed to the counselor's office, where you sit across from each other in comfortable chairs (no Freudian couches here). If you are like most first-time clients, your heart is now pounding and you half want to bolt out the door.

At the start of the session, the counselor typically asks you why you've come in for help. Though he or she then asks follow-up questions, offers some feedback and may explain some ground rules about counseling, usually from this point on it's you who does most of the talking. Opening up about personal concerns can feel strange at first, especially since you don't know this person. But often after a while you start feeling comfortable, and a sense of relief comes over you. It's good, you realize, to get these problems out at last.

Toward the end of the 45- to 50-minute session, you and the counselor decide if more visits would be helpful. If so, he or she explains who will work with you (often you will continue seeing the same person). Together you may agree on tentative goals for the sessions. Then you leave the office to schedule another appointment and to mull over what has happened.

Q: What then happens in the next session and the weeks to follow?

A: That depends largely on you and what you want to discuss. True, the counselor will no doubt inquire about certain areas—your family, your friendships and love life, your academic progress. He or she will ask questions, make observations, venture opinions. But much of counseling consists of you speaking your mind freely, bringing up whatever seems important to you, and therefore your discussions won't follow a predetermined course. The talk may shift from one problem to another, from deeply disturbing matters to seemingly trivial events, from current happenings to childhood memories to future plans. Even your feelings about counseling and the counselor are fair game for discussion. You and the counselor take up topics as they arise, and you both continue to make discoveries as you go along.

Q: But how does all this talking help?

A: That's a complicated issue, and by no means is every counselor in full agreement on the answer. Here is a very brief, partial explanation:

First of all, counseling helps because you discover things through talking—in a sense, you discover yourself. When you struggle to put your experiences into words and to express them to another human being, you clarify your thinking and come to realize your true wishes and feelings. Talking to the counselor also encourages you to take your thoughts seriously. On your own you may make discoveries yet dismiss them, but you give weight to the things you say in counseling.

Second, you learn through listening. Your counselor won't give you all the answers or tell you what to do, but his or her questions and observations may open up possibilities you hadn't previously considered.

Third, the relationship with the counselor can boost your self-esteem and morale. You realize you're not crazy, not immoral, not radically different from everyone else, but a person worth listening to and respecting. Ideally, the sense of acceptance the counselor conveys becomes generalized, and you start feeling acceptable in the eyes of other people as well.

And lastly, going to a counselor can inspire you to make positive changes. With support from the counselor, you may feel motivated to start studying, start speaking honestly to friends, start eating healthily. And once you get moving in the right direction, it's easier to keep up the constructive behavior.

Q: But if counseling is just talking and support, why can't I get it from my friends?

A: Up to a point you can, and if you're fortunate enough to have such friends, by all means do so. But very few people have friendships that allow them to reveal everything. In most friendships, people slant what they say and leave things out because they feel that otherwise their friends will disapprove or be bored or won't understand. With a counselor, you can tell all—you're *encouraged* to—and you're accepted and well understood whatever you say.

Also, in counseling all the attention is on you; you don't have to share. In no other relationship do you have this opportunity to focus entirely on self-understanding. And though friends may be wise and well-meaning, they're not objective about you, nor are they professionally trained. A counselor is able to see you with fewer distortions.

Q: But at least I know my friends care about me. Why should I talk to someone who's doing it as a job? That's not a real relationship.

A: Yes, counseling is a job. Talking to students is how your counselor earns a living. But remember that people enter the profession of counseling precisely because they want to help others. And even if they didn't feel this way originally, they'd soon find themselves caring because of the nature of counseling. You see, caring is almost inevitable when clients are opening up about private concerns and placing their trust in counseling. College counselors genuinely respond to the students they see. They do care.

Is the counselor-student relationship real? It's certainly *different*: exactly 45 or 50 minutes per week, always situated in an office, with the spotlight only on the client and the conversation mostly about the client's problems. Yet we would argue that this strange relationship is more genuine than most. Both persons are talking honestly, without putting on facades, about matters of substance. How many relationships are this real?

Q: You keep saying counseling, but what you're describing sounds like psychotherapy to me. Are they the same thing?

A: As we're using the terms, yes they are. Although we refer to counseling and counselors in these pages, we could as easily say psychotherapy and psychotherapists, or therapy and therapists.

Many professionals do draw a distinction between counseling and psychotherapy. The latter delves deeper, into the irrational, unconscious mind, and is more often considered a treatment for emotional disturbance. The term counseling, by contrast, is reserved for rational discussions rather than probes into the unconscious, and for "normal," not emotionally disturbed, clients. But in this book we're using counseling and psychotherapy interchangeably.

Q: Do you have to be crazy to see a counselor?

A: Not at all. In fact, truly crazy people often can't see anything is wrong and balk at getting help. Basically healthy people are more able to recognize a problem and take constructive action to correct it.

Did you know that approximately 10% of your classmates visit the college counseling center in any one year? As for the rest, many currently see private counselors, or have in the past, or will in the future. So not only aren't you crazy for going to a counselor, you're also in good company.

Q: Lots of people have worse problems than I do. Why should I go into counseling?

A: It depends on your own sense of need. The fact that somebody else is worse off is beside the point. If you are troubled about something, if there's a concern you'd like to discuss, and especially if you've been unable to handle the problem on your own, then the matter isn't trivial—we're talking about your life, after all—and you have every right to avail yourself of the counseling center.

Q: But I want to solve problems on my own. Isn't it a sign of weakness to depend on a counselor?

A: No. It takes courage to face up to a problem and ask for help. It takes courage to engage in self-examination and try to make personal changes. The "weaker" approach—it's called denial—is to sweep problems under the carpet and hope they don't reappear.

Mind you, we respect your desire to solve your own problems. Self-reliance is a valuable personal asset. But even self-reliant people have to take their cars to the mechanic and consult doctors when they're sick. Likewise, it's only sensible to ask for help when you can't solve a personal problem on your own.

Q: But what if I become too dependent on counseling?

A: That's very unlikely. Oh, you may look forward to your appointments, you may benefit greatly from them, you may like your counselor—we hope all this happens. But becoming dependent on counseling implies that you'll stop being able to manage on your own, whereas counseling is designed to accomplish exactly the opposite. Its aim is for you to conduct your own life better than you could before.

Q: How much will counseling cost?

A: Most counseling center services are free of charge to students, covered in full under their student health fee or student activity fee. Even if your college does impose a charge, it will probably be quite low.

Private counseling or psychotherapy is another matter. Depending on the region of the country and the credentials of the professional, the fees per session may range from $40 to a hefty $120 or more.

How then can you afford private psychotherapy if you want it? Your parents will have to help (if they can), you'll have to get a part-time job, or you'll need to be covered for psychotherapy under your parents' or your college's health insurance policy. With regard to insurance policies, be sure to read the fine print or ask the right person to find out exactly how much, if anything, you'll be reimbursed.

Fortunately, some private practitioners and most community mental health centers operate on a "sliding fee scale," which means that the fee depends on your ability to pay. So by doing some investigating you may find quite affordable psychotherapy. Your college counseling center can give you leads on where to look.

Q: I've been hesitating about counseling because I don't want to damage my college record.

A: There's no need to worry. Your appointments at the college counseling center are confidential; what you discuss stays between you and the counselor. No information about your sessions, not even the fact that you're in counseling, is passed on to deans, parents, faculty or anyone else outside the counseling center. Nor does your counseling experience show up on your official college record. So freely discuss anything you want; your secrets will be safeguarded.

There are a few things you should know about confidentiality. To assist in understanding you, your counselor will probably write some notes and keep them in a locked file (no one else will see them), and he or she may discuss your case with another counselor on staff. These are standard practices in the field, meant to help your counselor help you, and they don't compromise confidentiality. Also, some circumstances might arise where you'd *want* your counselor to communicate with a professor, dean, parent or a private therapist. If this comes up, your counselor would do so only after fully discussing it with you and receiving your written permission.

Are there exceptions to confidentiality? Yes, a few. According to the law in many states, your counselor has a duty to warn the appropriate parties if somebody's life is in danger, must report incidents of child abuse and must respond to court orders. But these exceptions come up very rarely and should not discourage you from getting help.

Q: When is the best time to go into counseling?

A: The sooner the better—but it's never too late. Sooner is usually better because tackling a small problem is easier than a problem that's grown big and complicated. So if you think you need counseling, go now rather than waiting until you're really in trouble. On the other hand, it's never too late; long-standing, seemingly desperate problems can be helped, too. Just because you've hesitated doesn't mean you have to give up on help now.

Here's a tip. College counselors' schedules tend to get filled up by the time of midterms. So if you have a choice, schedule your first appointment early in the term.

Q: My counselor has recommended group therapy, but I don't think I could tell my problems to a group of classmates.

A: Quite a few students are uncomfortable revealing their problems in a counseling group. In fact, many students are ill-at-ease and quiet in any kind of group, even a gathering of friends in the dormitory.

But your discomfort with groups is actually a strong argument to join one. Here is a safe opportunity to practice group interactions, with the support of the leader behind you and with the knowledge that every other member probably feels as you do. You are protected regarding confidentiality too; ground rules for the group stipulate that the identities of the members remain with the group. Chances are in a few weeks you'll feel surprisingly comfortable with these people. You'll talk with newfound freedom and look forward to the weekly meetings.

Some counseling groups are organized around a theme, such as eating disorders, assertiveness, sexual abuse survivors or children of alcoholic parents. In these groups you discover that you're not alone with your problem; others have had experiences and feelings like your own. Sometimes students attend one of these groups in conjunction with individual counseling; each therapeutic experience reinforces the other.

Q: If the counseling center at my college only has psychologists, should I go there? Wouldn't I be better off with a psychiatrist?

A: Uh oh, here we go. . . . Every several weeks, some student storms into our own counseling centers and demands to see a psychologist or a psychiatrist—a "real counselor," not an inferior substitute. But the truth is, both psychologists and psychiatrists are very well trained, and both do essentially the same kind of counseling. The same holds true for clinical social workers and for master's level counselors, the other main professions represented at college counseling centers.

Are these professions at all different? Yes, in certain ways, psychologists are specialists in psychological testing, psychiatrists in prescribing medication, and social workers in understanding community services. In terms of educational background, psychologists have a doctorate in psychology, psychiatrists are medical doctors, social workers have a master's degree or sometimes a doctorate in social work, and master's level counselors have (you guessed it) a master's degree in counseling.

But when it comes to talking to clients, these professions have much more in common than setting them apart. Good counseling is good counseling, whatever the counselor's profession.

Q: Then are you saying it doesn't matter who my counselor is?

A: No, we're not saying that. Your counselor matters a great deal. But the profession of your counselor counts far less than his or her personal qualities and the chemistry between you. When we speak of chemistry, we don't mean your feelings toward the counselor should be 100% positive. In fact, negative feelings that come up are important information that may shed light on your relationship difficulties with other people. All in all, though, you should feel positive about this person. Specifically, you should have the following reactions if counseling is to be successful:

- You generally feel that the counselor understands you.
- You generally feel accepted.
- You feel encouraged to speak candidly, to reveal yourself in depth.
- The counselor strikes you as competent, a professional who knows what he or she is doing.
- The counselor seems genuine and caring.
- On balance, you like and respect this person.

If your counseling relationship passes these tests, then you probably are working with the right person.

Q: My counselor says he's a gestalt therapist. Is that as good as a Freudian?

A: This is the psychologist vs. psychiatrist question in a different guise, and we have the same answer. There are good gestalt therapists—good for you, anyway—and less good ones. There are also more or less helpful Freudians, behavior therapists, cognitive therapists, Jungians and existential therapists. The label itself doesn't tell how well the counselor will work with you. The quality of the counselor, and of the relationship between you, is what decides.

There are dozens of counseling or therapy approaches on the market, each claiming to be the best. Some of them, notably Freudian psychoanalysis, dig deep into your past and uncover your unconscious conflicts. Others pay closest attention to the ways you behave, or to your thinking patterns, or to your unexpressed feelings, or to your personal relationships. Although these schools of counseling sound dissimilar in theory, good counselors tend to pick up on the same key issues no matter what their philosophy. And many counselors consider themselves "eclectic," which means that they draw on a variety of approaches rather than confining themselves to just one.

Q: I don't feel comfortable talking to a male counselor. If I ask, will the counseling center assign me to a woman?

A: Many counseling centers will try to satisfy your request. They'll also do their best to match you up with, say, an African-American counselor, or a young counselor, or a particular counselor a friend recommended. But bear in mind that your college's clinic may not have exactly the type of person you want. And even if that person exists, scheduling problems may make it difficult to match the two of you.

We appreciate that you may not like confiding in a male. Going into counseling can seem daunting enough without having an intimidating counselor thrust upon you. But sometimes you can benefit precisely because your counselor is the "wrong" kind. Much can be gained from learning to relate to people of the opposite sex or who are otherwise different from you.

Q: I don't feel comfortable with my counselor. Now what?

A: This happens sometimes. Counseling is a highly personal activity—it's a *relationship*—and sometimes the combination of personalities just doesn't click. However, before you give up on the counselor, try talking to him or her about your feelings, since your reaction may be rooted in your personal issues. If you can discover why you feel uncomfortable with this person, you may gain valuable insight into yourself. You may even start to feel differently and find that you can work with the counselor after all.

But after the discussion, you still may not want to continue with the counselor. That's okay; he or she will understand. Set up an appointment with somebody else. With luck, your second counseling relationship will work out fine.

Q: I sometimes feel worse after my sessions. Does that often happen?

A: Sometimes, yes. Counseling involves getting in touch with truths that you have pushed out of awareness. For example, you may finally admit to yourself that your childhood was unhappy, that you don't really love your boyfriend or girlfriend, or that you are unhappy with your current career path. Such realizations are disturbing. The pain they cause is the price you pay for authentic self-awareness.

But over the long haul, counseling should make you feel better, not worse—freer, not more burdened. If you continue to feel worse with no letup in sight, or if you sense that you're not making any progress at all toward your counseling goals, you need to discuss this problem with your counselor.

Q: I've been working on some difficult problems in counseling, but I'm feeling okay today and recently nothing bad has happened. Should I cancel my appointment?

A: It's probably best to keep it. Having a good week doesn't mean long-term problems have gone away. And even though you lack an immediate concern to bring up, you may be surprised at what you unearth during the session. Quiet times, when there's no crisis to resolve, often afford the best opportunity for self-exploration and reflection.

For counseling to be effective, it's necessary to maintain a certain continuity. Keeping appointments only when you feel upset is no more productive than taking an exercise class only when the mood strikes you.

Q: How will I know when I'm finished with counseling?

A: That depends on your goals, and these may change as you go along. Initially, for example, you may be concerned about anxiety attacks, whereas later, after your anxiety has abated, you may want to explore relationship difficulties. You never get to the endpoint of self-understanding. Problems and issues have a way of continuing to come up.

This is not to say you should be in counseling forever. The point is simply that you need to examine and reexamine your counseling goals. If there is pressing work still to do, then you should continue. If not, then maybe it's time to stop.

Q: My counseling center only offers short-term counseling. Should I see a counselor on the outside? Won't it be hard to start all over again with somebody new?

A: The decision about going in for long-term counseling is best made in consultation with your current counselor. It depends on your unfinished counseling goals and your motivation for continued work.

Is starting with someone new difficult? Yes, to a degree. You need to explain about yourself all over again, and you have to adjust to your new counselor's style. But the time spent in explanation is never a waste; each time you go over the same material you learn from the telling. And no matter how helpful your initial counselor was, it's almost always enlightening to work with someone new, who has fresh insights and a fresh perspective.

Q: What if I never go into counseling?

A: That's fine. Unless you have a problem that's too much for you, you certainly don't have to see a professional. Many persons lead a fulfilling life without ever consulting a counselor. All we ask is that you be honest with yourself about your difficulties and open-minded about receiving professional help. If you ever do need to consult a counselor, whether in college or in later life, we hope that you let yourself take that step.

FOR FURTHER READING

Fredda Bruckner-Gordon and Barbara K. Gangi, *Making Therapy Work: Your Guide to Choosing, Using and Ending Therapy.* New York: Harper & Row, 1988.

Judi Striano, *How to Find a Good Psychotherapist: A Consumer Guide.* Santa Barbara, Calif.: Professional SBcA, 1987.

IS THERE
LIFE AFTER
COLLEGE?

The final challenge of college is to learn how to leave it behind. Finishing up is not a simple matter of completing course requirements and sitting through the commencement ceremony. It is, like starting college, a major transition, a passage into the next developmental stage. Though some students are eager to move on, most greet the change with some uneasiness, a wistful looking back and an apprehensive looking ahead. It's not a small matter to pull up stakes and begin a new phase of life.

In this chapter we focus on career issues and other concerns you may have about graduating. There *is* life after college, but it's not surprising if you feel some ambivalence about getting there.

Q: I'm only a sophomore, but I'm worried because I don't know what I'll do when I graduate. How do I go about choosing a career?

A: Slow down a bit. You don't have to map out your entire life by the second year of college. Some of your classmates already do know their life's work, it's true, and that may work fine for them. But most undergraduates, especially those enrolled in liberal arts programs, need more time and experience to pick a career direction. Many still have not made a career decision even at graduation, and sometimes for several years afterward.

Choosing a career has to come about naturally. It's much more important to select wisely and when you're ready than to wrap up your career choice early.

Q: Then is sophomore year too early to think about careers?

A: No, it isn't. Now is a good time to discover interests, preferences and abilities that may lead to a career. To do this, we suggest the following:

- Pursue summer jobs, college internships, student activities and volunteer work. These experiences give you a taste of what it's like to work in various fields.
- Sample widely from your college's course offerings. In time, a pattern may emerge pointing in a given career direction. If, for example, you enjoy and excel in political science, history and international relations courses, then you may want to consider a career in law or the foreign service. If courses in visual studies and fine arts are your thing, a future in museum curatorship, architecture or commercial photography might follow.
- Bear in mind, however, that people enter careers from widely differing academic backgrounds. Your major doesn't commit you to any particular profession. Provided you fulfill the course requirements, you can major in biology and go to law school, or major in political science and enroll in medical school.
- Be sensitive to your own reactions. Try to discover jobs, activities and courses that really suit you rather than talking yourself into ones that don't fit. Jan, for example, decided early on to become a doctor based on her supposed interest in natural sciences. This plan comforted her; it felt good to be certain about her future and to impress family and friends that she'd be an M.D. some day. Trouble is, she didn't especially enjoy or do well in college-level biology and chemistry, and meanwhile she found deep satisfaction working part-time at a neighborhood day-care center. Only after repeatedly beating her head against the wall of pre-med courses did Jan finally level with herself. The truth, once she could admit it, was that elementary education suited her much better than medicine.
- Talk to professionals about the fields you are considering. Your college's career counseling office may have a list of alumni who can tell you about their jobs.
- You can also take advantage of the many other services provided at the career counseling office. These include consultations about careers, computerized guidance and written information about careers.

Q: In a few months I'll be graduating and getting a job, but somehow I don't feel ready to enter the work world. Why is that?

A: Many possibilities come to mind. One is lack of confidence in your abilities. Think back to when you took on previous challenges, such as entering college or starting a part-time job. Did you question yourself then? If so, it's not surprising that you're feeling uneasy at the prospect of this new challenge.

Maybe, too, you can't quite picture yourself as an adult professional. This is a common feeling that can last even into the first few years on the job. Many young professionals feel at work as if they're acting somehow, like children pretending to be grown-ups. They're not *really* accountants or salespersons or architects; those are just the roles they're playing. If you are feeling this way—if, understandably, your professional identity hasn't formed yet—then you may feel unready to enter the work world.

Family issues can also give you pause. If your career path has been staked out by your parents, now at the moment of truth you may not want to go forward. Or you may hesitate to start a career that has you professionally outdoing your parents, or that falls below their high standards.

Finally, you may feel that you haven't fully taken advantage of college, or haven't sampled enough of life. You don't want to get started on a career until you've fulfilled these other goals.

Q: Then if I don't feel ready to work, what should I do?

A: That depends on the strength of your ambivalence. You don't have to feel 100% positive about working to make a successful entry into the work world; almost everyone has some qualms at the beginning. But if your resistance is strong, then we suggest consulting a counselor to uncover the reasons and discuss sensible options. A professional can help you explore whether or not getting a job is now in your best interests.

Q: After the freedom and stimulation of college, I dread the idea of a nine-to-five routine and doing the same thing each day. How can a free spirit like me ever be happy with the same old grind?

A: Fortunately, the work world is a lot more varied than you imagine. Yes, there are many highly structured jobs, and many people who prefer them that way, but there are also looser company environments, freer careers such as college teaching, and the possibility of self-employment, where you set your own rules. Your college's career counseling office can give you leads on job and career opportunities where you'll enjoy freedom and variety.

No job will fit your needs to the letter. But just as some romantic partners are a good match for you, certain jobs are well-suited to your personality type. Rather than dismissing the work world as alien, be open-minded about working and look for a career compatible with your needs.

Q: But I can't imagine limiting myself to one profession and giving up other possibilities.

A: You're right, up to a point—pursuing a career does mean giving up options. You can't become, say, a nurse, while simultaneously pursuing full-time careers in teaching, administration and acting. You can either look at this negatively, as a terrible limitation, or you can see it positively, as a chance to specialize. For while it's true that in choosing a career you give up the unlimited horizons of childhood where any future seems possible, now you have the exciting opportunity to really know one area, to become an expert.

But let's not overstate the point about closing off options. Careers, after all, are multidimensional; they let you express different sides of yourself. So if you do go into nursing, you can still end up teaching nursing, being a hospital administrator, or being a health educator who draws on acting skills. You grow in careers, too; your duties change as you gain experience and expertise. Also, don't forget that you can pursue interests in your free time. If you have a glorious tenor voice that must be muzzled at the office, it can burst out in full song when you clock out at five.

Bear in mind, too, that a career decision isn't a lifetime sentence. If you want to try a new field in two, five or even twenty years, then you can switch careers, as millions have done.

Q: Can my college get me a job?

A: Getting a job will be your doing, but your college's career counseling office can equip you with skills to find jobs. This office has literature about professions and particular companies, and can show you how to prepare a résumé. Many career counseling offices also invite representatives from major corporations onto campus to interview students for jobs.

Q: I'm terrified of these job interviews. How can I cope with them?

A: They can be intimidating, at least at the beginning. Here are several ideas that may help:

- Attend workshops that the career counseling office may conduct on interviewing skills. You can also role-play interviews, having a friend or parent simulate an interviewer while you practice giving answers.
- Interview for several jobs. Experience at interviewing may increase your confidence.
- Consider several job possibilities rather than becoming fixated on one. An open-minded attitude about jobs reduces the pressure you'll feel on any one interview. Make sure, however, that you convey your sincere interest and knowledge about each position.
- Remember that interviewing isn't an exact science. Interviewers disagree on candidates, and the best candidate doesn't always land the job. So hone your interviewing skills, but don't torment yourself worrying about perfect answers, since you can never be sure how your answers will be perceived.
- While you shouldn't overdo second-guessing, it's a good idea after each interview to analyze what went well and what needs improving. A career counselor or a friend can help you objectively review your performance.
- If you do get rejected, take advantage of the experience by asking for feedback about your candidacy. And remember that sometimes organizations later recruit runners-up for other positions.

Q: How do I find out about graduate schools?

A: The first place to go is your college's career counseling office, where you can find catalogs and other information about programs. For the inside scoop on particular programs, you may also want to visit the schools and seek out officials and enrolled students there. Professors at your own college are another resource who can provide information about graduate training and professional opportunities.

If you plan to go to graduate school, you'll need to start about a year before you intend to enroll. An early start is necessary to learn about different kinds of programs, write to schools for applications, request letters of recommendation, and then apply. Application forms and required standardized tests must be completed by certain deadlines.

The entire process is involved, but no more so than the process that got you into college.

Once you've applied, be prepared to wait. Often graduate schools don't mail out notifications until mid-April. To ease your anxiety, it helps to apply to several programs rather than putting your fate in the hands of one or two admissions committees.

Q: There are two months left until I graduate. All my classmates have plans except me. What should I do?

A: As we said earlier, it's not unusual for college seniors to be undecided about their careers. In fact, since time is short, we recommend postponing ultimate career decisions. Much more important now is to make some immediate plans for after college. Consider your options: Is it best for you to look for a job, find volunteer work, help out in a family enterprise, or take time off to travel? Should you live alone, find a roommate, or move in with your parents? How will you pay for your room and board?

The sooner you make short-range plans, even if they're only for a few months or so, the better you'll feel about yourself and the future.

Q: My plans after graduation are to go home and work until I save enough for my own place. But how will I cope with living with my parents again?

A: Granted, the arrangement can be touchy, even if you generally get along well with them. Though different problems can arise, the most predictable are battles over privacy and control. You'll probably want to be treated as an independent adult, free to come and go and do as you please, while they may ask you where you're going at night, tell you to be home by midnight, and remind you to drive carefully. If you protest that they're treating you like a child, they can come back with the two classic arguments every parent uses: "We're still your parents" and "When you're in our house, you follow our rules."

One way to prevent power struggles is to come to an early agreement about ground rules. Discuss with your parents when you may come and leave, when you will and will not report your whereabouts, how often you may have visitors, and how much you will tell them about job hunting and your social life. For best results, present your side calmly and work toward compromise. You may not get all the privacy and freedom you want, but at least both you and your parents will know where matters stand and the atmosphere can stay cordial.

Some college graduates pay rent when they return home, or earn their keep by doing household chores. Paying your own way lets you feel less dependent on your parents while encouraging them to treat you like an adult.

Q: I'm looking forward to starting my new job and having an apartment when I graduate next month, yet I still feel somewhat anxious. Why?

A: Chances are you're more upset about moving on than you realize. Like any other major life transition, graduation from college involves an ending and a beginning. Both aspects can pack an emotional wallop.

Stop and consider how much of your life is coming to a close. You must say goodbye to classmates and professors; to classes, activities and social events; to places you've known; to the entire undergraduate life-style. Perhaps you have a boyfriend or girlfriend you won't see as easily now, or perhaps you haven't had a good college romance—and now you think you never will. Symbolically, you also bid farewell to the idea of being a student, or at least a college student. You leave behind, once and for all, the status of childhood. All this is a lot to give up, and it's no wonder if a part of you is grieving the losses.

Now consider what lies ahead of you. Starting next month, you'll be embarking on a new job, adjusting to becoming a full-time worker. Even though your position may sound desirable, it's only natural, as we said earlier, to have doubts and fears about the work world. Soon you'll also be looking for new friends, getting used to a new place to live and handling new living expenses. You can't fall back on old routines or on your college reputation; on all these fronts you have to establish yourself anew. And then, as the flip side to giving up childhood, you have to adjust to a more adult status. Thoughts like these are not unusual: "Now I'm supposed to be grown-up. My life is for real, not a preparation anymore. But am I ready for these responsibilities?"

When we discussed in Chapter 1 the transition into college, we counseled being patient with yourself. Now we echo that advice re-garding the transition out of college. Be patient if you have misgivings and apprehensions, if you have questions about yourself and what life has to offer. These are the normal reactions of any reflective human being to times of great change.

At the same time, remind yourself of your coping capacities. You made a successful entry into college, and now you can successfully navigate your way out of college. Remind yourself, too, that change is invigorating, the impetus to growth. Life is different after college, but it is, in its own way, every bit as rewarding.

Q: I burst into tears whenever I see one of my friends or think of leaving this place, and I feel totally overwhelmed. What can I do?

A: Though graduation is an inherently emotional experience, your reaction is evidence of irrational assumptions. You may be upsetting yourself by thinking: "I'll never have such good friends again." "The best years of my life are over." "I'll hate having a job."

As with any irrational thinking, our advice is to refute these assumptions and replace them with realistic alternatives. For example, you might challenge the first assumption by talking to yourself as follows: "Why can't I make good friends again? After all, I've always made new friends in the past. And besides, I don't have to lose my college friendships. Several of my closest friends will be living near me." Similar reasoning can be applied to the other faulty assumptions.

If this cognitive strategy fails to bring you relief, then the prudent course is to discuss your situation with a counselor.

Q: The problems of the world seem overwhelming. What difference can I make when I graduate?

A: No question, the newspapers are full of worrisome headlines. Whether you fix your attention on AIDS or drugs or the homeless, the greenhouse effect or the destruction of animal and plant species, regional strife or ethnic hatred or economic upheavals, the difficulties are immense. Granted, there's little that you can do, as one person, to change these global realities.

We would suggest, however, that a middle ground exists between saving the planet and giving up in despair. Single-handedly you can't rescue civilization, but you can have an influence through the work you choose and how you perform it, the people you touch, the energy and goodness of your daily actions. Thus you can't stamp out illiteracy, but you can, as a teacher or volunteer tutor, teach a few people to read. As a nurse or doctor, you can treat and bring comfort to the ill. In business or law or the civil service, you can serve your clients ably and ethically; in the arts, you can enlighten and entertain; as a parent, friend, neighbor and citizen, you can affect people positively. As the Jimmy Stewart character discovered in the movie classic *It's a Wonderful Life*, individual actions do add up. The part you play has an impact on the whole.

We would add that there never has been a time when problems were in short supply. Every age has enough bad news and dire predictions to justify pessimism for those who are so inclined. Indeed, how you view the world and your potential role in it says more about you than it does about the world. A gloomy and easily discouraged personal philosophy will see that darkness mirrored in the world. But if you can acquire a certain faith in yourself, then you will have faith that your own efforts can make a difference.

FOR FURTHER READING

Richard Nelson Bolles, *What Color Is Your Parachute?* Berkeley, Calif.: Ten Speed Press, 1986.

Clarke G. Carney and Cinda Field Wells, *Discover the Career Within You,* third edition. Pacific Grove, Calif.: Brooks/Coles, 1991.

Richard K. Irish, *Go Hire Yourself an Employer.* Garden City, N.Y.: Anchor Books, 1973.

Martha P. Leape and Susan M. Vacca, *The Harvard Guide to Careers.* Cambridge, Mass.: Harvard University Press, 1987.

H. Anthony Medley, *Sweaty Palms: The Neglected Art of Being Interviewed.* Berkeley, Calif.: Ten Speed Press, 1984.

Martin John Yate, *Resumes That Knock 'Em Dead.* Boston: Bob Adams, Inc., 1988.

APPENDIX 1
SOURCES OF
HELP ON
CAMPUS

Many offices at colleges and universities provide assistance and counseling for problems. Here, in thumbnail descriptions, are 11 sources of help if you run into a difficulty:

1) The *Counseling Center* (sometimes called the Mental Health Office or Personal Development Center) provides counseling for personal problems: anxiety, depression, substance abuse, sexual and relationship issues, family concerns, and all the rest. Most counseling centers offer short-term counseling (up to 10 or so sessions). Some also run one-session workshops and ongoing therapy groups. If you want long-term psychotherapy, the counseling center can refer you to private practitioners and community mental health agencies.

2) The *Study Skills Center* (also called the Academic Learning Center) specializes in academic difficulties. Professionals there may give tutoring and offer workshops on note-taking, studying techniques, test-taking strategies, reading skills, typing and time management. In addition, some study skills centers assess learning disabilities. There also may be a separate learning disabilities office on your campus.

3) *Academic Advisors.* Do you have questions about your academic program? Then contact an academic advisor, who can explain specific academic requirements ("How many science courses do I need to graduate?"), and, more broadly, help you find your way with important academic decisions ("Should I major in English or

213

business?"). At many colleges these advisors are faculty members—called, logically enough, faculty advisors. In addition to your official advisor, other faculty members may also be receptive to offering academic guidance.

4) The *Career Counseling Office* (also called the Career Advising or Career Development Office). This office helps you plan for life after graduation. When you first begin to think about careers, counselors there can help you clarify your values and vocational interests. Later in the process, they can help you secure a job through workshops on résumé writing, interviewing skills and job hunting, and through interviews they set up with company recruiters. Most career development offices have a library with information about career opportunities, graduate schools and short-term internships.

5) The *Financial Aid Office*. The role of this office is to assist you to find ways to pay for college if you and your family lack sufficient resources. The chief options available are scholarships and grants (provided by the government or the college itself), loans, part-time employment (either at the college or off campus) and deferred payment plans.

6) *Deans* and *Student Affairs Personnel* (exact titles depend on your college's administrative structure). These are individuals who wear many hats: academic advisors, organizers of social programs, informal personal counselors, and advisors to student government and activities. Deans also serve as ombudsmen, which is a fancy way of saying they can help you with a problem or complaint. Because they participate in the campus disciplinary process, deans sometimes have an intimidating reputation. However, most deans are decent human beings and caring counselors (they wanted us to tell you that).

7) The *Health Service* provides general medical assistance and possibly special treatment and counseling in areas like gynecology and nutrition. Many health services have contraceptive clinics as well. Like the counseling center, the health service also makes referrals to facilities and private practitioners off campus.

8) *Campus Ministers.* Do you have religious, ethical or spiritual questions? Then consult your campus ministers, who on many campuses include representatives from the Protestant, Catholic and Jewish faiths. Campus ministers also lead religious services and promote religious activities on campus.

9) *Residence Life Staff.* These are students, called Resident Assistants (RAs), and professionals, often called Residence Managers or Area Directors, who are in charge of life in the residence halls. At most colleges, residence life staff do far more than assign rooms and give out keys. They also provide informal counseling and put on social

and educational programs, and they are often the first people on the scene during psychological and medical emergencies.

10) *Other Professional Offices.* We include this catchall category because most campuses have additional resources serving special populations. For example, there may be offices that specialize in the needs of female students; African- American, Hispanic and Asian-American students; international students; disabled students; gay and lesbian students; and older, returning students. Check out the offerings at your school.

11) *Peer Counseling.* At many colleges, facilities have been set up for students to counsel students. Sometimes peer counselors specialize in particular areas such as alcohol use or sexuality. So if you want to consult with someone who can identify with the student's perspective, see if there's a peer counseling service on your campus.

APPENDIX 2
NATIONAL
SOURCES OF
HELP

In addition to sources of help on campus, national organizations can offer information and referrals for particular problems. Here are a few organizations and the services they provide:

AIDS AND OTHER SEXUALLY TRANSMITTED DISEASES

National HIV and AIDS Information Service 1-800-342-AIDS

Information about transmission of HIV, safer sex, etc. Referrals for counseling, treatment, testing, financial support, and related concerns. Spanish line: 1-800-344-SIDA; teletypewriter machine (for deaf callers): 1-800-AIDS-TTY.

National Sexually Transmitted Disease Hotline 1-800-227-8922.

Basic answers about sexually transmitted diseases, information about other hotlines, and free pamphlets on diseases and prevention. Referrals for local testing sites. No diagnoses over the phone.

ALCOHOL AND OTHER DRUGS

Adcare Hospital Alcohol and Drug Referral Hotline 1-800-ALCO-HOL

Telephone numbers for treatment programs and 12-step programs nationwide: AA, ACOA, Al-Anon, OA.

National Association for Children of Alcoholics 714-499-3889

Information about ACOA meetings over the phone, or in response to a stamped, self-addressed envelope sent to:

ACA
P.O. 3216
Torrance, CA 90505.

National Cocaine Hotline 1-800-COCAINE

Referrals to drug treatment centers and private practitioners throughout the nation.

Alcoholics Anonymous, Narcotics Anonymous: Check in your local telephone directory.

ANOREXIA, BULIMIA AND OVEREATING

American Anorexia/Bulimia Association 212-734-1114

Eating disorders information, and referrals for support groups, private therapists and treatment centers.

Center for the Study of Anorexia and Bulimia 212-595-3449

Information about eating disorders, how to talk to someone with an eating disorder, bibliography for further reading, and referral organizations.

Overeaters Anonymous: Check in your local telephone directory.

GAY AND LESBIAN ISSUES

Parents and Friends of Lesbians and Gays

Informational brochures and support for gays, lesbians, their families and friends. Call or write to:

Parents FLAG
1012 14th Street N.W., Suite 700
Washington, D.C. 20005
(202) 638-4200

STUDENT INFORMATION

American College Health Association 301-963-1100

Informational brochures on a variety of student health concerns, including AIDS, alcohol and sexually transmitted diseases. Call or write to:

ACHA
1300 Piccard Drive
Suite 200
Rockville, MD 20805.

The Chronicle of Higher Education 800-347-6969

A weekly newspaper that publishes news about all aspects of academia—finances, athletics, academics, student affairs, job openings.

National On-Campus Report 608-246-3580

A student-oriented newsletter about happenings on campuses around the United States. Call or write to:

National On-Campus Report
Magna Publications, Inc.
2718 Dryden Drive
Madison, WI 53704-3086.

SUICIDAL CONCERNS

American Association of Suicidology 303-692-0985

Referrals for self-help groups and counseling services across the nation.

Also, check your local telephone directory for a chapter of the **Samaritans** or **Contact**. These organizations have 24-hour phone services in which trained volunteers talk to persons who have suicidal concerns.

REFERENCES

We have avoided using excessive notes throughout this volume. The reader should refer to the list of suggested readings at the end of each chapter. Sources for specific quotations and references in the text are noted below, followed by sources of general information.

Chapter 1

[1]S.B. Cotler and J.J. Guerra, *Assertion Training* (Champaign, Ill.: Research Press, 1979).

[2]Karen Horney, *The Neurotic Personality of Our Time* (New York: W.W. Norton & Company, 1937), 89.

[3]E.B.Fiske, "Lesson," *The New York Times* (April 11, 1990): B8.

See also: J.L. Hopson, "The Unraveling of Insomnia," *Psychology Today* (June 1986): 43–49; M. Machlowitz, "As Millions Toss and Turn, Studies Pursue Secret of Sleep," *The New York Times* (April 21, 1981) C1–2; H. Molnar, "Of Dorms and Roommates," *The New York Times* (August 5, 1990) 10–11; J. Asher, "Born to be Shy?," *Psychology Today* (April 1987): 56–64; Jane E. Brody, "Personal Health," *The New York Times* (November 16, 1989): B19; S. Tifft, "Waging War on the Greeks," *Time* (April 16, 1990): 64–65; "Counseling on Religious Groups Encompasses Some Former Members," *The New York Times* (March 11, 1990): 43.

Chapter 2

[1]Barbara Scheiber and Jeanne Talpers, *Campus Access for Learning Disabled Students: A Comprehensive Guide* (New York: Closer Look: The Parents' Campaign for Handicapped Children and Youth, 1985).

[2]"Plagiarism is Rampant, A Survey Finds," *The New York Times* (April 1, 1990): A36–37.

See also: J.B. Burka and L.M. Yuen, "Mind Games Procrastinators Play," *Psychology Today* (January 1982): 32–41; W. Knaus, "Why People Procrastinate: Is There a Cure?,"*U.S. News & World Report* (October 24, 1983): 61–62; A. Lakein, *How to Get Control of Your Time and Your Life* (New York: New American Library, 1973); E. Kaye and J. Gardner, *College Bound* (The College Board, 1988); J. Gottleib, personal communication, May 2, 1990; *Fear of Studying*, (New York University, n.d.); S. Singular, "A Memory for All Seasonings," *Psychology Today* (October 1982): 54–63; G. Du Chossois, personal communication, May 1, 1990; "Dyslexics Learn to Believe, First, Then to Overcome," *The New York Times* (November, 11, 1990): A49.

Chapter 3

[1] E.E. Goode, "Beating Depression," *U.S. News & World Report* (March 5, 1990): 48–56.

[2] E.E. Goode, "Beating Depression."

[3] "The Nature and Causes of Depression," part 1, *The Harvard Medical School Mental Health Letter* (January 1988):1–4.

[4] M. McKay, M. Davis, and P. Fanning, *Thoughts and feelings: The art of cognitive stress intervention* (Richmond, Calif.: New Harbinger Publications, 1981): 17–45; H.B. Braiker, "The Power of Self-Talk," *Psychology Today* (December 1989): 23–27; D.B. Burns, *Feeling Good: The New Mood Therapy* (New York: Morrow, 1980);

A. Ellis, *Reason and Emotion in Psychotherapy* (New York: Lyle Stuart and Citadel Press, 1962); A. Ellis and R. Grieger, *Handbook of Rational-Emotive Therapy* (New York: Springer, 1977).

[5] E.H. Erikson, *Identity: Youth and Crisis* (New York: W.W. Norton & Company, 1968), 105.

See also: M. Terman and M. Link, "Fighting the Winter Blues with Bright Light," *Psychology Today* (February 1989): 18–21; E.H. Erikson, *Childhood and Society* (New York: W.W. Norton & Company, 1963), 247–269; L.C. Whitaker, personal communication, July 1, 1990; F. Schumer, "Bye-bye Blues," *New York Magazine* (December 18, 1989): 46–53; The State Education Department, The University of the State of New York, *Suicide among School Age Youth* (December 1984); E. Shneidman, "At the Point of No Return," *Psychology Today*, (March 1987): 53–58.

Chapter 4

[1] J.L. Rapoport, "The New Biology of Obsessive Compulsive Disorder," *The Harvard Medical School Mental Health Letter* (January 1989): 4–6.

[2] H. Benson and M.Z. Klipper, *The Relaxation Response* (New York: Avon Books, 1975).

See also: R.R. Wilson, *Don't Panic: Taking Control of Anxiety Attacks* (New York: Harper & Row, 1986); C.J. McCullough and R.W. Mann, *Managing Your Anxiety* (New York: St. Martin's Press, 1985); D. Goleman, "Doctors Cite Gains in Treating Panic Attacks," *New York Times* (January 30, 1990): C3; J.H. Greist, J.W. Jefferson, and I.M. Marks, *Anxiety and Its Treatment* (New York: Warner Books, 1987); F.R. Schneier, "Panic Disorder and Social Phobia Can Be Treated with Drugs, Therapy," *The Psychiatric Times* (July 1990): 16–17; M. Motlet, "Taking the Terror Out of Talk," *Psychology Today* (January 1988): 46–49; D. Goleman, "For Stage Fright, Rehearsal Helps," *New York Times* (June 12, 1991): C1, C10; American Psychiatric Association, *Diagnostic and Statistical Manual of Mental Disorders*, third edition, revised (Washington, D.C., 1987); D.M. Wegner, "Try Not to Think of a White Bear," *Psychology Today* (June 1989): 64–66; D. Goleman, "Study Finds Less Cause for Worry in

Nightmares," *New York Times* (March 15, 1990): B7; R. Williams, "The Trusting Heart," *Psychology Today* (January–February 1989): 36–42; N. Angier, "If Anger Ruins Your Day, It Can Shrink Your Life," *New York Times* (December 13, 1990): B23; C. Tavris, "Anger Defused," *Psychology Today* (November 1982): 25–35; E.A. Charlesworth and R.G. Nathan, *Stress Management* (New York: Ballantine, 1982); C.L. Otis and R. Goldingay, *Campus Health Guide* (New York: College Entrance Examination Board, 1989); A.S. Gentile, "Coping with Stress," unpublished manuscript; L.E. Kopolow, "Plain Talk About. . . Handling Stress" (Washington, D.C.: U.S. Government Printing Office, DHHS Publication No. [ADM] 85-502m, 1985).

Chapter 5

[1]K. Fisher, "Sexual Abuse Victims Suffer Into Adulthood," *APA Monitor* (June 1987): 25.

See also: L. Kutner, "Parent and Child: The First Visit to a Child at College Can Be Confusing," *New York Times* (November 16, 1989): C8; J.S. Wallerstein, "Children after Divorce," *New York Times Magazine* (January 22, 1989): 19–44; "Bereavement and Grief," part 1, *The Harvard Medical School Mental Health Letter* (March 1987): 1–4; R.J. Ackerman,"Interview: Robert J. Ackerman: A New Perspective on Adult Children of Alcoholics," *EAP Digest* (January/February 1987): 25–29; A. Kohn,"Shattered Innocence," *Psychology Today* (February 1987): 54–58.

Chapter 7

[1]"Sex Cools on Campus," *Psychology Today* (March 1989): 14.

[2]Statistics on the efficacy of birth control methods are from B.C. Sloane, *Partners in Health: Contraceptive and Reproductive Health Issues* (Columbus, Ohio: Charles E. Merrill Publishing Co., 1986).

[3]N.E. Macdonald, et al., "High-Risk STD/HIV Behavior Among College Students," *Journal of the American Medical Association* 263 (June 20, 1990): 3155–59.

[4]K. Kanthak and K. Nye, "Students Know AIDS Facts but May Not Follow Safe Sex Rules," *Columbia University Spectator AIDS Supplement* (October 29, 1990): 5.

[5]D. Johnson, "AIDS Clamor at College Muffling Older Dangers," *New York Times* (March 8, 1990): A10.

[6]P.H. Douglas and L. Pinsky, "Think You Know Everything About AIDS? Guess Again," *Columbia University Spectator AIDS Supplement* (October 29, 1990): 18.

[7]J.W. Chesebro, "Views of Homosexuality Among Social Scientists," in J.W. Chesebro (ed.), *Gay Speak: Gay Male and Lesbian Communication* (New York: Pilgrim Press, 1981), 175–88.

[8]J. Marmor, "Homosexuality: Nature vs. Nurture," *The Harvard Medical School Mental Health Newsletter* (October 1985): 5–6.

[9]T.H. Sauerman, *Coming Out to Your Parents* (Washington, D.C.: Federation of Parents and Friends of Lesbians and Gays, Inc., 1984).

See also: "Sexual Disorders," part 2, *Harvard Medical School Mental Health Letter* (January 1990): 1–4; S. Johanson, *Talk Sex* (New York: Penguin, 1988); Nancy Friday, *Men In Love* (New York: Delacorte Press, 1980) and *My Secret Garden* (New York: Pocket Books, 1973); Alfred Kinsey, et al., *Sexual Behavior in the Human Male*

(Philadelphia: W.B. Saunders, 1949) and *Sexual Behavior in the Human Female* (Philadelphia: W.B. Saunders, 1953); G.C. Higgins, "Sexual Problems," in P.A. Grayson and K. Cauley (eds.), *College Psychotherapy* (New York: Guilford, 1989); T. Bodde, *Why Is My Child Gay?* (Washington, D.C.: Federation of Parents and Friends of Lesbians and Gays, Inc., n.d.); *"Gay Student Wins Bid to Revise Anti-bias Policy,"* New York Times (April 15, 1990): 33; "Condom Jewelry Makes A Point for AIDS Alert," *New York Times* (December 17, 1989): 71.; G. Kolata, " For Those Concerned with Pill's Risk, a Look at the Choices," *New York Times* (January 12, 1989): B10; H.D. Gayle, et al., "Prevalence of the Human Immunodeficiency Virus Among University Students," *New England Journal of Medicine* (November 29, 1990): 1538–41; G. Cowley, "AIDS: The Next Ten Years," *Newsweek* (June 25, 1990): 20–27; G. Kolata, "Experts Debate if AIDS Epidemic Has at Last Crested in U.S.," *New York Times* (June 18, 1991): C1, C9. E.W. Johnson, *Love and Sex in Plain Language* (Toronto: Bantam, 1988); J.E. Kaplan, M. Meyer and J. Navin, "Chlamydia Trachomatis Infection in a Male College Student Population," *Journal of American College Health* (January 1989): 159–161; "Safe Sex," Charlottesville AIDS Resource Network for the American College Health Association, 1986.

Chapter 8

[1]D. Pace, "Acts of Intolerance on Campus: Focus on Date Rape." Unpublished manuscript, Grand Valley State University, Allendale, Michigan.

See also: NYU Committee on Safety, *Rape: Awareness, Prevention, Crisis Intervention* (New York University, 1990); W. Celis, "Students Trying to Draw Line Between Sex and an Assault," *New York Times* (January 2, 1991): A1, B8; J. Castelli, "Campus Crime 101," *New York Times* (November 4, 1990), Education Supplement: 34–36; N. Biggs, "When Is It Rape?," *Time* (June 3, 1991): 48–55.

Chapter 9

[1]*Drugs Drugs Drugs*, "Access" Series (Hanover, N.H.: Dartmouth College 1987): 2–7. See also "Marijuana," *The Harvard Medical School Mental Health Letter* (November 1987): 1–4.

[2]Office of Student Life, *Guide to Alcohol and Drug Policies, Procedures, Health Risks and Helping Networks* (New York: New York University, September 1990).

See also: *Alcohol Use and Health Risks* "Access" Series (Hanover, N.H.: Dartmouth College, 1988): 8; "Why Men Can Outdrink Women," *Time* (January 22, 1990): 61; M. Paulus, Personal communication, August 1, 1990; "Cocaine: Waking Up to a Nightmare," Phoenix, Ariz.: DIN Publications, 1989); "MDMA: Madness, not Ecstasy," *Psychology Today* (June 1986): 14; "Drug Abuse and Dependence—Part 1", *The Harvard Medical School Mental Health Letter* (October 1989): 1–4; "Amphetamines," *The Harvard Medical School Mental Health Letter* (April 1990): 1–4; C.L. Otis and R. Goldingay, *Campus Health Guide* (New York: College Entrance Examination Board, 1989); D. Goleman, "Breaking Bad Habits: New Therapy Focuses on the Relapse," *New York Times* (December 27, 1988): C1, C11; S. Peele, *Diseasing of America* (Boston: Houghton-Mifflin, 1989); "Freedom from Smoking," *Regarding Women and Health Care* (New Brunswick, N.J.: Robert Wood Johnson University Hospital, Summer 1990): 1; "Leaving the Pack Behind," *The Vigorous Violet* (New York University Office of Health Affairs, November 1990): 3; C.A. Presley and P.W. Meilman, "Alcohol and Drugs on the American College Campus: A Report to College Presidents" (Carbondale; Southern Illinois University, 1991); F.S. Stinson, B.D. Williams et al., "Demographic Trends, Alcohol Abuse and Alcoholism: 1985-1995" (Washington, D.C.: NIAAA. Division of Biometry and Epidemiology [Epidemiologic Bulletin No. 15], 1986).

Chapter 10

[1]Willard Gaylin, *Rediscovering Love* (New York: Penguin, 1986), 103.

[2]A.H. Rosenfeld, "New Treatment for Bulimia," *Psychology Today* (March 1989): 28.

[3]R.M. Lee, "Anorexia Nervosa and Bulimia Nervosa," in P.A. Grayson and K. Cauley, *College Psychotherapy* (New York: Guilford, 1989): 274–97.

[4]J.E. Brody, "Personal Health," *New York Times* (February 22, 1990): B9.

See also: S. Cunningham, "Bulimia's Cycle Shames Patient, Bests Therapists," *American Psychological Association Monitor* (January 1984): 16-17; Gina Kolata, "One Reason It's Hard to Keep Off Lost Weight," *New York Times* (April 12, 1990): B11; J. Gurin, "Leaner not Lighter," *Psychology Today* (June 1989): 32–36; J.E. Brody, " Secret of Successful Dieting," *New York Times* (July 3, 1991): C9; E. Hall, "PT Conversation—Judith Rodin: A Sense of Control," *Psychology Today* (December 1984): 38–45; M. O'Neill, "Dieters, Craving Balance, Are Battling Fears of Food," *New York Times* (April 1, 1990): 1, 22; M. Bloom, "Running Supports the Work of a Diet," *New York Times* (June 18, 1990): C11; K.D. Brownell, "When and How to Diet," *Psychology Today* (June 1989): 40–46; C. Simon, "The Triumphant Dieter," *Psychology Today* (June 1989): 48–52; American Psychiatric Association, *Diagnostic and Statistic Manual of Mental Disorders*, third edition, revised (Washington, D.C.: American Psychiatric Association, 1987); *Bulimia and Anorexia: A Sign of the Times* (Philadelphia: The Renfrew Center, n.d.); H.M. Weinstein and A. Richman, "The Group Treatment of Bulimia," *Journal of the American College Health Association* (April 1984): 208–15; H. Bruch, *The Golden Cage: The Enigma of Anorexia Nervosa* (New York: Vintage, 1979); C.L. Otis and R. Goldingay, *Campus Health Guide* (New York: College Entrance Examination Board, 1989); "What is Anorexia Nervosa?" Pamphlet. (New York, Gracie Square Hospital, undated).

INDEX

ABOUT THE AUTHORS

Dr. Paul Grayson and **Dr. Philip Meilman** attended graduate school in the clinical psychology program at the University of North Carolina at Chapel Hill. They have jointly authored numerous articles about college students.

Dr. Paul Grayson is now director of counseling services at New York University. Previously he counseled students at SUNY Purchase, Wesleyan University and the College of William and Mary. Dr. Grayson was the editor of *College Psychotherapy* (Guilford Press, 1989).

Dr. Philip Meilman is director of counseling at the College of William and Mary. His previous college counseling experience was at Dartmouth College and the University of Nebraska Medical Center.